Sunbelt Working Mothers

A volume in the series

Anthropology of Contemporary Issues

EDITED BY ROGER SANJEK

Sunbelt Working Mothers

RECONCILING FAMILY AND FACTORY

Louise Lamphere
Patricia Zavella
Felipe Gonzales
with Peter B. Evans

Cornell University Press

Ithaca and London

First published 1993 by Cornell University Press.

Library of Congress Cataloging-in-Publication Data

Lamphere, Louise.
    Sunbelt working mothers : reconciling family and factory / Louise Lamphere, Patricia Zavella, Felipe Gonzales; with Peter B. Evans.
        p.   cm. — (Anthropology of contemporary issues)
    Includes bibliographical references and index.
    ISBN 0-8014-2788-6. — ISBN 0-8014-8066-3 (pbk.)
        1. Working mothers—Sunbelt States. 2. Work and family—Sunbelt States. I. Zavella, Patricia. II. Gonzales, Felipe, 1946– . III. Evans, Peter B., 1944– . IV. Title. V. Series.
HQ759.48.L37 1993
306.87—dc20   92-56789
Printed in the United States of America

This book is dedicated to our mothers:

Miriam B. Johnson
Isabel Schnebelen
Angelita Sánchez Gonzales
Margaret Brandt Evans

Contents

Preface

When I get a job, I hang onto it. I'd rather hold a job than go look for a job. Even if it does frustrate me and get on my nerves. It isn't a bad job, so I don't seriously consider quitting. I never have.
—Mary Pike, age 22, stitcher, apparel plant

The hardest part of a working mother's life is trying to extend yourself over everything. You want to give 100 percent at work, you want to give 100 percent at home, you want to give 100 percent to your kids, and you can't do that always.
—Donna Garcia, age 28, skills trainer, electronics firm

Since 1960 an enormous number of mothers have entered the labor force in the United States, most of them in blue-collar, clerical, and service jobs. America's families are no longer typically composed of a working father, a housewife mother, and children. They are more flexible in form, ranging from traditional nuclear families to two-job families to families headed by single mothers, gay and lesbian couples, and single individuals (both young adults and senior citizens, primarily women). In 1991, in 58 percent of couples with children the women held paying jobs, and their wages made them substantial contributors to family income. In addition, in 17 percent of all households single mothers provided the primary support for their children (U.S. Bureau of Labor Statistics 1991). The increase in the numbers of working mothers has challenged our cultural notions about what family life and gender roles are about. With the growth in immigration since 1965 and the impact of the civil rights movements, more attention has been paid as well to cultural diversity among American families, which include white, African-American, Mexican-American, Japanese-American, Native American, and immigrant families from societies as diverse as Taiwan, Guatemala, Vietnam, Haiti, India, and Cuba.

Furthermore, the 1970s and 1980s were a period of profound change in the American economy. Industrial production declined in the East and Midwest as corporations moved production facilities abroad or located new plants in the South and West. Service industries became a greater part of the U.S. economy, manufacturing wages declined, and an increasing gap developed between the wealthy and working-class and low-income families.

In this context of demographic, cultural, and economic change, working mothers are at the center of what American families are becoming. In this book we focus on working mothers in Albuquerque, New Mexico, women from backgrounds we categorize as Anglo (or white) and Hispano (or Mexican-American). Some were married; others were single. In 1982–83, all were employed in electronics or apparel plants, workplaces that opened as a result of the economic shifts that brought about sunbelt industrialization in New Mexico. Most new branch plants of larger corporations were "sunbelt spillovers" from the Silicon Valley in California or "frostbelt refugees" from the Midwest and New England. Some were traditionally hierarchical in their organization; others, influenced by Japanese management practices, pursued a "high-involvement" philosophy. Together, they typify the kinds of transformations American workplaces began to make in the 1980s.

More than do supermom doctors, lawyers, and corporation executives, working-class working mothers and their households represent the kinds of diversity, flexibility, and change that are becoming characteristic of American working families. Mary Pike and Donna Garcia *were* committed workers. Being a working mother, however, meant bridging the separate domains of household and workplace and combining two roles, each assuming a full-time commitment. Like many women, they were struggling to reconcile the contradictions inherent in their dual lives.

These contradictions became apparent when Mary talked about frustration: having returned to work when her baby was six months old, she was having trouble learning a new job and had not been able to make the basic piece rate. She was also ambivalent about child care, worrying that the babysitter might replace her as "Mom" in her baby's eyes, yet believing that "she gets more attention from me coming home from work than she did when I was there with her all day." Despite her frustration and doubt, Mary did not consider quitting her job; her take-home pay was too important to the family when her husband was earning only $5.00 an hour in a warehouse job and there were monthly payments to make on their mobile home.

Donna Garcia saw the contradictions clearly, yet she too wanted to work, even though she had young children. "I don't think I could have stayed home. I was used to working; I've always worked. And I enjoyed my job, and there was no reason for me to quit."

The ways that working mothers mediate the contradictions they find both in the workplace and in combining work and family evolve through the "practice" of everyday life: they constitute a set of tactics, strategies, negotiations that differ among families and within and between different ethnic populations.

The hierarchical or participative organization of the workplace and the husband's job history and income also proved to be important sources of variability. Mary Pike, for instance, worked in a hierarchically managed plant with large departments, direct supervision, and a piece rate. Donna Garcia worked at a high-involvement plant with a team structure, job rotation, and an "open-door" style of management. Each presented its own set of contradictions.

While all our interviewees worked in new Albuquerque industrial plants, their husbands had a wider range of working-class jobs. In relation to their husbands' incomes, we found that some women were secondary providers (earning much less than their husbands), others were coproviders (earning about the same wages), and still others were mainstay providers (holding the steady job in the family). For example, Mary's husband, Don, laid off from a high-paying job, was working for wages similar to Mary's, whereas Donna's husband had worked his way up to a well-paid supervisory position. Don's vulnerability in the job market made Mary a coprovider, while Donna became a secondary provider as her husband rose higher in his company. These two providing roles in turn influenced the set of practices that Mary and Donna developed in negotiating the household division of labor and arranging for child care. Mary's husband did more than half the housework, Donna's husband much less.

Mary had no kin in the city to turn to for babysitting, but Donna's mother and younger sister helped her out.

Some of these contrasts fit ethnic stereotypes: for example, that Mexican Americans are more closely tied to kin. Others did not: for example, that Anglos have more stable economic situations. We found that simplistic generalizations failed to characterize the true complexity of the work and family lives of the women we studied. The contrasts between Donna's and Mary's experiences proliferate in additional directions as we consider the lives of our other interviewees.

To make sense of this diversity, one must analyze the mutual constitution of class, gender, and ethnicity and observe variability both within and between groups. Throughout this book we examine women's experiences in the workplace and the home, identify the social locations of Anglo and Hispano women, tease out both variations within each ethnic category and convergences that unite members of both groups. Where divergences occur, we argue, they are best accounted for by the different historical relationships of Anglos and Hispanos to the Albuquerque political economy. In other words, we have found that both convergence and difference characterize the lives of both Mexican-American and white women.

We have also learned that the new sunbelt industries have not been a panacea for the local economy or for the women who work in them. Because we conducted our research in the early 1980s, during a national recession that was particularly devastating for jobs in the mining, oil, and construction industries in New Mexico, the husbands in our sample were much more economically vulnerable than the wives. Since then, however, ups and downs in the apparel and electronics industries, both nationally and in Albuquerque, have demonstrated that women's jobs can be equally unstable. The pace of technological change, the impact of foreign competition, and the dependence on military contracts all make the electronics industry volatile, shifting, and subject to cycles. Moreover, the recession of 1990–92 created higher unemployment for working-class men so that dual-worker families are again facing the kinds of difficulties we found a decade ago. One electronics company announced a layoff of 300 workers in 1992, and another firm (formerly employing 1,000) will close by June 1993. Rather than a mini–Silicon Valley and a magnet for new industrial growth, Albuquerque may become a silicon desert.

Our research in Albuquerque became a team effort to understand the relationship between the workplace and the family and to place that relationship within the context of the local economy. Peter Evans, a sociologist who has studied industrial development and large corporations, was primarily responsible for researching the history and development of the local economy, with special attention to the relocation of new plants to Albuquerque. He interviewed plant managers for each firm established since 1971 and collected macro-level data on employment trends nationally, within New Mexico, and in the Albuquerque area.

The heart of the project consisted of intensive interviews with a sample of working mothers and their husbands, conducted during 1982–83. Peter Evans' interviews opened the door to cooperation from plant managers. They referred us to personnel managers (or, in one case, the plant nurse), who helped locate working mothers for possible interviews. We found other working mothers through friends and colleagues who could direct us to a sympathetic supervisor or other plant employee, and still other interviewees through union officers. In almost all cases, we had to rely on those who worked in a plant to ask women to participate. Even plant managers or personnel officers were not willing to give us a complete list of employees from which to draw a sample. One union provided a membership list, but it did not contain information on marital status or the age of children of women workers. Thus, even in the case of helpful union or management officials we relied on them to contact workers and ask for their participation. Once we began interviewing, working mothers themselves suggested co-workers who might be interested in talking with us. Overall, then, we had a "snowball sample" based on contacts with both workers and managers.

Our initial criteria were that the woman be a full-time employee in an apparel or electronics plant in an assembly-level job, that she have at least one child under school age, and that her husband be willing to be interviewed. As the study progressed, we found that although Mexican Americans constitute 35 percent of the Albuquerque population, it was easier to locate Hispano subjects than Anglo ones. We thus allowed our sample of Hispano working mothers to grow to approximately two-thirds of all the married women we interviewed. After hearing about the significant numbers of single parents in some of the plants, we began to develop a sample of single mothers as well, both Hispano and Anglo.

Louise Lamphere developed the interviews, based on her research in Rhode Island with the help of Felipe Gonzales and Patricia Zavella. Two interview schedules, covering both work and family life, were prepared in Spanish and English. Husbands and wives were interviewed separately, using the same questions, and the interviews were tape-recorded. Two sessions, each averaging one and a half to two hours, were usually needed to complete both interviews. The first interview included open-ended questions on the respondent's current job, work history, attitudes toward female participation in the labor force, typical daily schedule, day-care arrangements, allocation of housework and child-care chores, and family income and expenditures. The second focused on kin networks, the role of friends, and the importance of ethnicity, religion, and family values in the lives of the respondents.

Louise Lamphere and Gary Lemons conducted the interviews with Anglo couples. Patricia Zavella and Felipe Gonzales—with the help of Jennifer Martinez and Victor Mancha—interviewed Mexican-American wives and husbands respectively.

By the end of 1983 we had interviewed twenty-five couples in which the wife was a Mexican American, or Hispana (including three who were married to Anglo men); thirteen couples in which the working mother was an Anglo (including four married to Hispano men); and fifteen single mothers (twelve Hispanas and three Anglos). Of the 53 women interviewed, almost 70 percent were Mexican American (slightly over the proportion in the work force of local electronics plants and equal to the proportion in apparel plants). Approximately 70 percent of the women were married, and 30 percent were single parents.

Throughout the book we have used pseudonyms for our interviewees, and for the plants where they worked, in order to protect their anonymity.

In analyzing and writing up our data we adopted a collaborative mode of working. Often one of us took the responsibility of doing the initial data analysis, and another member of the team later reworked the chapter. Patricia Zavella, Felipe Gonzales, and Louise Lamphere spent long hours clarifying the argument or sharpening the case examples. All three together produced Chapter 1, which defines our project in the context of current theory and research.

Peter Evans took complete responsibility for Chapter 2, which surveys the growth of sunbelt industrialization within the Albuquerque economy, manufacturers' reasons for coming to Albuquerque during the 1970s and early 1980s, and the effects on the labor force—male and female, Hispano and Anglo.

Chapter 3, originated by Felipe Gonzales and Louise Lamphere, shows how the macrolevel processes outlined in Chapter 2 affected the lives of our informants. It presents work histories from women in each of four categories that we call "secondary providers," "co-providers," "mainstay providers," and "sole providers." In each category women's jobs solidified their commitment to being full-time workers and—to varying degrees—provided crucial support for their families.

Chapters 4 and 5, written by Louise Lamphere, move onto the shop floor to compare systems of control, wages, and work culture under the two types of organization we found in sunbelt plants: those that were "hierarchical," and those that used some version of "participative" management.

Chapter 6, Patricia Zavella's examination of the household division of labor, discusses how dual-worker and single-parent families mediated the contradictions that face working mothers in replacing their labor in the household. Factors important in negotiating household arrangements included day-care problems, women's economic roles, the shifts that men and women worked, and notions of gender roles.

Chapter 7, by Patricia Zavella and Felipe Gonzales, focuses on women's arrangements for day care, which are crucial to a mother's ability to work full time, particularly when the children are very young.

Felipe Gonzales and Louise Lamphere collaborated on Chapter 8, which examines the social networks women construct to meet their more occasional needs, both instrumental and emotional—networks that vary with the availability of kin and friends.

Finally, in Chapter 9 we argue that both convergence and difference characterize the lives of women who work in sunbelt plants. As they mediated contradictions in the workplace, where these women were not ethnically segregated and were all English-speaking high school graduates, their tactics and strategies for confronting control tended to converge; differences were a product of different management systems of control, as well as the historical and dialectical relationship between management and workers in a particular plant. In mediating contradictions between work and family roles, women had greater flexibility in creating support systems, but these in turn were shaped by their husbands' work situations, their kin networks, migration history, and so on.

Overall we argue for the salience of material conditions, rather than subjective differences, in shaping the effect of class, gender, and ethnicity on the situation of sunbelt working mothers. The insertion of high-paying industrial jobs for women into the Albuquerque political economy produced a range of patterns, which in turn had some impact on changes within the family itself. But Hispana and Anglo women's tactics, implicit negotiation, and response to both resistance on the part of husbands and systems of control at work were converging rather than diverging as we looked at new patterns of housework and child-care allocation. Where there were ethnic differences they seemed chiefly accounted for by the different historical relationships of Anglos and Hispanos to Albuquerque's political economy, Hispanos being local or at least in-state residents and Anglos being out-of-state migrants with relatively few kin residing in Albuquerque.

At work, Hispanas and Anglos faced the same systems of control in female jobs. If we take into account all aspects of the work situation, there is both a positive and a negative side of women's industrial experience in Albuquerque. On the negative side, plants have been successful in keeping out unions; in addition, a 1985 lawsuit brought by women at Southwest Electronics emphasized the impact of hazardous chemicals that can bring reproductive difficulties, central nervous system disorders, and cancer. On the positive side are the relatively high wages and good benefits that these jobs provide. Though jobs have been more stable since 1983 and some companies are expanding, sunbelt plants also experience layoffs and closures, or because of foreign competition may not expand as quickly as predicted. High technology is clearly not a panacea, but it has changed the lives of the working mothers employed in the new industrial plants that have come to Albuquerque.

This has been a collaborative book in more ways than indicated by its multiple authorship. The research was initially funded by a grant from the Anthropology Program of the National Science Foundation (BNS no. 8112726). A grant from the Russell Sage Foundation gave us time to analyze our data and write the first draft of the book. Additional financial support came to Felipe Gonzales from the Chicano Studies Program at the University of New Mexico. We are grateful to all three institutions for their assistance.

[xvi]

Many people have helped to bring this project to fruition. During the research stage Gary Lemons, Jennifer Martinez, and Victor Mancha spent many hours interviewing husbands and wives in our sample. We are also grateful to Lois Gonzales, our project research assistant, who patiently collected material from newspapers and periodicals and prepared a clipping file on each of the employing companies, tabulated some of the data on housework and child care, and examined the attitudes of husbands to their wives' employment. Carol Marron took on the tedious (and seemingly endless) task of transcribing the interviews, with the help of Barbara Bush-Stewart, Mary Lingenfelter, and Inge Van Buskirk. We also thank Maggie West for generously sharing her data from an earlier study of Computex.

During the writing phase of this project, our help came from many sources. Guillermo Grenier shared tapes and interviews with Louise Lamphere which contributed to Chapter 5. Louise's research assistants, Mary Jane McReynolds, Jocclyn DeHaas, and Art Martin, performed numerous word-processing chores, including putting the manuscript through a second program. Arlie Hochschild and Jane Hood read early drafts of Chapter 6 and made helpful suggestions for revisions. Patricia Zavella thanks Lynet Uttal and Josie Mendez-Negrete for their helpful comments on Chapter 7, and Micaela di Leonardo for discussions that helped her to clarify her thinking on social location and variation. We are grateful to Sam Tubiolo, who drew the map in Chapter 1. We also thank Roger Sanjek, editor of the Anthropology of Contemporary Issues series, and Peter Agree at Cornell University Press for their support and encouragement.

Finally, we gratefully acknowledge the women and men who participated in the project and gave of their precious time so that we could better understand the everyday lives of working-class families.

Louise Lamphere
Patricia Zavella
Felipe Gonzales

Albuquerque, New Mexico

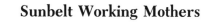

Sunbelt Working Mothers

[1]

Mediating Contradiction and Difference: The Everyday Construction of Work and Family

Feminist theory since the early 1980s has begun to be concerned with "difference," divisions not just between male and female but among women themselves. Rather than assuming a global notion of "Woman" implying that women from different national, cultural, and class backgrounds share experiences on the basis of their gender, theorists have begun to draw attention to the variability of women's experience and to the way in which it is differentially constituted depending on economic and cultural setting. In her introduction to *Theoretical Perspectives on Sexual Difference* (1990:2), Deborah L. Rhode observes:

> Feminism assumes a shared experience it seeks in large measure to challenge. What complicates the issue still further is the diversity of those experiences, a diversity that is gaining greater recognition within the women's movement. Over the last century, American feminists have centered theoretical and political attention on differences between men and women. Over the last decade, feminists have increasingly realized the importance of focusing also on differences among women, and on the way those differences mediate gender relations. A crucial contribution of recent theory has been its emphasis on diversity across class, race, ethnicity, age, and sexual orientation.

This insistence on the importance of understanding difference among women was initiated by women of color, lesbians, and women activists who confronted different interests among women in their political work. These women critiqued feminist theory and the institutions of women's studies, exposing their invisibility and exclusion and pushing for recognition of the multiple identities of women (Anzaldua 1990; Davis 1981; Glenn 1985; hooks 1984; Hurtado 1989; Moraga and Anzaldua 1981; Swerdlow and Lessinger 1983; Zinn et al. 1986). As Estelle Freedman reminds us, "The scholarly project of questioning gender salience follows the lead of activist feminist politics. A variety of writers engaged in grassroots politics since the 1970s have insisted that race, class, sexuality, age, and physical ability require a redefinition of the category 'woman' in every context in which a woman acts" (1990:259).

Feminists are now attempting to create a body of scholarship and conduct research in ways that will no longer "privilege" white, middle-class, or heterosexual women's concerns and that fully integrate all women. This viewpoint has produced an emphasis on women's "experience" and "identity." Proponents wish to recognize women's "many voices," that women of diverse class, ethnic or racial group, and sexual preference have very different perspectives on so-called universal feminine experiences. Yet the emphasis on identity as it derives from experience is not without difficulties. In an attempt to describe one woman's identity subjectively, there is a tendency to use an implicitly hyphenated string of categories. For example, Audre Lorde describes herself as a "forty-nine year old Black lesbian feminist socialist mother of two, including one boy, and a member of an interracial couple" (1984:114). Despite the apparent complexity, such a description can be limiting since it calls for multiple categories for those women who straddle boundaries—as many of us do—and throws into question which categories are most salient for each woman. Lorde's solution to this impasse is to hold on to the differences, to recognize how often they are infused with racism, sexism, heterosexism, and classism (creating categories of "others"), and to root out such distortions so that we can "recognize, reclaim, and define those differences" rather than having them imposed.

Nevertheless, capturing an individual identity through hyphenation can be problematic because experience is individual, and each woman can have a different perception of the same experience. We end up creating myriad categories with no means of bridging their differences, of understanding commonalities, or of reclaiming similarities in experience.

In a similar vein, theorizing "categories" of women in order to bring difference to the fore often begins with splitting the category "women" into such subcategories as "working-class women," "Chicana working-class single parents," and so on. Then using "identity" and "experience" as the further basis for analysis can become an essentialist project when the hyphenated category itself becomes an unexamined totality such as "the" working-class woman or "the" Chicana worker. Here we continue to ignore variation among members of the refined category and see "Chicana working-class women," for example, as having similar identities constructed out of the same unanalyzed "experience."

To move beyond essentialist pronouncements about groups of people, we need to acknowledge the constructed nature of categories and their embeddedness in power relations. Anthropologists now realize that "experience" itself, even the "raw" experience described in fieldnotes (Sanjek 1990), is socially constructed, mediated by historical, structural, and cultural constraints (Lamphere 1990; Rosaldo 1989). Furthermore, women's experiences and identities are constructed in a social context that includes power relations. These are constituted through the intersection of race, class, and gender and are often overlooked when the focus is on identity. That is, the ways in which the upper classes or white men or heterosexual women experience privilege, or the ways in which working-class women may share experiences of relative autonomy or powerlessness, can be important indications of power relations. As Freedman points out, power is a critical element often missing in the literature that emphasizes the valorization of women's differences (1990:259).

By developing a sense of the whole context and "attending to the waning as well as the waxing of gender saliency" (Thorne 1990:108)—and, we would add, the salience of race/ethnicity and class—we gain a more complex understanding of the dynamics of power and move away from simple binary oppositions and explanations of male versus female, or white women versus women of color (Thorne 1990; Yanagisako and Collier 1990). When we validate difference on the basis of "identity" or experience, it becomes difficult to understand commonality (not to be construed as sameness). We need an analysis that illustrates the plurality of experiences yet explains why one woman's experience can parallel that of another.

To overcome these difficulties yet to focus squarely on issues of difference, we propose a theoretical framework that embeds women's experience within historical conditions and examines how these shape women's strategies, rather than how women construct "identi-

[3]

ties." We use the notion of "social location" to specify the way in which regional and local political economy interact with class, ethnicity, culture, and sexual preference to condition the strategies and meanings that working mothers fashion through their agency.

We have chosen to examine issues of difference through the study of working-class working mothers because we believe that working mothers are at the heart of changing American families and that working-class families are often ignored in the larger debate of what is happening to American families. Further, particularly in the Southwest but in virtually every region of the country, American families are ethnically diverse. Our sample of Hispana and Anglo working mothers, both single and married, allows us to explore the way in which ethnicity/race and marital status create possibilities for differing strategies. While the experience of Anglo and Hispano husbands is an additional part of our story, particularly as it involves the knotty problems of housework and child care in dual-worker families, we have left exploration of gender differences as they relate to work and work culture for other publications (e.g., Lamphere 1991).

Within a framework that emphasizes the social location of working mothers, we see women as active agents. As Joan Scott has commented, "Subjects have agency. They are not unified, autonomous individuals exercising free will, but rather subjects whose agency is created through situations and statuses conferred on them" (1991:793). Becoming a working mother involves dealing with a host of contradictions in the workplace and in combining two roles. This effort is best thought of in terms of praxis or "practice," a cover term for the ways in which women mediate these contradictions through concrete behavioral strategies. Practice takes place within a structure, a workplace or a household, and each subject's differential set of practices and her engagement in the shaping, acceptance, or contestation of the meanings of a set of practices constitute her "experience." An emphasis on structure, agency, and practice opens up the possibility of variability within a category such as "women workers" or "Chicana single mothers." It also allows us to see when women of one subjective identity (Hispana working-class women, for example) do not act in terms of that identity alone but forge behavioral strategies that may converge with those of women in other categories or of men. Within a framework where both convergence and divergence are the outcome of the analysis, we can avoid either positing monolithic behavior for members of a category (Anglo working mothers) or ignor-

[4]

ing (or failing to conceptualize) common strategies, shared meanings, and converging practices.

The Class/Race Divide: Why Study Working-Class Families?

Since the mid-1980s increasing attention has been given to families in which the mother is employed. Yet there are still three problems with the state of our knowledge. First, the literature tends to ignore issues of class or to focus primarily on middle-class and upper-middle-class working women. Second, many studies still emphasize either the family *or* the workplace, rarely integrating the two within the covers of one book. Third, although we now have good studies of working-class women from nonwhite backgrounds, both in the United States and in the industrializing Third World, they seldom engage the issue of racial/ethnic differences within the working class through a comparison of at least two groups of women. Even more unusual are studies that focus on both single and married working mothers from either the same class or the same ethnic background.

As an example of the first issue, the lack of attention to class, Goldscheider and Waite's *New Families, No Families?* (1991), using large-scale survey data, provides an overview of changes in American families since the baby boom. The authors examine the impact of women's employment on men's housework and children's share of household responsibilities, yet we learn almost nothing about class differences (or similarities), and little about race or ethnic differences. The same can be said for a large number of sociological studies of the gender division of labor in dual-job families (Berk 1985; Berk and Berk 1979; Pleck 1985).

Arlie Hochschild's book *The Second Shift* (1989) presents wonderful and insightful portraits of the struggle over housework and child care in dual-job families. Because only 12 percent of her interviewees were blue-collar couples and 17 percent were in clerical and sales jobs, she profiles only three working-class fathers. They represent, however, three very different patterns. The first was a Latino factory worker who talked a traditional line but actually shared the housework with his wife, who provided child care for working parents in her home. The second was a black forklift driver who did very little at home except occasional play with his son and sporadic housecleaning, much to the distress of his wife, who contested his nonin-

[5]

volvement and finally left the marriage. The third example was a black working-class man who was more involved with his child and shared the housework with his wife more than anyone else in the entire study; this father was one of Hochschild's two examples of the "New Man" who shares the "second shift." The three cases suggest a good deal of variability within the working class and the need for a more thoroughgoing study of recent changes in dual-worker families. Hochschild's book, on the whole, follows a long line of studies that focus more clearly on middle-class and upper-middle-class dual-career families (Aldous 1982; Gallese 1985; Holmstrom 1972; Hood 1983; Rapaport and Rapaport 1971; Rapoport and Rapoport with Bumstead 1978).[1]

Judith Stacey's feminist ethnography, *Brave New Families* (1990), does focus on the working class. Her description of two family networks in California's Silicon Valley examines the impact of feminism and the "postindustrial" economy on two women, their husbands, adult children, and assorted grandchildren, boyfriends, and in-laws. She argues persuasively that working-class families are no longer traditional, and that divorce, remarriage, and cohabitation have created a postmodern family in which kin resources are important and family form is flexible and fluid. Not only has the Archie Bunker stereotype of the working-class family become invalid, but there is considerable variability within working-class families themselves.

The workplace, however, is conspicuously absent from both Hochschild's and Stacey's studies, and neither really engages the issue of racial/ethnic differences within a particular class. Their important contributions, particularly in providing rich ethnographic accounts of American families and suggesting variability and change within the working class, still leave much to be done in terms of understanding the dynamics within and among working-class families of differing ethnic and racial backgrounds.

The research that reports on working-class women of color has primarily examined the employment side of the work-family nexus, illuminating strategies of resistance on the job. Judith Rollins (1985) pre-

---

[1] To be fair, Hood's study (1983) includes blue-collar and professional husbands in equal proportion, although she does not use class as an important construct in her analysis; and some articles in the collection edited by Joan Aldous (1982) utilize data across a number of occupational categories. Yet, there is little attempt to focus on patterns that might contrast blue-collar working-class families with white-collar or professional dual-earner couples.

[6]

sents a nuanced commentary on northern black women domestics in Boston and their ways of dealing with the maternalism of white female employers. Karen Sacks's (1988) ethnographically based analysis shows how southern black women who do clerical work in hospitals bring family values concerning work, autonomy, respect, and conflict mediation to their jobs, enabling them to critique hierarchical hospital relations and to mount a union organizing drive. More analysis of the family side of women's lives is apparent in Evelyn Nakano Glenn's (1986) book on three generations of California Japanese domestic workers and in Mary Romero's (1992) discussion of southwest-born Chicana domestics. Both studies deal with the contradictions inherent in doing housework for pay in the home of an employer and for family members in one's own home. Yet as valuable as these works are, they do not provide comparative analyses of women from the same racial or ethnic groups in different contexts, nor of women from different racial or ethnic groups within the same context. Beatriz Pesquera's (1985) research on Chicana women in professional, white-collar, and blue-collar jobs does focus on the former issue; we have chosen to examine the latter.

Defining Social Location: The Political Economy

For us the study of diversity in women's experience entails an understanding of how race, ethnicity, class, and gender conjoin to constitute difference; we use the term "social location" to describe this conjuncture and the ways in which our Anglo and Hispano interviewees were differently positioned subjects (Zavella 1991a, 1991b). We think of social location as operating on two levels. At one level the term denotes the location of women in a particular political economy; here we focus on the larger political and economic forces that brought new industries to Albuquerque, as well as the patterns of growth and development that accounted for the residential position of Anglo and Hispano families within that city. At a second level, the term refers to a woman's social location not in a strictly spatial sense, but within a social structure where socially constructed categories— gender, class, race, ethnicity, sexual orientation—are linked to positions that in turn shape experience.

At the level of political economy, an important trend during the 1980s was the global restructuring of industry: the decline of manu-

[7]

facturing in the northeastern and midwestern United States and its relocation to the South and West and abroad. The U.S. economy has become more focused on service and clerical jobs, while some sectors of Third World economies are experiencing the creation of industrial workplaces. Women workers have been employed in areas of both industrial decline and expansion, particularly in electronics, apparel, and other light manufacturing industries. Social scientists have begun to focus on the implications of these trends and have given us a sense of the diverse lives of contemporary women pointing to class, racial, and even national differences as they have evolved in this restructuring.

An outpouring of research has examined the impact of global restructuring on women in the Third World countries to which "runaway" shops (particularly in electronics and apparel) have relocated: Jamaica, Taiwan, Hong Kong, the U.S.-Mexico border, and Malaysia (Nash and Fernández Kelly 1983; Ruiz and Tiano 1987; Safa 1986; Taplin 1986). Many of these women are single daughters whose wages are important to their parents' households (Kung 1983; Lim 1978, 1982, 1983; Salaff 1981; Tiano 1987a, 1987b). There is also a significant minority of married women in these labor forces, as well as a substantial number of single mothers, often 15–25 percent of the total (Tiano 1987a:27).

A recent study, sensitive to locating women within a political economy, is Aihwa Ong's *Spirits of Resistance* (1987), which describes the lives of Malay village women who have been incorporated into the Japanese-owned electronics industry. Ong discusses the "reconfiguration" of village life and changes in family and marriage patterns with the advent of free-trade zones. Then, turning to the workplace, she outlines the structure of power relations on the shop floor and tactics of resistance used by young, single women workers: from crying and seeking refuge in an Islamic prayer room to damaging electronic components. Most disruptive were attacks of spirit possession that actually stopped production until a spirit healer could be summoned to perform exorcistic rites. What attracts us to Ong's approach is not only her attempt to set women's experience within a political economy but her ability to link the home and the workplace and her attention to women's resistance at work.[2]

---

[2] Devon Peña (1987) writing about industrialization on the U.S.-Mexico border, is

Industrial restructuring has a domestic as well as an international side: in the Midwest and New England, working-class women have lost jobs as firms have moved branch plants abroad or closed facilities because of corporate buyouts or foreign competition (Rosen 1987). In the South and West, industrial employment expanded during the late 1970s and early 1980s, particularly in electronics but also in apparel and other light industries. Current research on the electronics industry has focused primarily on Silicon Valley, Los Angeles, and New York—three political economies that contrast with Albuquerque, New Mexico.

Silicon Valley includes the full range of the electronics industry: firms that specialize in research and development; firms whose headquarters as well as a large manufacturing facility are in Santa Clara County; and small subcontracting firms; and during the 1980s a proliferation of homework (Katz and Kemnitzer 1984:213–14). Employees in the industry thus range from high-level executives, engineers, and consultants to technicians and assemblers. At one end are affluent Anglo men and at the other a considerable number of immigrant women of Hispanic and Asian origins. Most studies of the electronics industry in California have used macrolevel data to establish the occupational segregation that has relegated immigrant women to relatively low-paying assembly jobs (Fernández Kelly and Garcia 1988; Green 1983; Katz and Kemnitzer 1983; Keller 1983; Snow 1983). Karen Hossfeld (1988a, 1988b) interviewed immigrant women employees in Silicon Valley to approach a microlevel analysis of their lives. Her anecdotes about women's tactics on the shop floor show reactions of resistance and quiescence, but she does not relate these to the overall production process and the characteristics of particular jobs. Many of the immigrant women Hossfeld interviewed held opinions about families and jobs similar to those of the women we studied in Albuquerque, but their location in more male-dominated immigrant families made their situation more like the immigrant women Lamphere studied in Rhode Island.[3] In comparison, Stacey's (1990) research on white working-class women emphasizes the interface be-

---

another of the few researchers who pay close attention to the importance of resistance among women workers.

[3] Some Asian immigrant husbands from middle-class backgrounds use electronics employment to launch themselves toward more middle-class jobs and English skills; see Hossfeld 1988a:15.

tween work and family, but her interviewees were among the small minority who became upwardly mobile in the expansion of the electronics industry during the late 1960s.

The electronics industry in the area surrounding New York City is much different. There were just over 300 firms in the New York metropolitan area in 1980, but their number had burgeoned to 680 by 1990. Most of the firms studied by Saskia Sassen and Maria Patricia Fernández Kelly were small, with work forces under 100, and independently owned (often having been started by engineers formerly employed in larger, more traditional firms). They tended to specialize in communications equipment and electronic components, designing and customizing their products. Some employed no women, but in about half of them the labor force was 50 percent female; very few Hispanics were employed by these companies; about one-third subcontracted to homeworkers (Fernández Kelly and Sassen 1991:129, 36–45).

In Los Angeles, by contrast, firms were much larger, and their labor forces were 60 to 70 percent female and 32 to 57 percent Hispanic. Furthermore, a significant proportion of workers (30 to 43 percent) were foreign-born Hispanics, and 10 to 20 percent were Asian.[4] They paid hourly wages ranging between $6.69 and $7.93. About half of the firms customized their products; some 40 percent subcontracted out to small independent companies or specialty houses; and about one-third had arrangements with offshore production plants in Mexico or Pacific Rim countries. Homeworkers were used by about 10 percent of the firms in a random sample of seventy-eight and by 30 percent of a smaller purposive sample (Fernández Kelly and Sassen 1991:58–67).[5] Fernández Kelly and Sassen argue that in both the small New York firms and the larger Los Angeles companies, flexibility and customizing are strategies for surviving in a fast-changing

---

[4] Fernández Kelly and Sassen use the term "Hispanic" to cover Spanish-surnamed women in both New York and California. We assume that most native-born Hispanic women workers in Los Angeles are Mexican Americans and that most foreign-born Hispanics are *Mexicanas*; in New York, Hispanics are likely to be Puerto Ricans, Dominicans, Colombians or other Latin Americans.

[5] The California sample of 100 firms contained a random sample of seventy-three, a purposive sample A of thirteen firms traced from the files of the Wage and Hour Division, where complaints had been lodged, and a purposive sample B of ten larger firms that were defense related. Our figures here indicate the range of data from these three very different subsamples.

[10]

market, where many firms specialize or are links between larger manufacturers and retail customers. The results are informalization of the labor market, increased homework, and a tendency to recruit Hispanic and Asian workers.

If Silicon Valley is one model, New York stands out as a second, a model in which the industry is in the early stages of development, and women—particularly new immigrant women—are yet to be fully incorporated in the labor force. Los Angeles, a third model, is a variant of the Silicon Valley model, though without the large commitment to research and development and its attendant highly paid male labor force. Some of the conclusions emphasized by those studying Los Angeles and the Silicon Valley (the exploitative, low-wage nature of electronics and apparel jobs, the paternalistic views of managers regarding women's work, and so on) may be a product of the particular nature of these industries in Los Angeles and Santa Clara County as much as of the theoretical perspectives of the authors. In addition, though wages of about $7.00 an hour may seem low in Los Angeles, Silicon Valley, or New York, in the Southwest they are substantially above the minimum and much better than wages available in the service sector.

Our data from Albuquerque suggest a fourth model, one in which women working in electronics and apparel production occupy a relatively privileged place in the local working class. In Albuquerque, industrial restructuring brought new branch plants of electronics and apparel firms to an economy otherwise largely dominated by government, military, and service employers. In the early 1980s these plants employed a predominantly female labor force, adding an industrial component to the increasing population of women workers. The 200 to 1,000 employees in each plant were largely involved in industrial production itself, rather than highly technical research and development. The work force was not an immigrant one but consisted primarily of high-school-educated, English-speaking Mexican-American and Anglo workers, the majority of whom were women. Within the larger Albuquerque economy, male jobs in construction and services were much more vulnerable than female jobs in new industrial plants, despite periods of layoffs and job instability.

The economic forces that encouraged firms to build new plants in Albuquerque in the 1970s and early 1980s not only created new work-places for women but pushed them to construct new arrangements within and understandings of family life. Technology changed

[11]

the nature of women's paid work, and "participative management" innovations in some plants created a new language of management-worker relations and a new organization of the work process. Our study particularly focuses on how women reacted to these new work-places.

Among Albuquerque's working families a woman's increasing full-time labor-force participation and her wage packet created the material base for a changing division of labor in the household. Families as well as work environments became "new places." Child care was no longer primarily the responsibility of mothers but was shared with husbands, grandmothers, or sisters or delegated to babysitters and formal child-care centers. Housework might remain chiefly in the hands of the wife (creating a double day) or, more typically, be shared with a husband. These new patterns of housework, child care, and social networking are the second major focus of this book.

Our study grows out of previous research on dual-worker families by Lamphere and Zavella. Lamphere (1987) examined the lives of immigrant women of Portuguese and Colombian background employed in industrial jobs in Central Falls, Rhode Island, during the 1970s; Zavella (1987) investigated the incorporation of Chicanas into the part-time, seasonal cannery labor force in the Santa Clara Valley of California. We still focus here on the relationship between work and family and view women as active agents; however, in Albuquerque we did not study immigrant or part-time women workers, and we found among younger mothers more commitment to the labor force and greater changes in family. Since we conducted this research in an area and within industries of expansion rather than decline, we have been able to examine new trends in the shaping of workplaces and home life that were not factors in our previous research. Finally, having built a comparison between Anglos and Mexican Americans into the study design and interviewed both men and women, we are much better able to theorize about the intersection of race/ethnicity, class, and gender than we were in our initial studies.

Refining the Social Location of Working Mothers

Our interviewees were working class in terms of their parents' occupations, their education, and their jobs at the time of our interviews; beyond these factors, however, their location within the working class was more complex. We selected working mothers who were semiskilled operatives, allowing the husbands' occupations to vary in the case of married couples and including a group of single mothers. One outcome of such a research strategy was to open up to investigation the issue of variability within the working class; another was to emphasize the importance of marital status in shaping women's lives.

We categorized households in four different segments of the working class, depending on the woman's level of income relative to the wages of her husband (if any). Most of the women we interviewed were earning between $5.00 and $6.50 an hour in 1982. In some families the husbands were earning almost twice as much, making women "secondary providers."[6] In others, women earned about the same wages as their husbands, making them "coproviders." In a third set of households wives were "mainstay providers," working at the more stable job with better benefits and often earning more than their husbands. Finally, single mothers were "sole providers" for themselves and their children. These differences gave women very different abilities to affect the household division of labor.

Although class and marital status combined to create real economic differences in women's situations, ethnicity did not always create divergent responses. We argue throughout this book that even when a woman's ethnic heritage places her in a social world composed of those of similar ethnic background, her behavioral strategies at work and at home often converge with and parallel those of women of different ethnic backgrounds. Albuquerque women workers in electronics and apparel plants were being recruited largely from populations of Spanish-surnamed natives of New Mexico (Hispanos) and of white Americans, many of whom were recent migrants to the state (Anglos).[7]

Working mothers in our study thus came from two very different cultural backgrounds. The Hispanas were, for the most part, mono-

---

[6] The term "secondary provider" is derived from Hood (1983) to indicate that women's contribution to family income is significantly (usually at least 30 percent) less than their spouses' income. We do not wish to imply that the women's wages were "pin money" or not important.

[7] New Mexico is regarded as a state with three traditions: "Spanish," "Anglo," and "Indian." Because blacks, Asians, and Native Americans—primarily Pueblo and Navajo—make up only a small proportion of these sunbelt women workers, however, we decided to focus on the two dominant populations.

[13]

lingual English speakers with a Spanish-speaking, Catholic heritage. Most had been raised in an urban environment, but many of their parents came from small rural communities where kin still lived. The Anglo women were primarily from English-speaking, Protestant, and non–New Mexican backgrounds. These differences were reinforced by the fact that their social networks were chiefly composed of people from their own ethnic heritage.[8] Thus, to some degree, there is a cultural and social basis for arguing that these are two distinct ethnic or racial populations within the Albuquerque working class.

We use the notion of social location to contextualize the position of our Anglo and Hispano interviewees as subjects. On the one hand, we emphasize the distinctiveness of the Albuquerque political economy, relative to Silicon Valley, New York, and Los Angeles; on the other, within the Albuquerque political economy we see how class, gender, ethnicity, and marital status come together to shape women's lives. Patterns thus generated are the structures within which women's contrasting experiences are constructed; conversely, where women and men of different ethnic backgrounds are brought together within the same occupational and class structures, the commonality of experience and the possibility of converging understandings are brought to the fore. The construction of difference is complex and problematic; if we are to understand the development of both diverging and converging behaviors and ideologies, we need to make explicit comparisons between women of different backgrounds as they interact within similar structural constraints. Our analytic strategy is to build a framework around an examination of the contradictions women face in combining work and family lives, emphasizing praxis or the behavioral strategies they have developed to put together these very separate spheres.

Contradictions: The Relationship between Work and Family

The increased incorporation of mothers into the paid labor force has brought with it a number of contradictions. Some shape the lives

---

[8] Seven of our couples were intermarried (one spouse being Hispano, the other Anglo), and their networks were more ethnically heterogeneous. Three Hispanas were married to Mexican immigrants; these women were better able to speak Spanish, and their networks comprised New Mexican Hispanos, Mexican immigrants, and their husband's kin in Mexico.

of working-class working mothers in general; others were particular to industrial workplaces as they developed in sunbelt economies in the 1980s. In other words, some processes we describe may be more generalized than those of "sunbelt industrialization," but they were being played out in a particular local economy which in turn generated other strategies and practices that may be found only in similar situations.

The contradictions faced by working women in Albuquerque plants were multilayered. In the first place, capitalist industrialization from the 1790s on created a disjunction between the domain of work and the world of the home. There are *two* domains, but workers, including women, live *one* life that must bridge and subvert those separate arenas. Work for wages takes place in one environment during a regulated period of time and under the control of others. Family life is situated primarily in another environment, the home. Although productive arrangements (the hours worked, the shift assigned, and so on) and the level of wages have a significant impact on the family schedule and budget, family life is constructed out of different relationships—those between husbands and wives, single mothers and their kin or roommates, parents and children. Thus our framework must encompass both domains, much as a woman's life as worker and mother is of one piece yet must be sensitive to two different organizational bases.

Second, the recent incorporation of mothers into the paid labor force has meant that women are trying to fulfill contradictory roles. Historically, this was not the case: different members of a family tended to focus their efforts on either productive or reproductive labor but did not try to combine the two in equal proportions.[9] Fathers and their unmarried children were usually the wage workers in the United States until World War II, with the very important exception of black mothers, who (along with some Asian and Mexican immigrants) have always engaged in productive labor. Productive and reproductive labor was allocated to different individuals within most families. Although working husbands, sons, and daughters did

---

[9] Productive labor involves the creation of goods or products for either use or exchange. In a capitalist system, workers produce goods in exchange for a wage paid by an employer who owns the means of production. Reproduction involves the labor needed to reproduce the means of production, a labor force, and the social relations of production. Contemporary families are the site of most of the reproductive labor involved in replacing the labor force, including housework and child care.

[15]

some reproductive labor, most was done by mothers (see Lamphere 1987). Since World War II, however, increasing numbers of mothers have entered the paid labor force, and during the 1980s the proportion of working mothers with preschool children grew dramatically. That the mothers in our Albuquerque study did not drop out of the labor force after their children were born indicates a new level of commitment to the world of work.

This generation of young working mothers has taken on two roles that are contradictory in that each assumes a full-time commitment: forty to forty-five hours in the workplace and a substantial number of hours for housework and the care of small children. An increased commitment to one role can undermine the the other. For example, if a woman leaves work early for a child's doctor's appointment, calls in sick to take care of a child, or worries about her home responsibilities while on the job, her paid work may suffer. Likewise, a full-time job may mean that housework does not get done, that women are not there to nurture a child's first steps, and that routine child care must be left to someone else. To mediate these contradictions, the women we interviewed were negotiating complex relationships with their husbands and other women, including mothers, babysitters, and friends. Often, a husband's or wife's explicit set of ideas surrounding the appropriate division of labor (an ideology about housework or child care) was in contradiction to actual practice. With day care, women felt the contradictory pull of both work and motherhood and this contradiction remained unresolved. But, once staying employed became a given, there was less of a contradiction between a woman's sense of ideal day-care and the practical arrangements she was able to make.

The participative management policies of some workplaces in Albuquerque created new contradictions. On the one hand, such policies call on American notions of participation and democracy, and often redefine management-worker relations as well. Plant managers have an "open door" to hear an employee's view of problems. Supervisors become "facilitators", rather than bosses, and workers become members of "teams" rather than employees of a "department." On the other hand, management still controls the major decisions about hiring and firing and continues to extract high levels of production from employees. As in the division of household labor, we found a contradiction between ideology and practice. In the household this contradiction was sometimes left intact, an inconsistency that re-

[16]

mained unresolved as couples sorted out their everyday lives. In the workplace, however, ideology often covered over and obscured hierarchical relations, and only through the practice of everyday life on the shop floor could workers see through management's conception of the firm and either accept or resist its various aspects.

This book explores these multiple layers of contradiction—between work and family, between the roles of worker and mother, between ideology and practice in constructing a household division of labor, and between management ideology and practice on the shop floor—in order to understand the complex ways in which working women construct their lives.

Practice Anthropology

Our approach is that of "practice anthropology," viewing women's behavior at work and at home as "praxis": the outcome of experience, of day-by-day trial and error in pushing against and coping with the requirements of a particular job, negotiating with a husband over housework, or dealing with the demands of a child. We see women as active agents who develop strategies for managing their everyday lives.

The emphasis on praxis in anthropological analysis derives from several sources. British anthropologists (Barth 1959; Firth 1962; Gluckman 1955; Leach 1954; Turner 1957) began to revise structural functionalism in the late 1950s and 1960s, viewing actors as using norms and rules in social situations to achieve political ends. Rather than seeing social structure as fully determining behavior, these theorists inserted human intentionality between social structure and actual decisions, events, and what Firth called the social organization: that is, social structure as actually worked out and practiced "on the ground." An emphasis on strategies, alliances, coalitions, and the creation of social networks were all part of the transactional anthropology that developed out of this break with traditional structural functionalism.

In addition, scholars have revived Marx's notion of praxis: "Praxis means man's [sic] conscious shaping of the changing historical conditions. . . . praxis revolutionizes existing reality through human action" (Avineri 1968:138–39). Or, as Marx himself put it: "The coincidence of the changing of circumstances and of human activity or

[17]

self-changing can only be grasped and rationally understood as revolutionary *practice*. . . . All social life is essentially *practical*. All the mysteries which lead theory towards mysticism find their rational solution in human practice and the comprehension of this practice" (1845:68–69). E. P. Thompson's classic study of the English working class shows class formation as an active, ongoing historical process in which the "we" forged by English workers came to stand united against "them": "The notion of class entails the notion of historical relationship. Like any other relationship, it is a fluency which evades analysis if we attempt to stop it dead at any given moment and anatomize its structure" (1966:9). Likewise, in proposing a theory of structuration as a way of understanding praxis or a treatment of "situated practices," Giddens argues for a mutual dependence of agency and structure: "Rules and resources are drawn upon by actors in the production of interaction, but are thereby also reconstituted through such interaction" (1979:71). Both these writers, a historian and a sociologist, have developed the idea of praxis through emphasizing the ongoing, processual nature of human interaction.

A third influence has been Pierre Bourdieu's theory of practice. Using the notion of "habitus" to describe the "durably installed generative principle of regulated improvisations," Bourdieu argues, like Giddens, that agency and structure have a dialectical relationship. "Through the habitus, the structure which has produced it governs practice, not by the processes of a mechanical determinism, but through the mediation of the orientations and limits it assigns to the habitus's operations of invention" (1977:78, 94).

Sherry Ortner, citing the work of Bourdieu, Sahlins, and others, calls practice anthropology a new trend that gathered "force and coherence" in the 1980s. Ortner acknowledges the influence of Marx: "The newer practice theorists . . . share a view that 'the system' . . . does in fact have very powerful, even 'determining' effect upon human action and the shape of events" (1984:146): hence the emphasis on constraint and hegemony. Yet there has also been an incorporation of the Weberian framework, placing the actor at the center of the model. The system shapes practice, but in Ortner's view, practice also shapes the system. Renato Rosaldo's *Culture and Truth* (1989) presents a recent vision of practice anthropology stressing the nuances of everyday life as worked out by members of a culture and "the border crossings" actors make, moving back and forth between different cultural and social milieus.

[18]

Feminist anthropologists have also had a role in developing a practice approach, beginning with Jane Collier's emphasis on women's strategies within family groups, which in patrilineal systems have the impact of undermining male power and creating a niche for women's interests. "Women are the worms within the apple of a patrilocal domestic group. They work to advance the fortunes of particular individuals—their sons and husbands—in a social system where men are taught to put group interests before private ones. . . . Men work to bind lineage mates together; women work to tear them apart" (1974:92). Wolf (1974) and Lamphere (1974), also noted women's strategies and the ways they may run counter to those of men.

More recently, Collier and Rosaldo (1981) and Ortner and Whitehead (1981) have developed this emphasis on practice by opening up the category of "women" to include women in different kin statuses (mothers, sisters, wives, daughters), and have more consciously examined the structures that shape gender relations in particular societies. Collier (1988) has paid particular attention to marriage systems as they shape the relations of different categories of women to a variety of males. Sylvia Yanagisako's research (1989) on capitalist firms also represents a newer emphasis on the importance of structure within which practice takes place. She sees male owners of Italian silk firms and their wives as having opposing sets of interests when firms are in the process of choosing a new generation of managers. Their strategies are not just individually forged by autonomous women and men, however; rather, they emerge from differing gender constructions of the family, the unit that owns the firm and must deal with the issue of inheritance and succession. Thus among feminist anthropologists there has been more recent attention to structure and system and to the variability of women's practice—their activities, strategies, "moves" and intentions, depending on their location in a particular structure.

This book encompasses both work and family but acknowledges their different bases of organization. The capitalist economic system structures the basic organization of industrial work life, since owners and managers hire the productive labor of their employees. Entering the labor force (that is, allocating one's productive labor to wage work) further structures one's reproductive labor: the particular times that can be allocated to eating, sleeping, child rearing, and other activities that reproduce one's own and one's family's labor power. Capitalist industry also separates the two spheres: the work-

[19]

place, where productive labor is utilized; and the home, where reproductive labor is allocated. Corporations and managers have more hegemonic control of the system that operates in the workplace. Workers (both men and women) have more flexibility in constructing the home and family. Thus, in building a practice approach to sunbelt industrialization, we emphasize notions of control and resistance in the workplace, and characterize by a wider range of strategies (negotiation, implicit understandings, passive resistance, and silence) the practice of constructing a dual-worker home life. This is not a strict dichotomy: we find some negotiations, implicit understandings, and consent in the workplace, and some use of the tactics of resistance in family life.

In the workplace, women confront a system of control. Their strategies involve, on the one hand, resisting efforts to extract labor from them and attempts to control the conditions of their work and, on the other, developing positive understandings about their work, often appreciating new participative management policies, for example, but weighing them together with other aspects of the job. For some women this means "buying into" and accepting management ideology: that is, the company's construction of work, management-worker relations, and the organization of the workplace. Other women retain more distance from management's viewpoint, positively evaluating some policies but constructing their view of work out of their own specific jobs, relations with particular supervisors, and the relevance of leisure activities, benefit packages, and organizational policies to their own circumstances. We argue that a language of resistance is appropriate to understanding women's reaction to contradiction in the workplace but that the dialectal relations between management and workers may take various forms. Resistance may involve primarily individual tactics, erupt into a union drive, or become subordinate to processes of consent to or distance from management.

At home, mediating the contradiction between their roles as mothers, wives, and workers involves replacing their reproductive labor. First and foremost this means finding someone to care for their children while they are at work. Some women, by working on shifts different from those of their spouses, rely on their husbands to provide parental care and nurturance. Other women reach out of the household toward mothers or mothers-in-law, babysitters, or day-care centers. The replacement of other reproductive labor—child-care tasks at home, cleaning, cooking, laundry, and other chores—evolves in relationship to husbands and children. For single mothers, it may entail relations with a coresident parent, sibling, or roommate rather than with a spouse. For working-class women, either tasks are reallocated within the household, or women continue to do them themselves in addition to their wage work. Our interviewees did not reach outside the household to hire others (domestic cleaners) or to pay for services (laundry, prepared foods) to replace their own household labor.

We have avoided viewing the family as an arena in which women confront a system of control (often labeled patriarchal control). Our interviewees were full-time participants in the labor force and thus stood in the same relationship to the political economy as their husbands. Most married women earned almost as much as their husbands (relatively few were "secondary" wage earners), and single mothers were the sole supporters of their children. These women were not struggling to wrest control from economically dominant husbands, but differences in their relative economic contribution to the household did influence the division of labor in housework and child care. We discovered a range of practices, from letting things "just happen" to open contestation with husbands.

Finally, we examined extra-household sources of occasional support. These working mothers used concrete exchanges among kin and friends to meet practical needs: borrowing money, obtaining transportation, trading clothes and babysitting—exchanges that may characterize the practice of women outside the paid labor force as well. Others, such as getting help for a sick child, obtaining a ride to work, and finding support in a work-related problem, were specific to the needs of working women. Emotional and general social support—finding someone to talk to about financial problems, marital concerns, child-care issues—was also a function of extra-household networks of female friends and kin. While most studies of working-class or minority women focus on the importance of kin networks (Bott 1957; Stack 1974), our study also reveals the importance of friends, particularly work-related friends, and particularly for the Hispanas in our sample.

The Context of Ethnicity

We debated long and hard about the appropriate term to use for the Spanish-surnamed interviewees in this study. No choice would

have satisfied all of our potential readers; there is no term that both
fits the labels our interviewees applied to themselves *and* places
them within the discourse of scholars who have studied Mexican-
American populations in the United States. Very few of our interviewees called themselves Chicano, *Mexicano*, or Mexican American. Most considered themselves "Spanish" or "Spanish American"
(terms they used interchangeably). But for most scholars those terms
erase the Indian and Mexican mestizo heritage of northern New
Mexican Hispano populations and carry a conservative political con-
notation. We were particularly uncomfortable with these terms because they highlight only the European aspects of a colonial system
which, in addition to being highly stratified, included a great deal of
cultural and racial mixing (see Dozier 1970). The label "Hispanic" has
been criticized as primarily a census category, a term applied to all
Spanish-surnamed individuals in the United States (including Puerto
Ricans, Cubans, Dominicans, and Nicaraguans) and implying a sense
of homogeneity that masks the diversity of national background, regional specificity, and class.[10] The anthropological and sociological literature typically uses Mexican American or Chicano, but our interviewees themselves felt uncomfortable with these terms.

We particularly want to stress the importance of regional diversity
in describing differences among Spanish-speaking populations of
Mexican heritage in the Southwest. The population of northern and
central New Mexico, as well as southern Colorado, is culturally distinct from those of Texas, Arizona, and California, partly because of
the historical roots of the Hispano population in New Mexico during
the colonial period are different and partly because migration from
Mexico has had less impact in the last forty years than in Texas and
California. Scholars of northern New Mexico have long used the
term "Hispano" to capture the regional distinctiveness of this area
(Arellano and Vigil 1985; Burma 1954; Galarza 1972; Perrigo 1985;
Winnie 1960).

In the end we decided to use the terms "Mexican American" and
"Hispano" interchangeably throughout the book to convey both the
regional distinctiveness of the heritage of most of our interviewees
and their class connection with other urban working-class popula-

---

[10] In 1991 the National Association for Chicano Studies passed a resolution con-
demning the use of "Hispanic" and advocating "Chicano" (*Noticias de NACS* 9(3),
1991). Neither term was used by many of our interviewees.

[22]

tions of Mexican heritage. The former is perhaps the most "neutral" etic term to denote New Mexicans of Spanish-Mexican heritage; the latter gives a sense of regional difference without invoking the Iberian-centered census category Hispanic.

In New Mexico, members of white ethnic groups that do not have a Spanish-speaking heritage are considered "Anglos" (Indians, blacks, and Asians are separately categorized). The term's meaning dates from the period of American rule, beginning in 1848, and the juxtaposition of this new dominant group to the Indian and Spanish-Mexican village dwellers. As the economy has been transformed and larger numbers of white Americans have been drawn to New Mexico from the Midwest, West, and Southeast, the population covered by the category "Anglo" has become increasingly heterogeneous. The term now collapses into one category ethnic distinctions that are often recognized in other parts of the country. Few of our Anglo interviewees were born in Albuquerque and, quite understandably, were often uncomfortable with the label, since it did not capture the content of their own submerged European ethnic histories. Yet in other parts of the West or Midwest, our interviewees would be considered white Americans, so we often use the term "white" interchangeably with "Anglo" to indicate the way white ethnicity is ambiguously constructed in the Southwest. To convey our interviewees' own sense of identity, however, we also we indicate how particular working mothers and their spouses label and identify themselves (see below).

Historically, the relationship between Anglos and Hispanos is what Lieberson calls migrant superordination and indigenous subordination (1961:904–5). Since the American defeat of Mexico in 1848, successive waves of American immigrants have gained increasing economic and political power within New Mexico as, first, a territory and later a state. The term "Hispano" designates not only a current population but the culture of the village system that dates back to the Spanish colonial settlement of the seventeenth and eighteenth centuries. Albuquerque was founded in 1706 by New Mexico's provincial governor and became the center of a string of villages along the Rio Grande, including Los Duranes, Los Candelarias, Los Griegos, Alameda, and Bernalillo to the north and Barelas, San Jose, Atrisco, Parajito, and Los Padillas to the south. The majority of the Spanish colonial population was centered in Santa Fe and Taos and in the villages located in the mountains and valleys of what are now Taos and Rio Arriba counties. The largely agrarian villages both in the

[23]

north and near Albuquerque survived through the 1930s. But during the Depression and World War II, many residents began to migrate from villages in the north, and those in the Albuquerque area became wage workers in sawmills, dairies, and meatpacking plants and on sheep ranches. After World War II, with the expansion of Anglo Albuquerque, the villages of the north and south Valley were engulfed by the city or brought into the sphere of its economic influence (Gonzales 1993a).

In the early twentieth century a fledgling Hispano middle class emerged. Excluded from the world of business, it took root in the professions: law, education, journalism, and politics. Hispanos adopted the term Spanish American not only to distance themselves from recent Mexican immigrants but to protest the discrimination and racism they experienced in education, politics, and the economy (Gonzales 1986, 1993b). Though Hispanos still hold important offices in state and city government and are a powerful voting block, particularly in northern New Mexico, they have less economic power than Anglos and are often in the position of a minority group in schools, universities, workplaces, and other institutions. With the twentieth-century growth of Albuquerque, Santa Fe, and Las Vegas, Hispanos have also become increasingly urbanized and acculturated to American norms and values, including the use of English in everyday life as well as in the schoolroom and workplace. Immigrants from Mexico and those who have relocated from California and Texas have had to adjust to the long-established relations between indigenous Hispano residents and Anglos.

Our Mexican-American sample reflects the Hispano history of New Mexico. The parents of working mothers and their spouses came largely from traditional Spanish village settlements.[11] Of the twenty-three Hispanas born in Albuquerque, thirteen of their mothers (57 percent) and fourteen of their fathers (61 percent) were born in small towns and villages in New Mexico, and one mother in a dominantly Hispano town in southern Colorado (an area considered part of the northern New Mexico or Hispano cultural region). Six mothers (26 percent) and six fathers (26 percent) were born in Albuquerque, and two mothers (9 percent) in other states. Although their parents came from rural areas, our interviewees were primarily urban. Be-

---

[11] For current perspectives on the Spanish-American village heritage, see Briggs (1988); Briggs and Van Ness (1987); deBuys (1985); Kutsche and Van Ness (1979).

sides the twenty-three of the thirty-seven Hispanas interviewed (62 percent) who were born in Albuquerque, five others were raised there.

In contrast to the Hispanas, eleven (69 percent) of the sixteen Anglo women interviewed were born outside New Mexico, mostly in states in the West and Midwest. Four (25 percent) were born in Albuquerque, and one in Gallup, New Mexico. Of the twelve not born in Albuquerque, three had spent a significant part of their childhood there; the other nine had come as adults. In other words, Anglo women were predominantly migrants to the state; Hispanas were primarily native to Albuquerque or migrants from rural New Mexico.

Yancey, Ericksen, and Juliani (1976:392) argue that ethnicity is not constituted in terms of a traditional culture existing through time but is rather a temporally variable and emergent product of group position in the social structure: Ethnic groups have been produced by structural conditions which are intimately linked to the changing technology of industrial production and transportation. . . . ethnicity, defined in terms of frequent patterns of association and identification with common origins, is crystallized under conditions which reinforce the maintenance of kinship and friendship networks." For the Mexican-American working mothers we interviewed, ethnicity was linked to a long, extensive Hispano background but significantly interwoven with working-class status and urban residence. Our white interviewees had no clear identity with a region or ethnic heritage, but their class situation and urban experiences as for our Hispano sample, were a common thread in the lives of these families. These differences and similarities were reflected in where the two groups lived, the language they used in everyday life, and their conceptions of ethnic identity.

Residential Location

Yancey, Ericksen, and Juliani (1976:392–94) point out that in an earlier phase of development in the northeastern part of the United States, European ethnic communities were reinforced by concentration in neighborhood enclaves that surrounded industrial work sites (see also Lamphere 1987). Later, with increasing dependence on automobile transportation, there was no longer a correlation between plant location and an immediately surrounding labor pool. Sunbelt plants are scattered throughout Albuquerque next to freeways, and

[25]

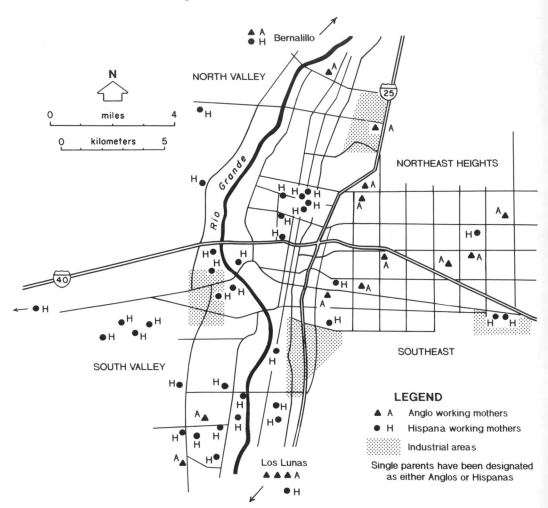

Map 1. Distribution of Hispana and Anglo working mothers in Albuquerque

they recruit from a citywide labor force. Although some women may eventually move to the same quadrant of the city as their employers, many drive 10 to 15 miles to work each day.

The Mexican Americans we interviewed lived primarily in areas of Albuquerque known as the North Valley and South Valley, the Anglos in the Northeast Heights, the northeastern quadrant of the city (see Map 1). But this was no clear-cut distinction. Some Hispano families lived in tight-knit, traditional Hispano communities along the Rio Grande such as Old Town (near the downtown), San José (in the South Valley) and Bernalillo (15 miles north of Albuquerque); others lived in mobile homes or apartments in the South Valley, small homes on the West Mesa, or occasionally in an apartment in the Southeast Heights. Some Anglos lived in the North or South Valley, in Los Lunas, or in the Southeast, usually in mobile homes or newer apartment complexes. Some were purchasing or building small houses, and two or three of the most affluent couples lived in substantial ranch-style homes. This dispersed pattern of residence for Hispanos and Anglos meant that few could identify with a neighborhood community.

The Importance of Language

Language usage and linguistic heritage more clearly demarcated the Hispano and Anglo samples than did residence patterns. Anglos were English speakers and used English at home. A small minority had parents or grandparents who spoke a different language, and one was a Greek immigrant. Thus, Anne Singleton's parents were French citizens, born in Paris, who migrated to Albuquerque, where their daughter was born and raised in an English-speaking environment. Vera Chandler was Greek and migrated to the United States to marry her husband, a second-generation Greek American. Both these women were raising their children as English speakers. For a few others, knowledge of a non-English language was a reality only for their grandparents.

Our Mexican-American sample was also primarily English-speaking: thirty-three of the 37 Hispanas interviewed (89 percent) either had only a slight ability to speak or understand Spanish, or did not speak it at all. Four women did speak Spanish at home and were fluent in the language; one of these was from Mexico, and the other three were married to Mexican immigrants. Only the Mexican immigrant was interviewed in Spanish. Yet Spanish was an important part of our interviewees' family and regional heritage. Thirty-two of fifty-one Hispano husbands and wives indicated that it was the primary language of parents or grandparents or was still spoken in the company of their kin. Most said that their children were learning some Spanish, often from grandparents or in the school system.

[27]

Manuel Perez, for example said, "We're leaving that up to . . . my parents. Their Spanish is better than ours." Thus, Spanish had more significance for them than any foreign language had for our Anglo interviewees.

Ethnic Identity

A plurality of our Hispano interviewees—twenty-three (62 percent) of the women and eight (31 percent) of the men—preferred to identify themselves ethnically as "Spanish" or "Spanish-American." "Spanish-Mexican," "New Mexican," "Mexican-American," and "Tex-Mex" were given by one woman each. "Hispanic," "Chicano," "Mexican," and "*Mexicana*" were selected by two interviewees. One husband emphasized that he was New Mexican. Four men each chose "Chicano"; three used "*Mexicano*"; and "Spanish-speaking," "Mexican-American" and "Mexican" were preferred by one husband each.[12]

Interviewees were sensitive about labeling themselves and uncomfortable about defining the meaning of ethnic terms (Gonzales 1991). Commonly, they asked for clarification of the question and then stumbled in the responses. Delores Baca, though active in the church-sponsored Bernalillo feast day celebrations and closely connected to Hispano village traditions, was reluctant to use any one label to identify herself: "Uh, I've never been asked that before. I'd say I'm 'Spanish-Mexican,' 'Mexican-Spanish,' whatever." When referring to the appropriate label for others, some interviewees indicated fear of saying the wrong thing. Daniel Leyba, who was born in Raton, New Mexico, and grew up in Albuquerque, identified himself as "Spanish" but expressed caution: "Uh, I don't know. I would play it by ear. Some people get offended real easy. I wouldn't know what to call 'em, there's so many different names, you know. There's some directly from Mexico. There's others from Spain. I guess I usually say Spanish people. That's a hard one. That's the best I can do."

Part of this sensitivity to labels seemed related to the fact that Mexicans and New Mexican Hispanos are often placed within the same social category. Deeper probing revealed that the term "Span-

---

[12] In New Mexico, public ethnic identification is voiced primarily by a small Hispano middle class (represented, for example, by the Hispano Chamber of Commerce) and by Spanish-surnamed ethnic entrepreneurs and politicians who articulate an ideology of affirmative action (Gonzales 1992b).

ish" first of all functioned to distinguish Hispanos from Mexican immigrants. Generally this contrast focused on cultural or socioeconomic differences such as language and place of birth. For example, Margaret Olguin, who identified herself as Spanish-speaking, said, "Spanish-American is born here in America. . . . I don't know how to say it. I don't know. Mexicans to me are different than what we are, because our language is different. I don't know how to explain." A small minority indicated that they felt superior to Mexicans. As Macky Garduño, who identified himself as Spanish and whose father comes from a Placitas land grant family, said, "Just the word 'Mexican' itself bugs me. . . . It makes me feel . . . low, I guess. I just don't like the word 'Mexican.'" (Macky, it might be mentioned, had an Anglo spouse.) His response conveyed the denigration of Mexicans within New Mexico that he wanted to avoid. Others felt some class identification with Mexicans. Albert Baca, who saw himself as a Chicano, said, "I feel like I'm part of the same people because I'm poor like them, you know, we're poor; we're not rich. [But] no, because I was born here, and we have different ways of living than they do in Mexico."

A second function of the label was to differentiate Mexican Americans from other ethnic or racial groups. Josephine Perez said, "[Spanish is] a person who's not Anglo or not Indian or not black." Sometimes this differentiation was made in terms of racial features or notions of "blood." Lucy Valdez, one of the many who identified herself as "Spanish" thought that the term "Mexican" meant "dark-complected people. I mean, not black, but brown-complected people— how should I put it?" Marta Ortiz, a self-identified Chicana, whose husband was born in Mexico, considered Spanish people those who had "Spanish blood." The term "Spanish-American" also referred to aspects of Hispano nativity and cultural heritage. Larry Valdez, another interviewee who was born in Raton and grew up in Albuquerque, identified himself as Spanish-American. He defined Spanish Americans as "born in the United States, and they're not true Mexicans, but I guess we're descendants from way back then . . . from Mexico or Spain."

Finally, several people could not or did not define what the terms meant. For example, Soccoro Peña, born and raised in Española, originally a northern New Mexican market center, could only say, "I am what I am, and I'm Spanish."

We interpret these findings to mean that Hispano sunbelt workers have an ethnic identity that is greatly mitigated by their working-

[29]

class position. They are aware of their membership in a non-Anglo social category and the possible disapprobation that may be thrust upon them. The use of "Spanish" or "Spanish-American" as a categorical marker, emphasizing difference and distinguishing Hispanos from Mexicans on the one hand and from Anglos, Indians, and blacks on the other, is similar in function to the use of "Mexican-American" in other regions of the United States. But equally important, New Mexicans explain the meaning of the category in a cultural and historical context that is particular to New Mexico.

Members of our Anglo sample gave us responses that also indicated their sensitivity to ethnic categories and how they might be applied. Our non-Hispanic sample was extremely diverse. We interviewed working mothers who identified themselves as Greek, French, German, Finnish, "hillbilly," and of other white ethnic backgrounds. Yet when asked if they had a distinctive ethnic heritage, apart from basic American customs and values, thirteen of the sixteen women (81 percent) said "no." Some women stressed the mixed nature of their ancestry. Karen Smith, who was born in Idaho and raised in a military family throughout twenty-two states, said, "The first time somebody asked me what my ethnic background was, I came home and asked Daddy, and he told me 'Heinz 57'." Mary Pike, born in Gallup, New Mexico, said, "We have a lot of ethnic heritage. I'm a little bit of everything. . . . I know that I'm German, Scottish, Irish, Italian, Danish, Slavic." Sally Hall, also from a military family, said, "I know I'm Irish and Swedish . . . blond-haired, green eyes or blue eyes . . . It's kind of obvious . . . fair-skinned and freckled here." Even the three women who expressed the greatest connection to ethnic customs said that it had been broken by migration or divorce.

Like their wives, few white American husbands emphasized an ethnic identity. Ten of the twelve men interviewed indicated that they had no specific heritage; one discussed his Greek-American background, and another stressed the importance of his identity as a Mormon. And although "Anglo" has a certain ideological resonance in the public arena of such states as New Mexico, Texas, and Arizona, many white Americans, especially those who have recently migrated to the Southwest, feel ambivalent about identifying as a member of this category.

Regardless of how they identified themselves, both Anglo and Mexican-American working mothers constructed their social networks—primarily female and composed of kin and friends—from members of their own ethnic category and class. Their daily experiences and social worlds revolved around family, kin, and work and church activities that were predominantly either Spanish *or* Anglo but not a mixture. The few exceptions were women who began to choose friends of a different ethnic background at work, and women who had married men from another ethnic heritage. Although there was some variability, then, working mothers were immersed in ethnic social worlds and had ethnically distinct support networks.

Throughout this book we compare the divergent and convergent strategies of Anglo and Hispana working mothers, being particularly concerned both with variability within each ethnic category and with similarities and differences across categories. We want to examine the way women mediate the contradictions of full-time employment and motherhood, not by creating a unidimensional contrast between Anglos, on the one hand, and Hispanas, on the other, but by exploring the full complexity and diversity of women's own ways of dealing with the problems they face on the job, the demands of housework, and the need for child care and social support.

Our interviews provide a rich sense of the diverse practices developed by working women and their husbands and by single mothers. From these data we work toward an analysis of the interpenetration of seemingly separate spheres, examining the construction of gender and ethnic difference as women's methods of coping with contradiction are shaped by the different social locations of Anglo and Mexican-American working mothers within Albuquerque's working class.

[2]

The Context of Sunbelt
Industrialization

By Peter Evans

To understand the contradictions working mothers face, one must begin with an analysis of the local political economy. It is this macroeconomic environment that shapes the availability of jobs for women and their husbands and sets the wage rates in particular occupations. The expansion and decline of different sectors of the local economy affects women and men differently, thus influencing dynamics inside a dual-worker household and setting the parameters for a stable income for single parents. First, in this chapter we examine the development of the Albuquerque economy since World War II, a period that brought increased manufacturing into an economy dominated by large government and service sectors. Then we analyze the reasons why manufacturers located new branch plants in Albuquerque during the 1970s and early 1980s. Finally, we explore the differential impact of this new industrialization on women and men, and on Mexican Americans and Anglos.

The location of electronics and apparel firms within a service economy and the economic recession of the early 1980s, which particularly affected the mining, transportation, and construction industries in New Mexico, set up their own contradictory forces. Firms moved to Albuquerque for a number of reasons, among them the relatively low wages that Albuquerque offered. Relying on a gender division of labor already in place throughout the wage and skill hierarchy of the electronics and apparel industries, managers hired women to fill a large number of the assembly jobs that were created as part of each new plant's production process. Mexican-American women, making up a greater proportion of the high school–educated labor force in Albuquerque, were recruited to these jobs in higher numbers than Anglo, black, or Indian women. At the same time, men were increasingly economically vulnerable as unemployment rose during 1982 and 1983. Jobs in mining and the oil industry (outside of Albuquerque) and jobs in construction and transportation (within Albuquerque) were declining or subject to seasonal layoffs.

From the point of view of the managers, sunbelt assembly jobs were low-paid relative to California or the Midwest. But from the point of view of women who had been working in low-wage service jobs, the new plants offered relatively high-pay and steady employment. Thus women moving into these plants were in economically stable positions at a time when men were becoming increasingly dislocated by the 1982–83 recession. These processes affected Mexican Americans more than Anglos and created a new group of female mainstay and sole providers, both well represented among the working mothers we interviewed.

Albuquerque as a Sunbelt City

At the beginning of World War II, New Mexico had been a state for only thirty years. Diverse Native-American cultures combined with three hundred years of Spanish-Mexican settlement gave the state a unique sociocultural mix. Its prospects for economic growth, however, had not changed substantially since the arrival of the railroad in Albuquerque in 1880. New Mexico had hardly participated in earlier waves of U.S. industrialization, remaining small, poor, and largely isolated. With a per capita income that was 63 percent of the national average, it ranked forty-sixth out of the forty-eight states. Its scattered population of half a million was insufficient to generate a local market for industrial production. Agriculture was the principal source of livelihood.

As the state's largest metropolitan area, Albuquerque contained about an eighth of the state's population and served as a service and commercial center for the surrounding agricultural areas. About half the population of what was to become the Albuquerque Standard Metropolitan Statistical Area (SMSA) was Mexican-American. About a quarter of the population was employed in wholesale and retail trade, most of the remainder in services or by the government. The

[33]

number working in agriculture-related jobs within the city was 60 percent greater than the number working in manufacturing (Brasher 1962:24). Of the 1,300 people working in manufacturing, the largest number (30 percent) were employed in processing lumber or making furniture. Then came food processing, which employed another 24 percent. Traditional heavy industries such as machinery, transportation equipment, and chemicals accounted for only 100 people in combination (Brasher 1962:35). All the firms involved were very small: a 1948 study found that the majority of manufacturing establishments employed less than ten workers, and most of these employed less than five. The largest firm in the city had 130 to 135 workers, and only eleven firms employed fifty or more (Bureau of Business Research 1949:35).

By the end of World War II, Albuquerque manufacturing still employed fewer people than agriculture, and lumber processing was still the most important industry (Bureau of Business Research 1949:19, 34). But a new factor had fundamentally altered the development of industry: once Los Alamos was selected as the site for the development of the atomic bomb, Albuquerque became a major center for research and development relating to nuclear weapons. The Sandia Corporation, which provided nonnuclear components, was located in Albuquerque. Kirtland Air Force Base, established at the beginning of the war, became the site of the Special Weapons Command in charge of nuclear weapons research and development for the air force (Oppenheimer 1969:A-3). ACF Industries, operating under contract to the Atomic Energy Commission, reputedly to construct the atomic bomb itself, grew eventually to employ "about half the basic workers in manufacturing" in Albuquerque (Brasher 1962:4).

Led in part by its new nuclear role, Albuquerque's overall growth during and after the war was rather spectacular. Population doubled between 1940 and 1950 and had increased by two-thirds again by 1960 for a total of 170,000, making it the sixtieth largest city in the United States. The manufacturing sector also expanded. The number of people it employed increased more than sixfold between 1940 and 1960. Yet because growth was so rapid, the overall importance of manufacturing in the city (and the state by extension) increased only slightly. Agriculture had shrunk to a level more consistent with an urban environment (1 percent of the work force), but the service and especially the government sector had expanded even more rapidly than industry, so that in 1960 manufacturing still employed only 8.8 percent of the city's work force (Brasher 1962:24).

The structure of the manufacturing sector as well as its size reflected Albuquerque's low level of industrialization. Classic heavy industries—primary and fabricated metals, chemicals, machinery, and transport equipment, which accounted in combination for the majority of U.S. manufacturing employment at the time—provided only about a sixth of the city's manufacturing jobs (Brasher 1962:35, table 15). More traditional categories of industry such as food, lumber and furniture, and stone, clay, and glass loomed large by default. The one exception to the generally traditional character of the manufacturing order was the nuclear weapons plant operated by ACF Industries, which was listed under "miscellaneous."

Those industries that provided the basis for highly paid, unionized blue-collar jobs in the industrial core of the United States were underrepresented in New Mexico, even taking into account the small overall scale of the manufacturing establishment. But equally important in its effect on women's roles and family structures was the fact that those industries with the highest proportions of women workers nationally were even more underrepresented in the state's manufacturing structure. The textile and apparel industries, which accounted for 30 percent of all women working in manufacturing in the United States at the time, were virtually nonexistent in New Mexico, employing less than 500 people in the entire state. Electrical and electronic equipment, by far the largest employer of women in the durable goods sector nationally, was also substantially underrepresented in the state. Given the kind of manufacturing jobs that were available, women's participation had to be exceptionally low. In the United States as a whole, more than a quarter of the labor force in manufacturing was female. In Albuquerque, the proportion was just over a sixth.

Albuquerque in 1960 was not a particularly promising prospect for new industries. Despite its spectacular growth overall, it had made only minimal progress in the direction of industrialization. It had a much smaller manufacturing base than its neighbors, Phoenix and El Paso (Luckingham 1982:96, 103–5), to say nothing of other sunbelt competitors in California, Texas, and the Southeast. The manufacturing structure that it did have focused on traditional industries or on very specialized defense production. The old problems of isolation and lack of local markets persisted.

With no large established blue-collar male work force to draw on, the existing labor force was not promising to American manufacturing. The median wage of the small male manufacturing work force

[35]

that did exist was above the national average, as it was for men in the Albuquerque service sector. Women working in manufacturing received substantially less than women in manufacturing in the country generally, but their numbers were quite small. In short, Albuquerque had neither a pool of skilled workers that a potential employer might capitalize on, nor a mass of low-paid workers that, relative to other locations, could lead to cost reductions.

Whether or not Albuquerque could attract a broader, more modern manufacturing base to complement the likely growth of its commercial and service activities remained an open question. Yet, in the early 1980s, Albuquerque doubled its manufacturing employment and tripled its manufacturing value added in real terms. This growth was accomplished despite severe setbacks during the 1960s when ACF Industries closed up shop and when the Sandia research complex cut back its activities. In 1982, the year our study began, Albuquerque was still a service and commercial center, but its industrial base had changed substantially. In order to trace this transformation and its consequences, it is necessary to look first at the thinking of the manufacturers who came to the city, and second at the response of women workers to the new opportunities.

Why Manufacturers Moved to Albuquerque

The conventional stereotype of sunbelt industrialization is that firms flock from the frostbelt looking for low energy costs and low wages. Like many stereotypes, this one has a grain of truth, but it misses the main dynamics of Albuquerque's industrialization. Traditional smokestack industry does not look at Albuquerque as a potential site. Because of transportation costs, manufacturers of heavy industrial goods need to be close to markets and suppliers, none of which are provided by Albuquerque. Producers of steel and other basic industrial goods, and manufacturers of autos and other consumer durables may have shrunk their payrolls in the north central states, but they have not brought them to Albuquerque and are not likely to in the future.

The firms that did move to Albuquerque after 1970 were mainly from newer industries such as electronics, whose output is very valuable relative to its weight and bulk, making transportation considerations largely irrelevant. Others came from less high-tech but more

[36]

labor-intensive industries where, again, the costs of shipping raw materials in and finished products out was not a primary consideration; among those in our study, medical supplies manufacturer Health-Tech and apparel manufacturer Leslie Pants are examples. Many of the newcomers grew up in the sun. One high-tech firm, Albuquerque's largest manufacturing employer in the early 1980s, came from Phoenix. SystemsPlus and Southwest Electronics were California companies. A fourth electronics plant came from San Jose via Phoenix. Their reasons for moving had more to do with the sense of crowding caused by the rapid industrialization in their original sunbelt homes than with escaping environments in which industrial growth was stagnating.

Electronics and aerospace firms have not abandoned previous growth centers, but there are real reasons for a company not to expand further in areas where explosive industrial growth has been going on for a long time. The legendary problems of Silicon Valley epitomize the disadvantages of operating in a high-growth environment. In the 1970s stories of workers turning around on their way to work because they noticed that the plant down the street was offering ten cents an hour more, or of employers forced to hire the same worker two or three times over the course of a year because labor markets were so tight, may be apocryphal, but that labor markets there were tight was quite true. This was especially a problem for firms with a substantial component of engineers or other technically trained personnel. Moreover, soaring housing prices may have made it more difficult to attract new professionals. Overstrained infrastructure, exemplified by traffic jams on the way to work, may have eroded the "quality of life" that these same professionals were looking for. The simple economics of finding a new industrial site in the Santa Clara Valley may have been sufficient to convince a firm that it should look for alternative expansion locations.

Most additions to Albuquerque's manufacturing establishment have resulted from general corporate strategies of geographic diversification. The dispersion of manufacturing facilities reflects current corporate thinking that smaller plants are more efficient. Corporate estimates of optimal work-force size vary from 300 to 2,000, but even estimates at the high end imply operations in a dozen different locations for a medium-sized to large corporation. The trend toward geographic dispersion may also be prompted by feelings that being too large a factor in the economy of any given community is more a

[37]

burden than an advantage. Setting up in a new location a bit removed from earlier operations may further be seen as offering a chance to introduce new managerial styles and new ways of organizing the labor process which might be resisted where other practices are already established.

Firms that agree with the principle of geographic dispersion vary as to the kind of location they need. An adequate supply of labor is a prime consideration. Small firms may be happy even in a tiny town, but for a major plant a reasonably sized metropolitan area is required. As a rule of thumb, firms like to have about 100 residents per employee: a plant that might eventually employ 2,000 workers would look for a city of some 200,000. A work force with industrial experience is some advantage, but at the same time large industrial cities may have some of the disadvantages of a Silicon Valley–style labor market: too much competition for the available work force. Having some preexisting industrial infrastructure is also an advantage, but again, the presence of too many other firms may place a strain on the existing infrastructure.

Geographic location is another factor. Albuquerque has grown more on the basis of sunbelt spillovers than frostbelt refugees. Although they may not worry about transporting their products, high-tech firms are concerned to maintain ties with the rest of the corporation. Manufacturing plants in industries undergoing rapid technological change require regular interchange with the kind of corporate services that normally remain in the original location. Research and development (R&D) and marketing do not move with manufacturing, yet they are essential to product development.

For firms looking outward from a base in California or Arizona, Albuquerque offers obvious advantages for maintaining corporate communication. Flights to Phoenix take only an hour, and there are direct flights to San Jose. Managers and materials can be moved back and forth between the plant and corporate headquarters with relative ease. For firms with home offices in the West, Albuquerque competes primarily with other western cities: Salt Lake City, Sacramento, Portland, Denver, Colorado Springs, and other medium to large urban areas. For firms with frostbelt homes (such as Howard Electronics and Computex), there is no special geographic advantage to a southwestern location. The geographic advantage that New Mexico offers a firm based in California or Arizona may go to New Hampshire or Vermont for a firm based in Massachusetts. Otherwise, the

[38]

logic of choice is very similar. Albuquerque is attractive to firms looking for a "semideveloped" medium-sized city, one that can already boast a reasonably developed infrastructure and a work force with a bit of industrial experience but a labor market that is still loose, dominated principally by low-paying service jobs rather than by other industrial employers.

Regardless of where a firm comes from, the principal issue in the location decision is labor. For the kinds of manufacturing facilities considering Albuquerque, locally specific costs are minor compared with the wage bill. In one location study, for example, the wage bill was four times the magnitude of taxes, utilities, and transportation costs combined. The fact that Albuquerque's manufacturing wages continue to be lower than those of cities in low-wage states such as Texas and Utah, and substantially below those in Portland, Seattle, Denver, and Phoenix, gives Albuquerque an obvious advantage.

It is a mistake, however, to focus exclusively on relative wages. Manufacturing operations in which the cost of unskilled labor is the primary element of competitive advantage have moved abroad. Those that remain in the United States involve an element of technological intensity based on some combination of the changing nature of the product, the complexity and expense of the equipment involved, and service relations with customers. This in turn implies that U.S. manufacturing operations will involve an important component of technical and professional personnel.

For most firms considering Albuquerque, dealing with the "labor question" means persuading professional personnel to transfer from the firm's previous location, or recruiting them on the national market, as much as it means worrying about the cost and availability of unskilled labor. For these firms, "quality of life" is a central issue in the location decision. If good engineering and design personnel are hard to attract to a given location, winning the battle for low-cost operatives is a pyrrhic victory. Consequently, such factors as the quality of the local education system, recreational and cultural possibilities, and the availability and cost of housing weigh more heavily in combination than relative wage rates. The fact that the people making the location decision can empathize with "quality of life" issues (indeed, some may themselves have to live in the environment they select) probably makes these issues even more important subjectively than they appear on official location study score cards (Malecki 1985:71).

[39]

If an attractive quality of life is the most important positive feature a city can have for manufacturers, politically powerful organized labor is the single most frightening feature. Whether in traditional labor-intensive manufacturing such as the apparel industry or in high-tech electronics firms, the opposition to unionization is consistent. Even corporations that have learned to live with union shops in other locations look for as securely nonunion an environment as they can find. Those that are not unionized in other locations, which includes most electronics firms, are determined to remain nonunion. Even in firms that express strong interest in worker participation, managers see unions as fundamentally impeding their ability to run their plants efficiently. They are also aware of the danger to their own prospects for corporate advancement. One put it bluntly: "If you come into a nonunion plant and it becomes unionized, you don't have a job."

Even though very few manufacturing firms in Albuquerque are unionized and any union organizer would consider the city a very difficult assignment, firms still see the fact that New Mexico has failed to produce a right-to-work law as a bad sign. Right-to-work is a symbolic issue more than a real one. Obviously, the absence of such a law has not made it easy to organize New Mexico manufacturing firms: less than 11 percent of its nonagricultural labor force was unionized in 1983. Nonetheless, the fact that the state has not been able to pass a right-to-work law suggests to would-be entrants that the local politicians care too much about the opinions of the labor movement.

Even so, New Mexico obviously has a strong advantage over the major northeastern and north central states, which are generally perceived—at least by those manufacturers who end up in the Southwest—as being hopelessly "anti-business" and politically dominated by forces tied to organized labor. In addition, several of New Mexico's western competitors (California, Colorado, Oregon, and Washington) not only are not right-to-work states but have higher rates of unionization (Grant 1982:42). New Mexico may lose a few points to southwestern competitors (Utah and Texas) or to southeastern states (the Carolinas and Florida), but it is still essentially a nonunion state, and that is an unquestionable advantage in attracting firms.

Other economic issues independent of labor also weigh in the decision. One is the availability at reasonable cost of adequate industrial sites; the existence of large tracts of undeveloped land close to the city works to Albuquerque's advantage here. A network of local suppliers may be important, although most major national corporations rely primarily on their own corporate sources for crucial inputs and depend on local suppliers only for routine general items. For some firms, local services (such as machine shops) may also be valuable, though here again it is smaller firms rather than branches of national corporations for whom this is likely to be an issue. A consideration of utility rates is usually not in Albuquerque's favor relative to its sunbelt competitors. Nor is New Mexico's 5 percent gross receipts tax, especially the fact that it applies to service activities (including R&D). On the other hand, the existence of industrial revenue bonds is a useful tax break.

Probably more important than those features of the political environment that can be translated easily into prospective balance sheet items, however, is the perceived general efficacy and enthusiasm of local government. Like attitudes toward labor, this is an amorphous but crucial issue for most companies. Firms like to have the feeling first of all that they are negotiating with a governmental apparatus that understands the needs of business and is agile enough to respond even to needs that require quick action and innovation. They also like to have confidence that future problems with government services such as roads or waste disposal, will be dealt with sympathetically and effectively. Albuquerque's inability to make or implement a decision regarding the construction of a badly needed additional bridge across the Rio Grande, for example, was considered a sign of "lack of leadership." On the other hand, the city's obvious enthusiasm for new firms and the existence of the long-established, professionally staffed Albuquerque Economic Development Service, have been advantages.

Most major manufacturers came to Albuquerque looking for abundant, relatively inexpensive, nonunion production workers in an environment that would also be attractive to professional personnel. As Malecki points out (1985:71,73), electronics firms have tended to locate branch plants in the sunbelt, "close to home," rather than overseas, and in urban areas rather than small towns because of the need for engineers on the site. Manufacturers did not look to the city to supply essential inputs or offer nearby markets for their products, but they did want a minimal level of local industrial infrastructure and sufficient transportation links to enable ready communication with their other facilities. For one important set of manufacturers, however, the logic of choosing Albuquerque was quite different: the defense-related firms that came because of Los Alamos, the Sandia labs, and Kirtland Air Force Base made the decision to move independent of economic considerations, and their arrival in turn helped make Albuquerque the sort of "semideveloped" city that could attract other manufacturers.

The impact of Albuquerque's defense establishment on its industrialization worked in several interrelated ways. Some firms arrived directly to service nuclear and other defense-related operations. For example, one firm that makes devices to monitor nuclear tests, came to Albuquerque in 1964 to do contract work for Sandia, and to Los Alamos under contract with the Atomic Energy Commission (see the *Wall Street Journal*, February 21, 1984, p. 1). It continues to do substantial business related to the development of nuclear weapons; it also has a civilian manufacturing operation that produces environmental data–collection equipment and other instrumentation.

Additionally, innovative ideas spun off into small companies by Sandia researchers were later bought up by national firms. One such Albuquerque plant had its origins in a small firm started by an innovative ceramist from Sandia; another now makes telemetry devices for missiles and satellites. Albuquerque's third largest manufacturing employer, Aerospace, Inc., came to Albuquerque in part to take advantage of a facility (and its trained workers) that had been owned by the Atomic Energy Commission. Finally, there are firms such as Sanders (now a branch of Howard Electronics), for whom the presence of a large air force base meant proximity to the customer for its principal product, the B-1 bomber.

The defense-related side of Albuquerque's industrialization is critical to explaining its initial transition from a small commercial and service center to a city capable of attracting major manufacturing operations. This side of the story is hardly novel in the chronicles of recent American industrialization, however: Glasmeier, Hall, and Markusen (1983:43) found per capita defense spending to be the single most powerful factor positively associated with the shift of high-tech jobs into metropolitan areas during the 1970s.

The Consequences of New Industrialization

Albuquerque's expansion of its industrial base was impressive by any standard: over 300 new manufacturing establishments were added to the city's industrial park between 1963 and 1982, more than doubling the previous number. While manufacturing employment in the country as a whole crept up only slightly during this twenty-year period, manufacturing employment in Albuquerque also more than doubled. Manufacturing value added increased 160% in Albuquerque (in constant dollars) while growing only 40 percent in the country as a whole (see Table 1). These figures are even more impressive, given the serious setback suffered by the city's manufacturing establishment because of defense cutbacks in the 1960s. In the 1970s Albuquerque outpaced even its sunbelt neighbors, Phoenix and El Paso, in the rate at which its manufacturing employment expanded (Luckingham 1982:103–5).

Still, an expanding manufacturing base does not automatically mean affluence. Despite the growth of industrial employment, New Mexico remained a poor state. In fact, the industrialization that occurred after 1960 did much less for New Mexico's standing relative to other states than had the war and the immediate postwar defense boom. In 1959 the median family income in New Mexico reached 95 percent of the national average; by 1979 it had dropped to 85 percent. Nor was there any evidence that manufacturing wages in the state as a whole were approaching the national average. Average production worker wages in New Mexico reached their peak relative to the national average (92 percent) in 1955. In 1982 they had increased from 1970 levels but were still less than 80 percent of the national average.

Table 1. Growth of manufacturing, U.S., 1963–1982

	1963	1982	Growth
Number of establishments			
Albuquerque	263	578	119%
U.S. (1,000s)	307	358	16%
Number of employees			
Albuquerque (1,000s)	8.2	18.0	120%
U.S. (millions)	16.2	19.1	17%
Value added (1982 $)			
Albuquerque (millions)	236	613	160%
U.S. (billions)	589	824	40%

Sources: U.S. Bureau of the Census 1963a: 6 (32-6), Table 4; 1963b:44, Table 1; 1982a:9, Table 6; 1987:723, Table 1303 (and 456, Table 766 for GNP price deflator).

[43]

Even in terms of the likelihood of finding a job, the results of industrialization were far from spectacular for the average New Mexican. At the beginning of the 1980s, unemployment rates were about equal to the national average: a rate of 9.1 percent in Albuquerque and 10.8 in New Mexico at the depth of the recession in June 1983, compared with 10.2 in the United States as a whole. The impact on the husbands in a number of families we interviewed was profound. In addition, the crisis in the semiconductor industry, which began in 1982 and intensified in succeeding years despite general economic recovery, provided a powerful reminder that the presence of high-tech industries is not necessarily a guarantee of prosperity or future growth.

In 1982–83, when our study was conducted, several plants were laying off workers and the opening of new ones was being delayed. But others were expanding, and the women we interviewed were able to hold on to their jobs or find others, as the layoffs were balanced by new positions. During 1984, however, the downturn accelerated, and the number of jobs in electronics as a whole decreased by 1,000. The industry began to recover in 1985, and in 1991 the number of electronics jobs was 2000 more than the 1982 level of 4,400 jobs in the state. The impact of the 1991 recession and military cutbacks began to be felt in 1992 as one plant announced layoffs and another closed its doors. Sunbelt industrialization has created important opportunities, but its overall impact on living standards should not be exaggerated.

The expansion of manufacturing did not make Albuquerque a "smokestack city." To the contrary, the experience of the 1960s and 1970s reconfirmed the city's emphasis on a service-oriented economy. Even though its proportion of total employment in manufacturing rose while falling in the United States as a whole, less than 10 percent of Albuquerque's labor force worked in manufacturing during those years, while the proportion nationally was more than 20 percent. Even in relation to its sunbelt sisters, the city's employment remained heavily skewed toward services: in Phoenix, about 17 percent of the work force was in manufacturing; in El Paso, over 20 percent. The dynamic character of Albuquerque's manufacturing sector and the multiplier effect from the industrial jobs created in the 1970s deserves, of course, at least part of the credit for the fact that nonmanufacturing employment was expanding twice as fast there as in the country as a whole. Still, not even those involved in the process of attracting new firms expected the proportion of manufacturing jobs in the city to exceed 15 percent.

The continued dominance of services, government, and commerce can be seen by looking at the city's major employers, as well as by examining overall employment figures. At the beginning of the 1980s only four of the top twenty employers were industrial firms. The city's large defense establishments, Kirtland and Sandia, continued to dominate the employment rolls, and almost all the other major employers were government or service organizations. Nonetheless, the list of top employers also provides a good indication of the extent of the changes in Albuquerque's industrial park. None of the four top industrial employers had been present at the beginning of the 1960s, and three of the four were involved in the production of electronic equipment, two of them for commercial rather than defense markets.

The importance of the electronics industry comes through equally clearly in an examination of changes in the overall structure of employment in the city. Forty percent of the growth of manufacturing employment between 1960 and 1980 was accounted for by the expansion of the electronics industry. Electronics employment grew from less than 5 percent to almost a quarter of the entire manufacturing labor force (see Table 2). Data on the value of output reveal even more strongly the importance of electronics. By 1982 electronics accounted for over one-third of Albuquerque's manufacturing value added (see Table 3).

Changes in most other categories were about as expected over the period, as Table 2 shows. "Food and tobacco" declined precipitously as Albuquerque became more integrated into national channels of distribution. The share of "stone, clay, and glass" shrank but did not decline absolutely, as it did in the country as a whole. Likewise, "lumber and furniture" grew substantially instead of stagnating as it did nationally. The departure of ACF (the nuclear/defense producer which the census apparently classified as a "fabricator of miscellaneous metal products") caused a severe drop in employment, but this was compensated for by the arrival of Aerospace, Inc. (which came under "transportation equipment" as a producer of airplanes). "Machinery" and "chemicals" grew only at the same rate as overall manufacturing. Without the arrival of the electronics plants, Albuquerque's industrial structure would have modernized slightly but not exceptionally.

The one somewhat surprising development was the growth of "tex-

[45]

Table 2. Structure of manufacturing employment in Albuquerque, 1960–1980

Industry	1960		1980		
	No. (in 1,000s)	%	No. (in 1,000s)	%	Growth
Lumber & furniture	435	5.2	1,499	8.1	244%
Stone, clay, glass	646	7.8	956	5.2	48%
Metal[a]	2,274	27.4	1,009	5.4	−56%
Machinery (nonelectrical)[b]	421	5.1	865	4.7	105%
Electrical and electronic[c]	375	4.5	4,336	23.4	1056%
Transportation equipment	176	2.1	2,412	13.0	1270%
Food and tobacco	1,719	20.7	1,176	6.4	−32%
Textiles and apparel	197	2.4	1,266	6.8	542%
Paper, printing, publishing	1,385	16.7	2,377	12.8	72%
Chemicals, rubber, petroleum	282	3.4	698	3.8	148%
Other	392	4.7	1,921	10.4	390%
TOTAL	8,302[d]	100	18,515	100	123%

Sources: U.S. Bureau of the Census 1960a:261, Table 127; 1980a:319, Table 228(B).
[a]Includes primary and fabricated metals.
[b]Does not include office machines and computing equipment.
[c]Includes office machines and computing equipment.
[d]Does not include nonspecified manufacturing industries.

tiles and apparel." While employment in apparel was stagnating nationally, it was the fastest-growing industry in Albuquerque outside of defense and electronics—principally because of the arrival of Leslie Pants.[1] Apparel and electronics both represented a shift in Albuquerque manufacturing from production for local markets to production for national ones. And both industries were heavy employers of low-wage female operatives.

These changes in the structure of Albuquerque's manufacturing structure were far from gender blind. The trend toward the feminization of the manufacturing work force, which could be observed in the United States overall during this period, took an unusually dramatic form in Albuquerque. As Table 4 shows, women moved from exceptionally low participation in manufacturing in 1960 to substantially above the national average in 1980. Women constituted only about a

[1] Transportation equipment (with the most rapid growth outside of electronics) is primarily a defense industry, since it consists in New Mexico of aviation equipment rather than ground transportation equipment.

Table 3. Share of electronics in the manufacturing sector,
Albuquerque, 1982

	All Manufacturing	Electronics	Share of Total
Number of establishments	578	32	5.5%
Number of employees	18,000	4,500	25.1%
Value added (in $ millions)	613.2	209.0	34.1%

Source: U.S. Bureau of the Census 1982a:9, Table 6.

Table 4. Growth of manufacturing employment by gender, Albuquerque and
U.S., 1960–1980

	1960	1980	New Entrants	Growth
Albuquerque				
Total	8,341	18,515	10,174	123%
Men	6,860	11,848	4,988	73%
Women	1,481	6,667	5,186	350%
% women	17.8	36.0	51.0	
U.S. (in 1,000s)				
Total	17,513	21,915	4,402	25%
Men	13,112	14,919	1,807	14%
Women	4,401	6,996	2,595	59%
% women	25.1	31.9	58.9	

Sources: U.S. Bureau of the Census 1960a:261, Table 127; 1970b:798–800,
Table 235; 1980a:319, Table 228(B); 1980b:365, Table 285.

sixth of the manufacturing work force when the period began, but
they were an absolute majority of the new recruits to manufacturing.

The scope of these trends becomes even clearer when they are
examined in specific industries (Table 5). Electronics, a highly dynamic industry, began the period with a predominantly male work
force. Apparel has traditionally been a female industry. Stone, clay,
and glass made up a relatively stagnant industrial segment whose
work force was traditionally male dominated. While the national
work force in electronics moved toward feminization, in Albuquerque the move was even more rapid: from just over a quarter of the
work force in 1960, women constituted the majority by 1980. Like

[47]

Table 5. Growth of women's participation in selected industries, Albuquerque, 1960–1980

	1960	1980	New Entrants	Growth
Electronics[a]				
Total	375	4,336	3,961	1056%
Men	271	2,042	1,771	654%
Women	104	2,294	2,190	2106%
% women	27.7	52.9	55.2	
Apparel				
Total	139	1,127	988	711%
Men	34	163	129	379%
Women	105	964	859	818%
% women	75.5	85.5	86.9	
Stone, clay, and glass				
Total	646	956	310	48%
Men	618	830	212	34%
Women	28	126	98	350%
% women	4.3	13.2	31.6	

Sources: U.S. Bureau of the Census 1960a:261, Table 127; 1980a:319, Table 228(B).
[a]Includes machinery plus office, computing, and accounting equipment.

electronics, the apparel industry in Albuquerque started the period with a lower proportion (about 75 percent) of women workers than characterized the industry nationally and ended it with a higher one (over 85 percent). Even in stone, clay, and glass the proportion of women increased: women, only 4 percent of the labor force at the beginning of the period, accounted for almost a third of the new entrants.

Greater participation of women in the labor force was not limited to the manufacturing sector. In Albuquerque, as in the United States in general, the proportion of women workers also rose substantially in the service sector; indeed, the vast majority of women added to the labor force were added in the service sector. Nationally, however (as Table 6 indicates), the proportion of women increased more rapidly in services than in manufacturing, and the gap between the two percentages had grown wider by 1980; in Albuquerque the increase was smaller in service than in manufacturing, and the gap became smaller. The divergence between local and national trends had obvious implications for the effect of women's rising participation on working-class (as opposed to middle-class) households.

[48]

Table 6. Women's employment in manufacturing and nonmanufacturing, Albuquerque and U.S., 1960–1980

	% of Labor Force	
	1960	1980
Manufacturing		
Albuquerque	17.8	36.0
U.S.	25.1	31.9
Nonmanufacturing		
Albuquerque	34.6	43.5
U.S.	35.6	47.5

Sources: U.S. Bureau of the Census 1960a:261, Table 127; 1980a:319, Table 228(B).

Middle-class and working-class families were affected by general national trends toward the increased labor-force participation of wives and mothers. In Albuquerque as in the country as a whole, women increasingly took advantage of new employment opportunities, irrespective of the family structures in which they found themselves. The most radical changes—again, as in the country generally—occurred among married women with children. As Table 7 indicates, married women with children under six years of age more than doubled their participation in the labor force. Married women

Table 7. Female labor force participation, Albuquerque, 1960–1980

Family Situation	% in Labor Force		
	1960	1970	1980
All women	35.0	40.9	51.6
Married (husband present)	30.7	37.6	47.7
no minor children	—	41.5	44.9
children under 6	19.1	27.3	43.1
children 6 to 18	—	42.8	56.5
Others[a]	45.1	46.1	56.5
children under 6	—	44.9	57.7

Sources: U.S. Bureau of the Census 1960a:206, Table 116; 1970a:151, Table 85; 1980a:138–41, Table 216.
[a]Single, widowed, and divorced.

[49]

with children between six and eighteen were, by 1980, more likely to join the labor force than women without minor children.

The reasons Albuquerque's new industrialization created an employment structure with gender implications different from those of the traditional industrial structure in the United States as a whole had in good part to do with the different industrial mix that prevailed in Albuquerque, most specifically with the relative absence of jobs in traditional "smokestack" industries and the high union wages associated with them. The differences also had to do, however, with the different structures of employment within industries.

Looking at the wage structure of the electronics and apparel industries in 1979 shows that within each industry differences between Albuquerque wages and the national median wage were greater for men than for women, leaving men's and women's earning within each industry less far apart in Albuquerque than in the country as a whole (see Table 8). In electronics in Albuquerque, men made only 80 percent of the national median male wage. Women electronics workers also made less than the national median, but the differences were not as great, so the discrepancy between male and female wages in Albuquerque was less than in the nation as a whole. Apparel showed a more dramatic version of the same phenomenon. While women's wages were less than 60 percent of men's nationally, Albuquerque was different. Albuquerque men made only a little more than half the national median male wage, but women made more than the national median for female workers. Consequently, women apparel workers in Albuquerque ended up making more than their male counterparts.

In sum, the overall effect of the new industrialization on working people in Albuquerque has been incremental rather than revolutionary. The growth of industry has been an important but not the central element in Albuquerque's growth. Manufacturing continues to provide only a minor share of employment, and Albuquerque still retains chiefly a government and service economy. The expansion of the electronics and apparel industries, however, has created new employment opportunities for women and increased earnings. In addition, more and more women with children, particularly those with children under six years of age, are remaining in the labor force. If the new industrialization changed nothing else, it should have affected the work patterns of working-class women and the ways in which they integrate their work and family responsibilities.

[50]

Table 8. Wage differences by gender in electronics and apparel, Albuquerque and U.S., 1979

	Men		Women	
	ABQ	U.S.	ABQ	U.S.
Electronics[a]				
Wage distribution				
> $14,999	41%	58%	3%	12%
> $10,000[b]	27%	21%	21%	31%
< $10,000	33%	20%	75%	57%
Median earnings	$13,195	$16,486	$8,348	$9,325
ABQ median as % of U.S.	80		90	
Women's median as % of men's in U.S.		56		
Women's median as % of men's in ABQ		63		
Apparel[c]				
Wage distribution				
> $14,999	16%	32%	2%	3%
> $10,000[b]	14%	21%	14%	9%
< $10,000	71%	46%	84%	88%
Median earnings	$5,868	$10,682	$6,174	$6,135
ABQ median as % of U.S.	55		101	
Women's median as % of men's in U.S.		57		
Women's median as % of men's in ABQ		105		

Sources: U.S. Bureau of the Census 1980a:365, 362, Table 231; 1980b:396, 398, Table 290.
[a]Electrical machinery equipment and supplies.
[b]But less than or equal to $14,999.
[c]Apparel and other finished textile products.

Albuquerque offers a particularly striking example of the kinds of employment structures with which the American working class as a whole will be increasingly confronted over the coming years. First of all, because it *is* a service economy, most working-class people must find jobs in the service sector. Yet for those without middle-class credentials, manufacturing jobs remain economically more attractive than those available at the bottom end of the service sector (as epitomized by the low median wages in retail trade). Manufacturing jobs, though a minority, are becoming increasingly important to working-class families.

Second, Albuquerque exemplifies the relative feminization of the manufacturing sector. Few cities in the United States have witnessed as rapid a rise in the proportion of factory jobs held by women. Men in Albuquerque, even more than men nationwide, have had an increasingly difficult time finding jobs in manufacturing (in fact, the

[51]

proportion of men working in industry actually declined between 1960 and 1980). Those who do find such jobs are not likely to get the high-paying ones traditionally associated with the unionized blue-collar work force. They may still be better than the jobs available to their wives, but the *difference* in pay will be less than it was in 1960.

Women's Work in Manufacturing

Sunbelt employment opportunities make women's wages of central importance to the family economy. Since the time when the gap between male and female earnings was greater in Albuquerque than in the United States as a whole, adaptation by the family to the changing position of women in the labor force has been compelled with particular rapidity. Moreover, because the jobs they offer are more attractive than those at the bottom end of the service sectors, manufacturing firms in Albuquerque have the pick of the local labor force. And because they are primarily nonunion, no countervailing institutional force constrains management in setting productivity goals.

For women workers, all these factors combine to ensure that the new industrialization comes with imperative demands as well as opportunities. If they do not perform well individually, there are numerous women working in low-paid service-sector jobs who could move up economically if manufacturing jobs became available. If they do not perform well collectively, there are other localities to which the branch plant could be moved. Corporate headquarters as well as local managers are aware of how various locales compare in terms of labor costs, productivity, absenteeism, and quality of output. In this, as in the overall shape of employment opportunities, Albuquerque reflects trends that are increasingly characteristic of the manufacturing sector overall.

The impact of the new industrialization on the potential relative earning power of men and women in dual-worker families is reflected in the changes that took place in Albuquerque and in the United States between 1960 and 1980: nationwide, women's wages in manufacturing remained constant relative to men's, but there was a sharp change in Albuquerque. Table 9 shows the disparate trends. Median male wages in Albuquerque manufacturing, substantially higher than the national average in 1960, had fallen well behind by 1980. Women

Table 9. Trends in manufacturing wages by gender, U.S. and Albuquerque, 1959–1979

	Median Annual Earnings	
	1959	1979
Women		
U.S.	$2,439	$8,296
Albuquerque	$2,285	$7,518
ABQ as % of U.S.	93	91
Men		
U.S.	$4,447	$15,945
Albuquerque	$5,325	$12,232
ABQ as % of U.S.	120	77

Sources: U.S. Bureau of the Census 1960a:274, Table 130; 1960b:554–55, Table 208; 1980a:362, Table 231; 1980b:396, 398, Table 290.

factory workers, on the other hand, maintained their position relative to national averages.[2]

These changes in the manufacturing sector were all the more important for women in Albuquerque because they were not mirrored in nonmanufacturing jobs. As Table 10 shows, women's increased participation in manufacturing was the key to improving their relative earning power in Albuquerque, while men in manufacturing fared poorly relative to their counterparts in nonmanufacturing jobs. In 1960, men were making more in manufacturing than outside it; by 1980, they were earning less. For women the evolution was the reverse: women's manufacturing wages were lower than nonmanufacturing at the beginning of the period and higher at the end.

The different structures of the electronics and apparel industries show substantial difference between Albuquerque and the nation overall, which in turn has implications for how husbands and wives who work in these same industries might fare (Table 8). Nationwide and in Albuquerque, of course, women were more concentrated at the bottom end of the distribution, and the apparel industry had

[2] It is important to keep in mind that median, as opposed to average, earnings are determined by the earnings of those in the bottom half of the wage distribution. Insofar as we are concerned with working-class as opposed to middle-class men and women, the figures for median earnings are the appropriate ones.

Table 10. Trends in median annual earnings by gender, Albuquerque, 1960–1980

	1960	1980
All employment		
Men	$5,158	$12,617
Women	$2,336	$ 7,055
Female as % of male	45	56
Manufacturing		
Men	$5,325	$12,232
Women	$2,285	$ 7,518
Female as % of male	43	61

Sources: U.S. Bureau of the Census 1960a:274, Table 130; 1980a:362, Table 231; 1980b:396, 398, Table 290.

more workers at the bottom end than did electronics. Also, as would be expected, there were more people at the bottom end of the distribution in Albuquerque than in the United States as a whole. In addition to these obvious differences, however, there was an interesting interaction of gender and location effects. In general, men were more disadvantaged by the Albuquerque location than women. The top-heavy distribution of male earnings that characterized electronics in the country as a whole did not characterize Albuquerque, and men working in apparel in Albuquerque were much more heavily concentrated at the bottom of the income distribution than in industry nationally. For women, however, the Albuquerque distributions in both industries took roughly the same shape as the national ones. In apparel, in fact, in Albuquerque in 1980, there was a higher proportion of women concentrated in the middle of the distribution, and their median earnings were higher than those of men in the industry.

None of this should be taken to suggest that women in Albuquerque had become a new aristocracy of labor. They were still making only 65 percent of male wages in manufacturing and even less in the service sector. But the data do indicate that Albuquerque is a city in which the importance of wives' earnings to the economy of the working-class family has increased substantially. Women are now more, rather than less, likely to be employed in manufacturing in Albuquerque than in the United States in general. If wives and husbands are both employed in manufacturing, their wages will more closely approach equality than in many other cities. Given the continued small size of the city's manufacturing sector overall, the possibility that the wife will work in industry while the husband is forced to take a lower-paying service-sector job is greater in Albuquerque than in the United States in general, again raising the relative importance of the wife's income.

Another significant factor was the impact of the 1982–83 recession on men's jobs, particularly outside of manufacturing. The peak of the recession occurred in the first six months of 1983; as noted, unemployment hit 10.8 percent in New Mexico and 9.1 percent in Albuquerque during June. Construction jobs were reduced by 3,400 between May 1980 and May 1983. Construction is a highly seasonal industry, and jobs fluctuate from a peak during June and July to a low point (usually of approximately 2,000 fewer jobs) in January and February. The industry began to pick up during the summer of 1983, but compared with the nationwide expansion in construction, New Mexico did poorly (*New Mexico Labor Market Review*, September 1989, p. 7): jobs in New Mexico peaked in 1985 and then fell, so that by 1991 construction positions in Albuquerque were still below 1980 levels. Mining jobs were particularly hard hit during the early 1980s; the industry lost 7,800 jobs or 25 percent of its payroll between March 1982 and March 1983 (*New Mexico Labor Market Review*, March 1983, p. 1).[3] Finally, the transportation sector (which also fluctuates seasonally because school bus drivers are laid off in the summer) lost about 900 jobs in Albuquerque between 1980 and 1983. Because men are the predominant wage earners in all these sectors, the job decline in 1982–83 had a severe impact on a number of men in the families we interviewed. At a time when working-class women were moving into better-paid manufacturing jobs, working-class men were increasingly vulnerable to longer layoffs and unemployment.

All these effects were probably particularly important to the Mexican-American community, which makes up more than one-third of the city's population. As Table 11 shows, Hispanic women participated in the labor force in 1980 in about the same proportion as non-Hispanic women.[4] Hispanic women and men, however, were both

[3] The *New Mexico Labor Market Review* is published monthly by the state's Employment Security Department, Research and Statistics Section, P.O. Box 1928, Albuquerque, NM 87103.

[4] In this section we use the term Hispanic rather than Mexican American or Hispano since Hispanic is the category employed by the U.S. Bureau of the Census.

Table 11. Hispanic men and women as proportion of labor force, Albuquerque, 1980

	Hispanic Men as % of Male Labor Force	Hispanic Women as % of Female Labor Force
Managers/professionals	18.2	15.3
Service workers	46.9	44.2
Craft workers	39.0	38.2
Operators	48.2	52.5
Total employed	32.6	31.7

Sources: U.S. Bureau of the Census 1980a:115, Table 214; 319, Table 228.

concentrated in working-class occupations within the labor force. Hispanic men, 32.6 percent of the male labor force in 1980, were only 18.2 percent of professionals and managers but 46.9 percent of service workers, 39 percent of craft workers, and 48.2 percent of operators. Hispanic women were even more concentrated in blue-collar and lower-paying white-collar jobs: 31.7 percent of the Albuquerque SMSA labor force in 1980, they were only 15.3 percent of managers and professionals but 44.2 percent of service workers, 38.2 percent of craft workers, and 52.5 percent of operators—the category from which our interviewees were drawn. This concentration is further indicated by the data on median annual income in Albuquerque. In 1980 Hispanic men had a median income of $10,197 per year, more than $1,500 less than that of the general population; Hispanic women earned a median income of $5,684, compared with $6,356 for the working female population as a whole (U.S. Bureau of the Census 1980a: 384, Table 236).

In other words, Hispanic men and women were located in working-class jobs throughout the Albuquerque economy, but the fact that Hispanic women are being pulled into the manufacturing labor force is dramatically illustrated if one examines the electronics and apparel industries in particular. Table 12 shows that while Hispanic women were only a third of the female labor force, they were 45 percent of the labor force in manufacturing generally, 50 percent of the women workers in electrical machinery and electronic equip-

Table 12. Hispanic women in the labor force, Albuquerque, 1980

	Number	% of All Women	% of All Hispanics
Population	58,239	33.1	51.9
Labor force	28,982	31.9	42.1
Manufacturing	3,016	45.2	42.4
Electrical & electronic	966	50.8	69.5
Apparel	627	65.0	88.4

Sources: U.S. Bureau of the Census 1980a:115, Table 214; 319, Table 228.

ment, and almost two-thirds of the women workers in apparel.[5] Hispanic men were not drawn into either manufacturing in general or electronics and apparel in particular to the same extent as Hispanic women. Thus, the chances that a working-class Hispanic wife would work in industry while the husband held a service-sector job or blue-collar position in construction, transportation, mining, or even farm work were even greater than for the working class in general.

Speculating on the basis of data from the state as a whole (data for Albuquerque are not available), it would seem that Hispanic women differentially benefited from the new industrialization not only in terms of opportunities for participation but also in terms of their relative wages. Table 13 shows that they did relatively better in manufacturing than in other jobs in 1980, and relatively better in electronics and apparel than in manufacturing overall. This does not change the fact that Hispanic women were the worst-paid group in the population, but it does mean that in working-class Hispanic families in which both the husband and wife worked in industry, the wife's income was likely to be even more important than it was for non-Hispanic couples who both worked in industry.

Sunbelt working mothers were thus the benefactors of an interesting contradiction. From a national perspective, manufacturers were attracted to Albuquerque partly because of its relatively low wage

[5] These figures are slightly different from those in the previous paragraph because they are based on the percentage of women in an industry rather than the percentages of women and men in specific occupational categories.

Table 13. Median earnings of Hispanic women in New Mexico, 1980

	Earnings	% of All Male Wages	% of Hispanic Male Wages	% of All Female Wages
All jobs	$5,965	47.2	56.1	91.2
Manufacturing	$6,843	57.0	67.5	100.5
Electrical & electronic	$8,119	60.6	67.4	97.0
Apparel	$6,185	76.9	81.2	103.8

Source: U.S. Bureau of the Census 1980a:356–59, Table 231.

rates; from the point of view of women who had held low-paying service-sector jobs in Albuquerque, the new plants offered higher wages and the possibility of stable employment and good benefit packages. At the same time, men's jobs were particularly vulnerable to the downturn of 1982–83, especially in mining, construction, and transportation.

The growth of industry in Albuquerque during the 1970s and 1980s took place in the context of a service economy heavily dependent on government and military spending. Albuquerque was an attractive location for branch plants in the electronics and apparel industry because it was a medium-sized city with good airline links to corporate headquarters, a good service infrastructure, and a responsive city and state government. The wage rates were low relative to Silicon Valley, Denver, and Phoenix; and New Mexico, despite its lack of a right-to-work law, was not perceived to be a pro-union state. The electronics and apparel industries have traditionally hired women for semiskilled assembly jobs, and the new plants located in Albuquerque contained a mix of jobs that also focused on a relatively low-paid female labor force. Yet for the women who were hired to work in these new plants, industrial jobs were likely to be the best they had ever held.

[3]

Women's Industrial Work
in the Family Economy

Although the economic forces that brought sunbelt industries to Albuquerque in turn helped shape the lives of the couples and single parents we interviewed, we take the position that women and men are not passive pawns of history but active agents engaged in the "practice" of forging a stable economic situation for themselves and their children. To make the link between the larger Albuquerque political economy described in Chapter 2 and what we call the "family economy," this chapter focuses on the work and marriage histories of nine couples and three single mothers—twelve stories that illustrate the range of variability among our interviewees. What we saw during our interviews in 1982 was the end product of the work histories of husbands and wives as they had interacted over the years of marriage, or the end product of a single mother's relationships with boyfriends, a husband or other male partners.

Since the job histories of wives are constructed in relationship to their husbands' employment, women find themselves in very different situations as couples build their family lives. A woman may be an equal wage earner (often in the early stages of marriage), a secondary provider in a couple where the husband earns more than the wife (usually later in the marriage), or the economic mainstay (if her husband has an erratic job history). Or she may become the sole support of children through divorce or by remaining a single parent.

We divided our sample into four categories, each of which represents a different relationship of a woman's employment to the overall family economy in 1982. Our case examples in this chapter introduce women in each of these categories, which also constitute four locations within the Albuquerque working class: each represents a different level of income earned by those with high school educations employed in blue-collar jobs. Like Jane Hood (1983) in her research on two-job families, we have focused on the working mother's providing role. Hood relied partly on a couple's subjective feelings about the importance of a wife's income; we have used a more objective or external set of criteria in assigning provider roles.

Nineteen women (36 percent) of our sample of 53 working mothers) had relatively equal jobs with their husbands and were "coproviders" (see Table 14). Eleven other wives (21 percent) held industrial jobs that were more stable and often better paid than those of their husbands; we have considered these wives "mainstay providers." For eight women (15 percent) the husband's job history was more stable, he had a higher-paying "male job," and the wife's wages provided about one-third of the family income; we have called these wives "secondary providers." In comparison with couples, the fifteen single mothers in our sample (28 percent) represent a very different kind of family economy. Some single mothers we interviewed had become pregnant as teenagers and never married their partners; others had been married, had had children, and were subsequently divorced. Unlike married working mothers, all were the primary or "sole providers" for their children, though they may have lived with parents, siblings, or roommates to cut housing and food costs.

The income and benefits provided by jobs in the new Albuquerque plants created a committed female labor force. All the women in our study were working in an apparel or electronics plant full-time. Their wages did not vary greatly; most ranged from $5.00 to $6.50 an hour. These wages placed our interviewees (both Mexican-American and Anglo) in the elite of Albuquerque's employed females. Most of them were earning between $10,000 and $12,000 a year. In 1979

Table 14. Women's contribution to family income

	Secondary Providers	Coproviders	Mainstay Providers	Sole Providers	Total
Hispana	7 (19%)	11 (30%)	7 (19%)	12 (32%)	37
Anglo	1 (6%)	8 (50%)	4 (25%)	3 (19%)	16
TOTAL	8 (15%)	19 (36%)	11 (21%)	15 (28%)	53

[60]

only 23.7 percent of women with income in Albuquerque had been making more than $10,000 (U.S. Bureau of the Census 1980:375, Table 234), and forty percent were making less. Obtaining a full-time industrial job placed these women in a good income-producing category, clearly above the position women tended to have in the service sector.

In Chapter 2 we cited macrolevel statistics to argue that Mexican-American women were pulled into sunbelt manufacturing jobs in greater proportion than white women. The greater number of Mexican-American working mothers in our sample reflects that fact. Of the fifty-three working mothers we interviewed, thirty-seven (70 percent) were Hispanas; in the thirty-eight couples, twenty-five (66 percent) of the wives were Mexican Americans. These percentages are slightly higher than the proportion of Spanish-surnamed women in the electronics labor force but about the same as the proportion in the apparel labor force.

Hispano and Anglo families were evenly distributed, however, within the range of family incomes. Since we focused on finding working mothers in sunbelt industries, the jobs of the husbands were allowed to vary. All but two husbands had blue-collar jobs. Both Hispano and Anglo men worked in low-paying jobs as maintenance men, shipping clerks, stockers, and laborers; others held jobs in the same manufacturing plants as their wives; a few (again, both Hispano and Anglo) held high-paying male jobs in larger corporations, such as machinist, engineer specialist, technician, maintenance foreman, and supervisor. Thus, husbands' wages ranged from $3.35 an hour to $15 an hour. Hispano and Anglo family incomes varied within the same range: Hispano couples from $13,452 to $43,440; Anglo couples from $12,438 to $44,500. In short, Hispano families were not noticeably either poorer or better off than Anglo families, and Hispano and Anglo couples were relatively evenly distributed within our four categories summarizing the wives' provider roles.

Depending on the income level and stability of the husband's job, the impact of the wife's employment in manufacturing ranged from "crucial to the payment of essential bills" to "significant in maintaining a family's life-style." In no case could the wife's wages be considered mere pin money; even for the few families with high male wages, a wife's income provided the possibility of a better standard of living within the working class.

Single mothers had significantly lower incomes than couples, reflecting both the lack of a second income and the low wages of women workers relative to men, especially those men whose earnings of $9.00 or $10.00 an hour placed their families in the top end of the income distribution in our sample.

Families of Coproviders

We first examine the work and family histories of five coprovider families (three Hispano and two Anglo). Just under half of our Mexican-American couples (eleven of twenty-five) and slightly over half of our white couples (eight of thirteen) were in coprovider relationships. Incomes for Mexican-American couples in this category ranged from $13,600 to $29,300 and for Anglo couples from $15,300 to $28,340.[1] The Senas, Bacas, and Pikes are examples of families in the lower half of this range; the Smiths and Riveras represent families in the upper half. These five cases show how women and their husbands coped with the ups and downs of the New Mexico economy and how the woman's manufacturing job became an important stabilizing force in each family. The Senas (a Hispano couple) and the Pikes (an Anglo couple) illustrate the impact of the 1980–82 recession on male wages. Leo Sena lost a high-paying job at a uranium mine when it closed in 1980, and in 1982 Don Pike was laid off from his $11.95-an-hour job on an oil-drilling rig in Hobbs, New Mexico, after oil prices started to fall. The Bacas are an example of a family in which the husband never had held a very high-paying job and the wife's steady work kept the family afloat over the entire span of their marriage. For the Smiths and the Riveras, by contrast, two well-paying jobs in the same sunbelt plant gave each family a steady income at the upper end of the coprovider range.

In all categories of our sample, women had obtained their manufacturing jobs either by entering industrial work shortly after high school or by finding work in an apparel or electronics plant after holding lower-wage service or clerical jobs. Among the coprovider cases, Toni Sena and Delores Baca both began work at Leslie Pants

---

[1] We estimated incomes from both the husband's and wife's interviews; each was asked to give data on weekly or monthly gross and take-home pay for self and spouse. Husbands tended, we thought, to be more accurate. We based the estimate of annual income on 1982, which often included several months of unemployment for a husband during the 1982 recession.

shortly after leaving school; at the time of our interviews Toni had been employed at the plant for four years and Delores for eight. Mary Pike, in contrast, had worked in her father's advertising agency and as a waitress before she became a stitcher in an apparel plant. Karen Smith, at age thirty-nine, had an even more extensive employment history: a series of positions—waitress, credit clerk, stock clerk, manager of a bingo hall—characterized her work experience before she obtained a high-paying union job at Aerospace, Inc., five years before our interview. Deborah Rivera was an exception to these two patterns. She (and one other working mother we interviewed) had received electronics training in the armed services and with this background was able to find an electronics job when she arrived in Albuquerque.

Each case illustrates the kinds of decisions women and their husbands made "in practice" as they learned to cope with the economic vulnerability of male work in the Albuquerque economy of the early 1980s. For these five couples and the other coproviders in our sample, by 1982 the husbands had located relatively stable jobs but with pay that only equaled that of their wives. We can see in these cases why couples have come to value women's continued employment—employment that puts working women in the position of holding in tension the contradictions of being simultaneously a worker and mother.

The Senas

Like several other coproviding wives, Toni Sena already had her manufacturing job by the time she was married. Toni was twenty-four years old, a few years below the average age of the women we interviewed. Her parents were from two small towns within twenty-five miles of Albuquerque; Toni said her father's family came from Spain, but on her mother's side "there's Indian in our blood." Toni grew up in the South Valley of Albuquerque, speaking English rather than Spanish (the language in which both parents were raised), and identifying herself as "Spanish." Toni went to New Mexico State University in Las Cruces after high school and held a half-time work-study job at a mental health halfway house, where she was paid $3.10 an hour. Toni said she had enjoyed that job because she was a psychology major; nevertheless, after a while "I was homesick so bad."

For one thing, her boyfriend, Leo, lived in Albuquerque. The 150-mile drive one or the other made to be together caused financial and academic strains. Toni quit college after a year and got hired as a stitcher at Leslie Pants. She and Leo married five months later, when she was twenty and he was twenty-three.

Leo's father was born in a Hispano village near Grants, but like Toni, Leo grew up in the South Valley. His parents raised a family of ten children, with Leo among the younger ones. He saw himself as either Spanish American or Chicano. His first job after high school was as a part-time bus driver. Following six months in this line of work, his brother helped him get a janitorial job at a large uranium mine near Cebolleta, eighty miles west of Albuquerque. Leo progressed steadily at the mine, going in the next five years to assistant toplander, toplander, assistant hoistman, hoistman, truck driver, and finally assistant miner. At this point he was making $10.00 an hour, and Toni close to $5.00, enabling them to have the big traditional wedding that Toni said she had always dreamed of. They were also able to close the deal on a small two-bedroom home ten days before the wedding. The place was four blocks from her mother's house in the South Valley area where they had lived all their lives.

Toni said that she did not have to work at the time of her marriage but that she did not want to stay home, at least for a while. Besides her paid job, she did considerable volunteer work at a couple of hospitals in Albuquerque, hoping for an employment opportunity in a health-related field. For two years the couple did well financially. Then, one month after the birth of their first daughter in 1980, Leo lost his job when the mine closed in the recession that hit New Mexico's entire western mining district. Leo was hired two months later as a tractor operator at $9 an hour. This job lasted a year, until a fight with the foreman caused him to resign. Toni had been wanting to quit work during this period, but Leo feared the building tension with his foreman would result in his leaving his job. As he said, "I talked to her about it, and I told her that the job was not secure enough for her to quit . . . I told her why and she understood." Recalling the situation herself, Toni said, "My husband lost his job, or was laid off at that time, so I didn't quit. Kind of fortunate."

Leo drew unemployment benefits for close to a year and despaired that there were no jobs to be had in Albuquerque. Two weeks after his unemployment ran out, he was informed by his brother-in-law of an opening at a plant that made portable heaters and coolers. Leo became a sheet-metal worker at $5.10 an hour. Toni was still a seamstress making $5.00 an hour, piece rate, when we interviewed them. Both jobs provided minimum health and life insurance benefits, and their yearly income of $19,584 allowed them easily to make the $252 monthly payment on their house and meet weekly expenses. Toni said she would have liked to get back into the mental health field, but in her words "there's nothing there. . . . I had the training, and that didn't even help, you know. It's really hard to get into a job like that, but I did try." Leo emphasized his desire to have Toni finish her schooling, but given the immediate importance of her income, he said that dream would have to wait until he got a better job. Since the recession in the mining industry had eliminated high-paying jobs like the one he had held, and since he had difficulty in getting a good blue-collar job in Albuquerque, it seemed unlikely that he would regain his previous earning level.

In 1982, the Senas were "managing," mainly because Toni's job was a stable and relatively well-paid one that she had maintained throughout her husband's period of unemployment. While working at Leslie Pants, Toni had been by turns a secondary provider while Leo was a miner, a mainstay provider while he was unemployed, and finally a coprovider while Leo was a sheet-metal worker. At the time of our interview, both felt that their jobs paid too little to satisfy them, and that there was virtually no opportunity for promotion in either workplace.

The Bacas

Like Toni Sena, Delores Baca, twenty-five, had already been working steadily—for six years— when she married Albert, also twenty-five. Delores grew up in Bernalillo, a town seven miles north of Albuquerque, although her father was from a small Hispano village about fifteen miles farther to the northwest. Her family was heavily involved in the annual Bernalillo fiesta for San Lorenzo, held in August and featuring *matachines* dances. Of all the families we interviewed, Delores and her relatives were perhaps closest to traditional Hispano village life, which centered on a local parish and its religious customs. Delores spoke both English and Spanish and identified herself as "Spanish-Mexican or Mexican-Spanish." She graduated in June 1974 and got her sewing job at Leslie Pants a month later. She met Albert, who grew up in Albuquerque in a large family headed by his divorced mother, that same year, and they started

[65]

"going out." Albert said they wanted to get married, "but at that time, you know, I didn't have nothing to my name. I didn't even have a good steady job or nothing."

Feeling generally alienated, Albert joined the army in 1976, and he and Delores decided to "ease up" on their relationship, though they occasionally corresponded. After his discharge in 1979, however, Albert deliberately set out to court Delores. She was receptive because of the problems she had been having with her boyfriend at the time. Albert had already lost one job after coming home when he asked Delores to marry him. By the time they did marry, seven months later, he was working at a tire sales and repair shop. This job lasted only a few months, but soon he was working at another tire shop.

Finally, Albert secured a job as a stocker for a discount grocery store, his fourth job in the year and a half since he had returned from the armed services. Making $4.25 an hour, however, his contribution was still not sufficient to cover the $200 a month rent on the one-bedroom apartment they had found in a middle-class section of Albuquerque. At the time of our interview, Delores and Albert were renting a one-bedroom house across the street from her parents' home in Bernalillo, for $165 a month. Delores's mother took care of their daughter at no cost; in return, Albert occasionally brought his mother-in-law surplus groceries.

The Bacas reported that in 1981 Delores had earned between $8,000 and $9,000, while Albert made between $11,000 and $12,000. Part of the difference was due to the reduced hours Delores incurred as a result of the 1982 recession in the apparel industry. Despite the temporary difference, however, the Bacas were clearly a coproviding couple, as Albert's attitude toward Delores's working made evident. In response to the question of whether or not they had debated her returning to work after the birth of the baby, he said, "We really didn't talk about it, you know. It came up one time, but I told her, the way it is now, I told her, we need you to work . . . because we wanted to have kids, you know, and without her working and our little girl, we wouldn't make it, not just with my income coming in by itself." And again, when asked how he felt about the amount of time Delores spent away from home, Albert said, "The way I feel about it, you know, if it really bothers her to work and to come home and take care of Cathy, she can quit. But we're just not going to be able to have the nice things that we've been getting. We're going to be living on a strict budget and that's it, not more and no less."

The Riveras

The Senas and the Bacas exemplify the effect on the household economy when the husband's job history is problematic but family income is relatively stabilized by the wife's manufacturing job. Five other couples were also in the lower half of the income distribution within the coprovider category, earning between $18,000 and $23,000. In some households the women were making more than their husbands, whose jobs in service, distribution, or agriculture nevertheless seemed relatively stable. At the upper end of the coprovider category were six additional Hispanic couples in which *both* the husband and wife had stable jobs, the husband either being employed in the same electronics plant or working for a large corporation, or holding a blue-collar job with the City of Albuquerque. The Riveras are a good example of couples in the top end of the coprovider category, those with annual incomes of between $23,000 and $30,000.

Sabine and Deborah Rivera met in the army, where both had trained in basic electronics and communications repair. Once engaged, they planned that each would return home—he to Washington state, she to New Mexico—and as soon as one got a job, the other would move so that they could marry. Deborah was the first to be hired; she got a job at Southwest Electronics. Sabine arrived in Albuquerque and was also hired at Southwest a month later. They were married a month after that. Sabine received several promotions and had been working steadily; it was in fact Deborah who had been laid off and then rehired. In the meantime, they had had a child. At the time of our interview she was making $6.25 an hour and Sabine $7.74. Their combined salary of $26,860 in 1982 enabled them to make the $411 monthly payments on their two-bedroom home in an expanding section of West Albuquerque.

Sabine Rivera, like most husbands in these coproviding couples, was positive about his wife's employment. "I like it. It helps quite a bit. Her income is not the same as mine, but at the same time her income is quite a bit more than what I would say the average [is for] New Mexico people. And without her it would be really tight for me to make the bills." "The bills" in the Riveras' case involved a higher than average house payment and a new pickup truck. Sabine emphasized that "without her working, we wouldn't be doing as good as we're actually doing, and be able to afford some extra things, if we want them. We're doing pretty good, let's just say."

The Pikes

Like the Senas, some Anglo couples had been affected by the husband's loss of a high-paying male job, which made the wife's employment all the more important in the family economy. Mary Pike, twenty-two at the time of our interview, graduated from Gallup High School in western New Mexico in 1981. Her father was in journalism and public relations; her mother was an administrator in a nursing home. It was Mary who described her ethnic heritage as "a little bit of everything. . . . I know that I'm German, Scottish, Irish, Italian, Danish, Slavic." During high school she had worked in a fast food restaurant and for a nursing home, and after graduation she was employed full time in her father's advertising agency at minimum wage for about a year and a half. She said she liked the job but found it difficult to work for her alcoholic father. She then married a young man she had met three years previously. Don, a high school dropout who had taken an equivalency diploma (GED), worked a minimum wage as a janitor for the local Holiday Inn until he broke his leg. Then he went to Albuquerque and worked on commission as a knife salesman for two weeks before returning to Gallup, where he and Mary lived with her father.

Don and Mary next moved to Lovington in southeastern New Mexico, where he began work as an oil driller at $11.95 an hour, and Mary got a job as a cocktail waitress making the minimum wage plus tips. "My husband wasn't thrilled about my job," she recalled, but "it was money, so he didn't complain too much." Mary did not care for her work either: "I didn't like the smell of the bar, the smoke and the alcohol, and spilled drinks splashed on you, [and the customers complaining] 'You gave me the wrong change.'"

Before long Don lost his oil drilling job when he misplaced a ring of important keys. Mary had been a barmaid for two months when she heard a radio announcement that an apparel plant in Hobbs needed stitchers, Even though she lived twenty miles away, she said, "I jumped out. I was there the next morning. They were looking for operators and didn't need any experience, which was good

[68]

because I'd never even, you know, sat down at a sewing machine. And they hired me right there." Don had been out of work three months when he also applied and was hired at the same plant.

The Pikes worked at the Hobbs plant three months before it closed down. They had bought a house trailer while Don was working on the oil rig, and Mary was three months pregnant when the news of the plant closing came: "I was in tears . . . thought I was losing all the insurance, and both my husband and I were losing jobs. I was really scared." The Pikes applied for transfers, however, and felt lucky that both were placed in the Albuquerque plant where they were working when we interviewed them. Their daughter was born four months after they moved to Albuquerque, and Mary returned to work when the baby was six weeks old. Since she had not worked a full year for Leslie Pants, she was not eligible for maternity pay, so "I had to go back and start getting the paychecks . . . I was off completely. It was real hard on us." Mary sees herself as someone who hangs on to a job, even if there are frustrations. Of course, financial considerations were paramount: "We do need the money to get by. We have a lot of real high payments on this trailer. Which has caused us a lot of anguish."

Mary's work history exemplifies the pattern of a woman who moves through a series of low-paying service or low-level clerical jobs that do not usually provide benefits and that accompany a husband's generally erratic job history. A manufacturing job at the end of this series offered basic security with a salary higher than that of previous jobs. The position at Leslie Pants also came with the health benefits that mothers regarded as crucial.

The Smiths

Another Anglo couple presented an interesting job history that was also marked by change over the years but during which the couple made a gallant entrepreneurial attempt to enter middle-class life. Karen Smith, thirty-nine, and Rex, forty-three, were originally from Utah. Karen first married while in high school but was widowed when her son was a year old. She was a waitress when she met Rex, a department store credit clerk when she married him a year later. Karen was not raised a Mormon, but Rex traced his ancestry back to the Mormon families who crossed the plains as pioneers.

Karen stayed home as a housewife the first two years of her marriage, while Rex held down a well-paid job as a fireman for the railroad. In 1965 he became a professional photographer and then a training specialist at Hill Air Force Base in Utah. After the birth of another child, Karen reentered the job market in 1965; she started as a retail stock clerk, then got secretarial training in the manpower program and became an auditor for the Internal Revenue Service. A third child was born during this period, and so her child-care demands led her to get a second-shift job as office clerk at Hill Air Force Base.

Rex quit his job in 1974 because he felt that the affirmative action appointment of a black person had circumvented his own promotion to supervisor of his unit. At this point he set up his own photo studio and women's boutique. More important, the Smiths bought into a statewide cosmetics distributorship that was tied to the "Dare to Be Great" program of Samson Enterprises. Rex and Karen were immediately successful. They expanded their market throughout the western states and supervised ten area directors, who in turn supervised a hundred door-to-door salespersons. Symbolizing their status, Rex said, "Me and my wife . . . would go in Lear Jets, traveling all over the western states, giving conferences . . . [and] training programs . . . and showed them how to build their organizations."

The Smiths' difficulties began when the parent organization ran into tax problems with the Utah attorney general and went bankrupt in Utah; as a result the Smiths lost the $150,000 they had tied up in the company and their home as well. They moved to Tucson, where Rex was hired by one of his own former area directors in the cosmetics business. Karen was pregnant at the time and did not work. They moved to Albuquerque when they were awarded the New Mexico distributorship. But when the supervisor who had made the arrangements with the New Mexico office was killed in a car accident, the Smiths were out of work once again. Then Rex got a job training employees in one of Albuquerque's major new car dealerships—his take-home pay varing considerably with sales. Karen managed a bingo hall from 5:00 to 11:00 P.M. and on weekends at $25 a night.

In 1977 Rex got a temporary job as a photographer and audiovisual coordinator at Kirtland Air Force Base. Karen had had her fourth child in 1976 and was out of the job market for two years. Then Rex was laid off. Karen applied at many places but was especially interested in Aerospace, Inc., because a friend had told her that it paid well. She said, "I just went out and put my application in, and then I kept calling back till they got tired [and hired] me." In time, Karen helped Rex get hired at Aerospace as well. Rex recalled that the wife of a friend of his landed a job there first:

> She got in the door out there and of course she really liked it, the benefits and the programs; well, she got her husband on out there, and eventually she got my wife on, and eventually after I left the government . . . had no job, and so I just says, "Hey, I'll just go out there." Decent money. Started working out there sweeping the floors, got seven dollars an hour for it, you know. You could go anywhere in this town and couldn't get that. So, you know, that was one of the big things I went out there [for].

With his ambitions, Rex said that he put forth his own case at Aerospace, and "I thought things was going to move ahead pretty fast for me . . . building on up to management, but it hasn't happened so far."

The Smiths had been working five years at Aerospace when we interviewed them. She was a line inspector making $10.41 an hour; he was a lathe operator at $10.04. Reflecting the equality of their contributions to the household economy, their budget was set up so that the basic monthly bills came out of her check, and his was used for groceries, clothes, savings, and trips. They were renting a three-bedroom home in a predominantly Anglo section of Albuquerque for $470 a month and were making payments on two vehicles.

The Smiths' income was the highest among the coproviding Anglo couples. There were four couples whose income, ranged like the Riveras', between $23,000 and $30,000. Two households at the lower end of the scale resembled the Pikes in their income level and the husband's steady but not very highly paid wage job.

In all the coproviding couples, both Anglo and Hispano, women had stable jobs in an electronics or apparel plant, had often worked for the same firm for several years, and were earning wages about equal to that of the husband, or even more in some cases. Some husbands had suffered layoffs or unemployment in the recent past, but by the time of our interviews they had been working steadily at a job that perhaps paid only $5.00 or $6.00 an hour but at least put the family on a stable financial footing. The cases we have discussed illustrate that at critical junctures in their history as a couple, the wife's employment represented a contribution equal to the husband's. Both husbands and wives came to recognize that living with the contradictions of a family with a working mother was a necessity in the 1980s.

Mainstay Providers

In the seven Hispano and four Anglo households in which we have classified the wife as a mainstay provider, the husband had not been able to acquire a stable job. Often his skills were fewer and his work history filled with even more layoffs and disruptions than those of coproviding husbands. The household incomes ranged from $15,000 to $19,680 for the Mexican Americans, and from $12,500 to $17,000 for the Anglo couples. In several cases, either the husband had been laid off during the year previous to our interview or the wife had not worked full time. Male vulnerability in the Albuquerque economy, especially in the recession years of 1980–82, emerges even more clearly in the work histories of these families. For most of these working mothers, finding and keeping a job was an important aspect of family economic stability, given their husbands' difficulties in the labor market. Like the women who were coproviders, some of these wives entered an industrial job just after high school and stayed in this kind of work because of the relatively good pay and benefits; others found higher-paying industrial employment after a succession of low-level clerical and service jobs. Facing and living through the contradiction of combining work and family roles was an even greater necessity for these mothers.

The Mondragons

A typical case history among mainstay households is that of Valerie and Roberto Mondragon, both twenty-two at the time of the interview. Both were Albuquerque-born Hispanos. Valerie was raised in the area of Los Padillas in the South Valley, while Robert's family was located in Old Town, an active and very old Hispano community centering on the San Felipe Church. Though neither spoke Spanish at home, they identified themselves as Spanish rather than Mexican American or Chicano. Valerie's first job after high school was as office secretary for Youth Development Incorporated, where she helped place teenagers in jobs. She was working there full-time (at $3.90 an hour) when she met Roberto, and they started going out "every day until we got married." They were married eleven months later when Valerie was two and a half months pregnant. By this time, she had gotten a job on the production line of a dingy leather goods plant.

Roberto's adult work history was delayed nine months because of a foot operation after high school. He was unemployed when he met Valerie and had had difficulty securing steady work from then on. He and Valerie lived with his parents until their daughter was two months old. By the time the child arrived, Roberto was working in construction at a petroleum plant in Barber, Texas, but was laid off after five months. Valerie went back to work again when her daughter was three months old. Asked if she and her husband had discussed her returning to work after the birth of the baby, Valerie said, "He said I had to work. 'If we want to make it and buy a house, you have to work.'"

Valerie was willing, as long as she did not have to manufacture leather products again. Friends in the youth program where she had previously worked informed her of possible openings at a plant that manufactured generators and motors for a space shuttle, but this job was little better than the leather place. The work was strenuous and the environment raucous. Anyway, Valerie was laid off after three months. Roberto managed through a family referral to get a job at a company that manufactured cement slabs for constructing farm buildings. But he was injured again not long after starting, and the resulting operation on his hand laid him up another eight months.

Then Valerie "heard they were hiring" at HealthTech, which had just opened its Albuquerque plant. She applied in May 1981 and was hired the following September at $5.30 an hour on the day shift and $5.50 on the night shift. Valerie's manufacturing job gave the Mondragons' household economy a stability it had not had since their marriage. Meanwhile, Roberto had started as a framer for a construction company at $4.50 an hour, but shortly before we interviewed the couple he was again laid off. By this time, the Mondragons had moved back in with his parents. Asked why, Valerie said, "We were tired of paying rent and utilities and we wanted to save up for our own house." There had been monthly rent payments of $205 and car payments of $175, in addition to the other regular expenses for a family of three.

In the middle of our second interview with her, Valerie said that Roberto had just gotten a job as a "financial adviser or something like that." She was not sure what this job was about; it was "for some kind of broker," she said. It was unclear whether or not Roberto's new

[73]

work would be sufficient to make the Mondragons a stable coproviding couple. If it depended on sales commissions, his lack of experience would likely have meant another period without income following our interview.

Four other Hispano husbands whose wives were mainstay providers had histories of personal difficulties or handicaps. Lorenzo Peña and Felipe Ortiz were alcoholics, which caused much personal and financial disruption in their marriages; Larry Valdez had suffered a back injury; and Allen Griego had a history of epilepsy and memory loss. All four of these men were employed in jobs that paid only $4.00 to $5.60 an hour; it was their wives' industrial jobs that provided each family with a measure of financial stability.

The Phillipses

In the Anglo couples where the wife was a mainstay provider, the husbands suffered a lack of skills or a history of unstable jobs rather than personal or physical disabilities. The fact that in four of our thirteen Anglo couples the husband lacked a steady job paying "male wages" indicates that the economic vulnerability of men in the Albuquerque economy was not just a Mexican-American phenomenon.

Jesse Phillips, age twenty-one, at the time of our interview, provides the best example of a young husband whose lack of skills was the major reason for his distinctly secondary role in the family economy. Jesse was born in Texas, the youngest of six children whose father was employed in the construction industry. The family moved around the West before settling in Albuquerque. Like several other husbands married to mainstay wives, Jesse had dropped out of school. At the time he quit he thought he was "just not getting enough out of high school," but by 1982 he regretted this decision: "If I had stayed in longer, I probably could have learned a lot more." Even his equivalency diploma (GED) had had little impact on his employability. He had held three jobs before going to work in 1982 as a farmer's helper, milking cows and cleaning up on the dairy farm owned by the father of a high school friend. He was earning $3.35 an hour working mornings and evenings, but he had earned only $3.50 at his two previous jobs and $4.00 at his first job after leaving high school. He had apparently been unemployed for the three years between 1978 and 1981.

[74]

It was Jenny Phillips's job at HealthTech that kept the family financially anchored. She and Jesse had been married three months before our interview, and they had a fourteen-month-old son. Jenny was ninteen, the daughter of an Anglo father and a Navajo mother, but she had virtually no contact with her relatives on the Navajo reservation because of her inability to speak the language. She had worked at various jobs while still in high school and living at home. Jesse had been largely unemployed throughout the time that Jenny lived with him before their marriage. As he said, "Well, I had jobs, but nothing you can really put your finger on, call a job, you know, not where you can bring in money and raise a family." Indeed, Jesse was unemployed when Jenny decided to look for work when her child was ten months old. She said that she and her mother went job hunting together and had heard from several sources that Health-Tech hired periodically. Jenny considered herself fortunate: "I know a whole bunch of people that applied but they never heard nothing. And I just came down here one day, with my mom. . . . She was actually looking for a job, and I just applied too, and they called me up, and I didn't even know who they were."

At the time of our interview, Jenny had been working at Health-Tech for five months, but this was enough to make evident her primary providing role. The couple still lived with his mother in her mobile home. His work on the farm was irregular, and he received no fringe benefits whatever. Jesse's wish, classic among the working class in the West and understandable given his lack of skills, was to land a job as a roughneck in an oil field, simply because he knew that the pay was good. More realistically, he said he hoped to get a grant to attend vocational school and take up welding. Expressing his predicament, he said, "God, I can't see doing what I'm doing now, you know. It's getting bad; you have to have a skill." Meanwhile, Jenny's take-home pay of $160 a week guaranteed the $150 a month rent they paid to his mother as well as the basic necessities of life for a family of three.

The three other Anglo couples in the mainstay grouping showed that husbands could earn greater hourly wages than their wives and still contribute less to the family economy overall. Jack Mead had been laid off from his job at a radio station. Brett Anderson, a cement truck driver, had been unemployed for several months because of the recession in construction. Gary Hall was a mechanic at Leslie Pants but had an unstable job history. The precarious nature of the

[75]

Halls' household economy may have been a result of their youth and lack of financial responsibility. Sally Hall recognized a problem in their attitude toward money: "Well, if we had it in the bank, had it organized, paid the bills, and this and that and the other, you know. As it is, we blow it on this and that and the other, and we never have any."

On the other hand, the situation of many of these husbands, both Anglo and Hispano, reflected the economic vulnerability of many working-class men in New Mexico during the early 1980s when mining, construction, and some industrial jobs were disappearing. Men in coproviding families were also affected by the recession, of course. But for many men whose wives were mainstay providers, the combination of the recession with personal problems, lack of skills, or perhaps just bad luck meant that only the wife's manufacturing job made it possible for the couple to cover their housing, food, and transportation costs.

Wives as Secondary Providers

Our study suggests that perhaps not enough attention has been paid to the nuances of economic stratification within sectors of the working class. Though most working wives were either coproviders or mainstay providers, there were some, whose contribution was "secondary" in the sense that the wife typically earned about half as much as her husband or one-third of the family income. This small proportion of the thirty-seven couples (eight, or twenty-two percent) were doing exceptionally well relative to other sunbelt couples we interviewed.

The Sandovals

The dominant pattern in the secondary provider category was for a working-class woman to marry a working-class man who was able to rise through the ranks of a company that provided advancement opportunities.

Geri Sandoval was originally from the small, impoverished town of Mora in northeastern New Mexico and was going to high school in nearby Las Vegas, New Mexico, when she met Ray. Ray was from Albuquerque but was attending Highlands University in Las Vegas.

Before enrolling in college he had been a grocery sacker and a movie usher, both jobs paying less than $2.00 an hour. Ray considered himself a native New Mexican: "I think I'm still carrying on when the conquistadors were conquering. I'm still conquering and this and that . . . I mean I'm battling this and that through jobs and new horizons. Maybe I still carry that type of tradition."

Ray had been at Highlands only one year when he decided to move back to Albuquerque, where he worked first in a lumber mill for $2.00 an hour and then as a plumber's helper for $3.65. Geri stayed in Las Vegas after high school and worked as a babysitter and then a cafe waitress. Their relationship flourished, despite the distance, but their wedding plans were canceled when conflicts arose with both their parents—some having to do with his Catholic and her Presbyterian affiliations. In 1973 Ray was laid off. At the office of the plumbers' union, waiting for a job call, he heard that the telephone company was hiring. He applied and was made a cable splicer, working outdoors.

For some time, Ray's employment history at the phone company was filled with problems. Four months into the job, he was affected by a cutback and was down-graded. As he described it:

> I . . . got booted down to supply attendant, due to [a] forced adjustment type situation. Back in '73, they had this big oil embargo, so they cut off all the oil, and everything started tightening up back there, so they laid off tons of people. I ended up being on the borderline. They offered me a job to work graveyard in supply. I was desperate to work, since I'd been on the [plumbers' union] bench for a month.

Ray and Geri were married in 1974. She did not work during the first year of their marriage but then got a job as a dishwasher at a fast food restaurant. As Ray put it, "The bills, the rent and food, and a simple luxury like going out to eat dinner—we couldn't do it on my check." After three months she was referred by the state employment office to Southwest Electronics, where she got a job as a repair person. She continued working for Southwest, and in 1980 the Sandovals bought a large two-bedroom house in Albuquerque's west end; their payments were $521 a month. In 1981 their son was born, and Geri went back to work at Southwest when he was four months old.

Ray remained a supply attendant for five years before the com-

[77]

pany's fortunes started, as he put it, "blooming again," and he was made a frame attendant in 1979. From there, he hoped to move back to cable splicing, but he encountered what he considered were problems of discrimination: "They would pass me by. I would get pissed off because they would bring in people from New York and New Jersey, and they would call in all these exceptionally qualified people from the East, and I said, 'Hey, I don't believe that's right. There's talent right here in New Mexico.'"

As a result of his threat to go to the Equal Employment Opportunity Commission (EEOC), the phone company made him a "technical assistant" in the central office with slightly better pay. Fortunately for Ray, this position was upgraded significantly to "engineering specialist" a month later, and he started "zooming right up," as he put it. As an engineering specialist he supervised and coordinated the operation of large telephone equipment throughout the state.

In the eight years between his initial hiring and our interview, Ray had moved from wages of just over $5.00 to just over $10.00 an hour. Geri, meanwhile, had moved up to a higher-paid assembly job and was earning $5.96 an hour plus incentive pay.

The Thomases

The Thomas family history was quite similar to that of the Sandovals. Leona identified herself as Spanish; Carl was born in Texas to white parents; both grew up in Albuquerque's South Valley in working-class families. After graduating from high school in 1972, Carl worked less than a year as a gas station attendant and as a truck driver. Then he was hired in the mail room of the gas company at $2.66 an hour. Within a year he became a laborer making $3.20, and a few months later was promoted to skilled crewman at $4.00 an hour.

In 1975 Carl married Leona, who had already been working at an electronics plant for four years. After nine months they built a house next door to Leona's parents and became part of her Hispano extended family network on a day-to-day basis. Carl continued to advance at the gas company, moving up to backhoe operator at $4.66 an hour. In 1977, just before giving birth to their first child and while she was making $7.40 an hour, Leona was laid off and stayed out of the labor force a year and a half before getting a job at another electronics plant. This job lasted only four months, but she was able

[78]

to find work at Computex right away. Starting in 1979 at $3.65, by 1982 she was earning $6.30 an hour. In 1981 they had their second child. In the meantime, Carl had been promoted to construction crew foreman and, after nine years with the company, was making $11.21 an hour. Over the years with Carl's raises and promotions, the Thomas household had become financially comfortable; their house payments were only $142 a month. They also purchased two and a half acres of mountain property, a boat, and a pickup truck and were able to spend weekends away from Albuquerque.

Two other men in these exceptional couples had also made their way from low-paying to relatively high-paying jobs in sunbelt industries. Ronald Gilbert was an Anglo married to an Hispana. After taking vocational classes at the local technical institute, he obtained a job assembling aircraft instruments, and then worked at a plant that produced cash registers, which was taken over by Computex. Promoted from Technician I to levels II and III, by 1982 he was earning $10.80 an hour. His wife, Jeanette, had also had five years' experience at Computex and was making $6.25 at the time of our interview.

José Garcia, from Texas, had been hired in 1976 as a production supervisor for HealthTech and was transferred to Albuquerque when its new plant opened there. He had met and married Donna, a single parent who worked as a personnel clerk at the same Texas plant. In Albuquerque she was able to get a personnel job at the new Systems-Plus plant and then became a skills trainer for $7.00 an hour. Taking advantage of new jobs in Albuquerque had placed the Garcias in the top income earning position of all the couples in our sample. (See the Appendix for occupational and wage data on the other four couples in which wives were secondary providers.)

In sum, these eight couples found themselves in an exceptional position within Albuquerque's working class, primarily because the husbands had been able to get jobs in large industrial firms, public utilities, or city management. Though several of these men had some college or technical training, their education for the most part did not fit their subsequent job situation. Rather, their ability to move up within the same organization, often into better blue-collar jobs but sometimes to managerial positions, meant steady pay raises over a period of five to ten years. In addition, their wives or female partners—though not coproviders—had stable jobs with apparel or electronics firms. Most were making wages above the average for the women in our study.

Single Mothers as Sole Providers

The place of a single mother's job in the household economy is radically different from that of a married woman. The single mothers we interviewed were earning much the same wages as married women (most between $5.00 and $6.00 an hour, with a median of $5.56, but their jobs were the primary means of support for themselves and one or more children. Without a partner who could earn male wages, they were at a distinct disadvantage.

We interviewed fifteen single mothers. Like our married women, their average age was 28.7 years, and most had either one or two children. Their hourly wages ranged from $3.35 per hour (a seamstress at Leslie Pants) to $10.40 per hour (an inspector at Aerospace, Inc.). The three single parents (two Anglos and one Hispana) who earned over $9.00 per hour were all employed at Aerospace, Inc., the plant that paid the highest wages in the city. Their income range was $19,500 to $20,280 per year, totals comparable with those of households in which wives were mainstay providers but unusual among single parents. The other twelve women (ten Hispanas, one *Mexicana*, one Anglo) were earning an average wage of $5.25 per hour and had annual incomes ranging from $4,800 to $12,000—below those of our mainstay couples. Clearly, a woman in a household with a male wage earner, even one with an unstable work history or low-paying job, had the advantage over a woman supporting children on female wages alone.

The work and family histories of these single mothers not only illustrated women's interaction within the Albuquerque economy and the crucial role of their industrial jobs, but also showed how relationships with men and male wages had entered their adult lives at various times. As a group, they represented a wide range of past relationships, marriages, divorces, and living arrangements. Five women had never married the fathers of their children; eight were divorced; one was separated; one was a young widow. Only four received any kind of support from their divorced husbands or the fathers of their children; hence, all these women were the primary providers for themselves and their offspring.

Six (40 percent) of these single parents could not afford to live alone with their children; the other nine (60 percent), including three who worked at Aerospace, had separate households, but their work and personal histories showed that "in practice" women often oscillate between living with relatives or roommates and a growing ability to establish an independent household. Those women who had been in the labor force for several years before the birth of their first child or women who became single mothers through divorce during their late twenties or early thirties were more often able to live on their own. Women who had been teenage mothers and whom we interviewed when they were in their early twenties were often still living with kin. Only a few of the older women in our sample had been able to secure a higher-paying job or even a house of their own. Inez Luna and Lorraine Delgado had formed new relationships and were living with their partners in 1982, thus changing their status from sole to secondary provider. Jeanette Gilbert and Donna Garcia had made this transition several years earlier and had had additional children by their second husbands. Finding a male provider had clearly brought greater financial stability to these women's lives, but not all women can or want to achieve this solution to the dilemmas of single parenthood.

Three cases show how women's work and personal trajectories were shaped by a set of practices and concrete decisions. Susan Anaya had worked several years after high school before having a child and was living on her own with her son at the time of our interview. Her job at Southwest Electronics allowed some independence, but she had often lived with her mother or sisters during periods of financial difficulty, illustrating the dialectical, oscillating quality of a single mother's household economy. Grace Estrada, a teenage working mother who had returned to live with her parents after her divorce, had not yet been able to achieve a separate household like Susan, though she was hoping to do so. Christina Espinosa, divorced later in her life, had been able to find a high-paying sunbelt industrial job and had inherited her mother's house. Each of these cases represents a point on the line from relative dependence to relative independence though in practice women's experiences often swing back and forth between the ends of this continuum as they attempt to deal with the contradictions of being mothers yet supporting their children solely on women's wages.

Susan Anaya: A Fragile Independence

Susan was twenty-eight at the time of our interview with her. Born to working-class parents, she was exactly in the middle of a family of fifteen children, including seven brothers and seven sisters. Like Toni Sena, Valerie Mondragon, and Leona Thomas, Susan was born and raised in Albuquerque; she too spoke only English at home and identified herself as "Spanish." When she graduated from high school in 1972, one of her sisters encouraged her to apply to a training school called the Skills Center, operated by the Concentrated Employment Program (CEP). After eight weeks of instruction in electronics, Susan found a job at a firm that produced business machines, one of Albuquerque's early industrial plants, where she worked nights assembling calculators and cash registers for $3.00 an hour. She continued to live at home, and her salary helped to pay her family's monthly bills.

Susan worked at this job for three years and relished it: "Really, I just loved it. I liked it so much, the people. It was a new building, sometimes it was kind of cold in the winter, but that's natural. I got along with the supervisors, all the way, I mean you didn't even have to know the big shots; they'd go introduce themselves to . . . everybody. And they'd have meetings all the time showing you how production was doing." During this time she moved twice, first to share a place with her sister Elena and a girlfriend, and then to live with another sister, Ramona. By the time she moved to a third apartment with another girlfriend, she was unemployed: in 1975 her firm shut down its Albuquerque plant. Susan received $700 in severance pay and went on unemployment for eight months. Meanwhile, she began "going with" Mike, later the father of her child. After Susan's father died, she and some of her single siblings moved back home to keep their mother from being alone.

In 1976 Susan "just went and applied" and got a job as a Grade 1 assembler at Southwest Electronics. She built wiring for cables, and after a year she was moved up to Grade 2 assembly, doing circuit board touchup. In 1978 she transferred to the progressive assembly line, where she was still working in 1982.

Between 1976 and 1981 Susan moved another three times, the last two times to live with different sisters. In 1981, at the age of twenty-six, she found herself pregnant. She had been seeing her boyfriend for seven years but felt she could not marry him because of his "love of freedom" and his lack, from her point of view, of a sense of responsibility: "A lot of times, he was like a kid." Discussing her decision to manage alone, she said, "I've always been very independent and I just faced it and I thought, well I could do it. I mean, there's younger girls that do it. And I'm an adult; I could do it." By the time of her son's birth, Susan had her own apartment, and a niece came to help with the baby for a few days. When the niece returned to school, Susan moved in with her sister Elena for six weeks and helped by taking care of Elena's children plus the children of another sister, Josephine. Her mother was important during this period as a source of advice and help.

Susan returned to work in November 1981 and found an apartment for herself and her son. At the time of our interview, she said Mike was still waiting for her to call him to resume the relationship, perhaps to get married, and she said she just might follow up on this suggestion. Meanwhile, bringing home $760 a month, she was able to manage rent and utilities payments of $135 a month and other expenses. She felt lucky that a mother of a close friend had volunteered to care for her child during working hours for only $20 a week. Susan's stable job at Southwest Electronics, her long history of participation in the labor force, and her supportive network of sisters and mother were important factors in her ability to maintain an independent household. And since she had several times lived with sisters or her mother, that option was probably open if future financial difficulties warranted a move to a cheaper housing arrangement.

Among the remaining five single mothers who were able to maintain independent households even on women's wages, four could count on help from female kin or in-laws in finding jobs, housing, or child care. Their independence was relative and often achieved only after a period of living with relatives and after continued experience in the labor force.

Grace Estrada: Living with Kin

Most of the six women who were living with kin were also women who had had their first child between the ages of sixteen and nineteen. They had not experienced many years in the labor force before becoming a mother (as had Susan Anaya, for example) or their marriages were very brief, pulling them back into kin relationships and dependence on a mother or sister for help and assistance. Grace Estrada is a good example of the difficulties these young mothers had in combining early parenthood and a job that would eventually provide the kinds of resources necessary to live independently.

Grace was born in Albuquerque, the fifth of seven children; she was raised there and also in Los Lunas, twenty miles south of Albuquerque. Her parents were both from Belen, the largest town to the south of Los Lunas. She grew up speaking English, though her parents spoke Spanish, and like most of our other interviewees she identified herself as "Spanish." Her father was a construction worker, and at the time of our interview her mother was employed at a training center for mentally retarded youth. Right after graduating from high school in 1979, Grace worked at Kmart as a cashier for $2.90 an hour and met her future husband, who also was employed there. By December of the year she graduated, she found herself pregnant. She married quickly, starting family life in an Albuquerque apartment. Her daughter was born in 1980. The marriage soon deteriorated, however, when her husband's drinking problem grew and he began to abuse her physically. She left him when her daughter was five months old and immediately went on welfare.

In 1981 Grace worked as a cook in a fast food restaurant for $3.35 an hour. By this time she had moved into her mother's house, and her mother began providing child care. Grace quit this job in order to focus on the details of obtaining a divorce. Later in 1981 she heard through her cousin that there were openings at the Leslie Pants plant, and she was able to get a job as a seamstress. She worked there eight months, making $5.50 an hour. This relatively high wage meant she was doing well on the piece rate, and at first Grace liked her job. Then major problems arose. One was that her supervisors were rotated rapidly—"so they could know the different departments," she said—and in the confusion of changing supervisors she was falsely accused of having sewed some pants that had been rejected. Also, the plant did not have enough work to assure her of a full week, and her job seemed more and more insecure: "The hours were lousy. . . . I'd come all the way from Los Lunas to work, and they'd send me home at 11:00 a.m. It was a lot of pressure, too. I didn't even know if they were going to lay me off for good until they got a new contract in or what."

In the meantime, one of her previous supervisors moved to the new HealthTech plant and encouraged her to apply there for a job. She did and was hired in late 1981, eleven months before our interview. The HealthTech job paid only $5.00 per hour when she worked days and $5.20 when she worked evenings, but it was less demanding than the job at Leslie Pants and had good benefits. Its major disadvantage was the alternating shifts, two weeks on days and two weeks on evenings. Since her mother was taking care of her daughter, however, Grace was able to manage the rotation. When we interviewed her, she was still living with her parents, even though she did not feel particularly close to them. Her mother cared for Grace's sister's two daughters after school, as well as Grace's daughter. Since the mother herself worked nights (from 11:00 P.M. to 7:00 A.M.), Grace could get home before her mother left for work, even when she was working the evening shift. "I give her what I can a week," Grace said of the cost of child care. "There's times when she won't take it, but I make her take it."

That Grace was looking for more independence was reflected in her consideration of a day-care center for her daughter. Her mother insisted that this was not necessary, but Grace felt that the time put into child care overburdened her mother: "My mom gets home from work, and Nicole's already awake and everything . . . she hardly ever sleeps." Even more telling was her attitude toward her new job at HealthTech. She found the work boring sometimes, but it provided her with job security and good pay and was thus a much better position than she had had at Leslie Pants.

The five other single mothers living with kin were all Hispanas. Four—Annette Griego, Corrine Maldonado, Rosa Gomez, and Regina Armenta—also married young, had relationships that were broken by divorce or death, and then moved in with relatives. Regina Armenta, for example, moved to Albuquerque from Cebolla in northern New Mexico and worked at both Leslie Pants and HealthTech. Her finances were such that she shared an apartment first with her sister and later with her cousin, and sent her son back to Cebolla to live with his grandparents. Carmen Archuleta, the sixth single mother in this group, had her child when she was in her twenties and did not marry the father. She had tried living on her own, but could not meet her expenses, partly because she was having difficulty making the piece rate at Leslie Pants and earned only $3.35 an hour. She thus found it necessary to move back in with her parents.

These single parents who were living with kin had not yet managed to become financially independent, but they did not contrast significantly with the group living independently, many of whom had moved in with parents, siblings, or roommates at some time in the course of their lives as working mothers. This shows a real oscillation between these two states, between independence and dependence on kin. As women became older, however, they were often able to secure the resources (through either a better job or a low-cost housing subsidy) to become head of an independent household.

Christina Espinosa: An Older Sole Provider

Christina Espinosa, a Hispana, and two Anglo women were in a more comfortable financial situation than the other single mothers because they worked at Aerospace, Inc., a unionized plant, and averaged $9.81 an hour. All three had been married and divorced and were in their thirties. Evelyn Thompson and Laura Davidson were still in contact with their husbands, who regularly saw the children. Christina and her brother had inherited her mother's house, and she later purchased her brother's half-interest; home ownership provided her with a measure of financial stability.

The work and marriage histories of these women were in some respects similar to those of the younger, more financially precarious single parents: difficulties with an alcoholic husband, going on welfare after the breakup of a marriage, a long series of low-paying jobs. For all three, however, obtaining (and keeping) a job at Aerospace had been the turning point in their financial histories and the key factor in allowing them to maintain an independent life-style.

Christina Espinosa was born in Albuquerque, the second of three children. Her mother, a New Mexican Hispana, was born in a small village about two hours' drive from the city. Christina never really knew her father, who was of German heritage, because he left the family when she was five years old. Although she celebrated holidays and Hispano traditions with her mother's extended family, Christina preferred to call herself an "Albuquerquian" rather than identify with either her Spanish or her German roots. She saw her own life as parallel to that of her mother: "See, my mom was divorced, raising three kids also [and working full time]. So it's been a family history." At the time of her death the year before our interview with Christina, her mother had been an inspector at Computex. Mother and daughter were both single mothers who had benefited from sunbelt industrialization.

In 1967, at the age of fifteen, Christina became pregnant while dating a *Mexicano* truck driver who was also a neighbor in California, where Christina's mother had moved. She married him; they had a son and moved to their own apartment. When she was seventeen, her second son was born. She took a job as a janitor for six months in order to help out a friend, but her husband opposed her working for wages outside the home. Given his opposition, she expected to become a housewife after the job ended, but her husband's alcoholism and physical abuse caused Christina to leave him and return to Albuquerque in 1972; she and her sons moved in with her mother (who had already come back). Two months later, she got an assembly job at a plant that assembled business machines, where her mother also worked. Because her mother worked days and Christina worked evenings, one could always be home with the children. After the plant closed in 1976, Christina was able to get a job at Aerospace Inc. and her mother at Computex, which took over the plant where the business machines had been made. In 1979 Christina tried living alone with her sons and then with a female roommate. Neither arrangement lasted more than a year, and in 1981 she and her sons moved back to her mother's house.

During this period Christina progressed through several promotions at Aerospace. She started at just over $5.00 an hour in 1976; after several job changes she was making $9.75 in 1983. In 1982, her mother died, and after buying her brother out, Christina was able to use what would otherwise have been rent money for home improvements. At the time of our interview her sons were thirteen and fifteen years old and no longer needed day care. Like many of the other single parents, Christina's life as a mother had started with a teenage pregnancy. When her marriage broke up, she became a working single parent supporting two children but relying heavily on her mother for housing and child care. Financial independence had been made possible only by her relatively high-paying job at Aerospace, Inc., and the fact that she had inherited her house.

The working mothers we interviewed forged an economic position for themselves through their decisions to enter and stay in the labor force and through their varied relationships with male partners and husbands. We have emphasized variations among the household economies of working-class families, both Hispanic and Anglo. The majority of the women we interviewed were either coproviders or mainstay providers, earning half or more of the family income; over a quarter were single mothers and sole providers for their children; only a minority of 15 percent were married to men who earned twice as much as they did and had family incomes that placed them at the comfortable end of the working class.

We have also stressed the processual and dialectical nature of the interface between the family economy and the larger Albuquerque political economy. Family and work histories demonstrate that women often move from one position within the family economy to another as their marital relationships, their husband's jobs, and their own employment change. For some, like the Sandovals, the wife was a coprovider during the early years of their marriage but, as the husband's job trajectory progressed upward, became a secondary provider. For others, like the Senas, the husband's history was full of "ups and downs" that mirrored the New Mexico economy, and the wife was by turns a secondary provider, a mainstay provider, and a coprovider.

The single mothers were in a particularly difficult position, since industrial wages—though better than service-sector wages—were often not enough to support children in an independent household. Examining the histories of single mothers in a processual and dialectical fashion indicates that residential and financial independence is often a fragile state. Those who had been married often moved from being coproviders or mainstay providers in unstable relationships to being sole providers after a divorce. Some lived with parents or sisters before obtaining an apartment of their own; others who had tried to establish their own households, and been forced to move back into shared quarters.

Thus the issue of gender difference loomed large in the constitution of the household economy. Men and women hold very different jobs in a segregated labor market, and women's pay is often much lower in female-dominated occupations compared with that of male-dominated positions. The relative position of the household within our four different segments of the working class often rose and fell in relation to a husband's job stability and earning power, but women's well-paying jobs in the electronics and apparel industries acted as a stabilizing and even critical force.

Ethnic differences were less important. Although more Hispanas were being pulled into industrial jobs—a fact reflected in their larger number in our sample—both Anglo and Hispano couples were distributed among secondary-provider, coprovider, and mainstay-provider categories. Anglo as well as Hispano men lost jobs and were laid off in the 1982–1983 recession. Both Anglo and Hispano males often lacked skills and had personal or health-related problems that contributed to an unstable work history. On the other hand, both Anglo and Hispano men were among those earning wages of $10 or $11 an hour, which, along with a wife's wages, placed the family in a more comfortable position within the Albuquerque working class.

[88]

The biggest contrast was between women who could count on male wages, no matter how unstable, and single mothers. A woman's status as working wife or single mother made a bigger difference in her economic situation than did her ethnic background.

On the whole these women were highly committed to their jobs. Their commitment meant facing a set of contradictions in the workplace and mediating the contradictions between the necessary roles of mother and worker. Contradictions in the workplace centered on the relationship between managers and workers and the role of management policy in keeping productivity high. To understand these everyday struggles on the shop floor, we need to explore two different kinds of sunbelt plants: those that had a traditional hierarchical management structure, and those that were exploring participative management structures.

[4]

Mediating Contradictions
in Hierarchical Plants

The major contradiction in industrial workplaces stems from the fact that firms own the means of production but must employ workers to produce the plant's output through their own labor. For their part, workers use their labor to produce goods that are not under their control but are the property of the firm. In exchange, employees earn a wage to provide for their own subsistence and that of their children, reproducing the labor force on a daily and generational basis. Because managers are always pushing to extract surplus labor from their workers in order to actualize a profit, employees in any workplace are confronted with a system of control. An understanding of the varieties of control systems operating in sunbelt plants provides a starting place for an analysis of the processual and dialectic relations between management and women workers on the shop floor.

We have been influenced by Richard Edward's analysis of managerial control in American industry (1979) but have constructed a set of categories that better reflect the complexities of contemporary Albuquerque workplaces. We describe three interconnected aspects of management control. The first is the labor process itself, the cutting up of production into particular jobs that together result in a product, whether a pair of pants, a video terminal, or an automatic thermostat. The second is the organization of these jobs under a system of supervision. The third is the system of monetary incentives: a wage system (based on hourly rates, a quota/bonus system, and/or piece rates), benefits, and profit sharing.

[90]

These three aspects of control are intertwined in complex ways in any particular plant. Our analysis cross-cuts the categories of simple, technical, and bureaucratic control used by Edwards, since aspects of all three are often found in the same plant, or two types may be combined in a particular department where one segment of the production takes place.[1] Within a hierarchical structure, for example, an apparel plant may use a labor process based on the bundle system (a form of batch processing), determine wages by a piece rate, and put evaluation and discipline in the hands of a supervisor. Here control is exerted primarily through the wage system and the simple control exercised by supervisors. In other hierarchical plants, an assembly line (a form of technical control) might be the center-piece of the control system. In contrast, in participative plants the "debureaucratization" of control (Grenier 1988), or the apparent attempt to break down hierarchy and rigid procedures, is part of reorganizing the labor process, the wage system, and supervisor-worker relations. Thus a "high involvement" plant may use an assembly line but allow workers to rotate jobs. Management may debureaucratize control through worker participation in teams or employee votes on shift rotation and holiday schedules. Plant managers may initiate equal benefits for blue-collar and white-collar employees, or pay workers by the hour with little attention to quotas and without the complicated calculations involved in a piece-rate system.

In addition to the labor process, supervisory structure, and wage system, there is a fourth and very important component: nonmonetary rewards. These are crucial in creating a plant "culture," both within a department or team and at the plantwide level. The character of this plant culture may be determined by a union, may buttress a traditional hierarchy, or may build loyal company employees in a nonunion environment. In addition, participative policies and plant culture together can help to persuade workers to accept the management's vision of the firm, rather than encouraging workers to

---

[1] Control systems involve the direction of tasks in the work-place, the evaluation of the work itself, and the discipline and rewards meted out to workers as a result. Edwards (1979:18–21) defines simple control as the ability to exercise power personally, to reward good performance and discipline workers on the spot. Technical control is embedded in the labor process itself, usually in the way machines control the pace and direction of work; the assembly line is the classic example. Bureaucratic control is institutionalized hierarchical power through the firm's rule of law or company policy.

shape their own vision of what worker-management relations are like.

Each one of these aspects—labor process, supervisory system, wage system, and plant culture—can be thought of as organized along a continuum: more to less fragmented, more to less hierarchical, more to less based on incentives, and more to less controlled by management. The particular combination of practices used in each plant is critical to an understanding of the framework for "practical" relations on the shop floor.

Our analysis examines two contrasting kinds of plant organization. The three plants described in this chapter had hierarchical management structures; the four plants described in Chapter 5 utilized various components of high-involvement—less hierarchical, more participative—organization, reflecting the impact of Japanese management policy on American corporations in the early 1980s. Each plant's control system brought about a variety of responses among workers, ranging from acquiescence (successful co-optation by management) to individual coping tactics and various forms of collective resistance. We argue that whether women's tactics take the form of resistance or acquiescence on the shop floor, they are not easily understandable in terms of ethnic and cultural background but are more clearly the result of the dialectical relationship between management policies and workers' attempt to retain control of their labor and their own vision of their work.

Difference and Dialectical Relations in the Workplace

Management's attempts to extract greater productivity from workers and at the same time pay as low a wage as possible have created a division of labor in the industrial workplace which emphasizes gender difference. Historically, women have been recruited for semiskilled jobs that emphasize manual dexterity, hand-eye coordination, and patience. From the early nineteenth century until World War II, they were recruited as daughters from families where their reproductive labor could be absorbed by others. Daughters' relatively weak position in the productive family economy and early wage economy meant that they could be hired in wage jobs at much lower pay than could their brothers and fathers. Ideological notions about women's place in the home, their ability to do work that required "nimble fingers," and their presumed inability to do "heavy male work" may have encouraged employers to place women in particular jobs. Alternatively, such cultural notions may have been a post hoc justification of women's weak economic position. In either case, lower female wages and a set of ideas justifying women's appropriateness for certain jobs have gone hand in hand in the creation of gender-based difference in industrial jobs.

In the industries we studied in Albuquerque, where jobs were segregated by gender, the proportion of female to male workers varied considerably from plant to plant. Apparel and health products plants were predominantly female. At Leslie Pants, of 488 direct production workers, all 450 stitchers were female (92 percent); one of sixteen machine repair workers was female; all twenty-two cutters were male. At the other extreme was Aerospace, Inc., whose work force of over 1,600 was 80 percent male (primarily skilled machinists); there were approximately 320 female production workers in three assembly departments. In between were many of the electronics plants with a ratio of about 60 percent females to 40 percent males. For example, the Southwest Electronics plant had a work force of 1,006 in 1982; of the 888 Hispano and Anglo names that could be identified from union records, 586 (66 percent) were female and 302 (34 percent) were male. Men were platers, machine setters, and technicians; women worked on the assembly line or were testers and materials handlers.

Aspects of control, especially the production process and the wage system, varied within these gender-segregated work forces. Batch processing and piece rates characterized the organization of women's work as stitchers in the apparel industry, and "stuffing boards" on an assembly line was a typical electronics job for women. Men in these same plants (such as mechanics and cutters in an apparel shop, and machine setters and techs in an electronics firm) did not usually work under piece rates or on a quota/bonus system. Further, their jobs were more individualized and not regulated by an assembly line.

Men in other industries, of course, often do work on assembly lines, as in the auto industry (Shaiken and Herzenberg, 1988), or are paid on the piece rate, as in a machine shop (Burawoy, 1979). But these are male-dominated industries characterized by higher wages and a different history of management-worker conflict and unionization. Thus, on their own, the labor process, management supervision, and a wage system are "gender neutral." As they are combined

[93]

in any particular industry or plant, however, they are experienced differently by male and female workers because job categories are so gender specific.

In some instances, management has used ethnicity as well as gender to divide workers. For example, in the textile industry in Rhode Island, waves of immigrants were recruited to different job levels within a gender-segregated division of labor: English, Irish, and French Canadian men who arrived as the industry was expanding occupied the best jobs; Portuguese and Polish men were confined to the lower-paying male jobs in the picking and carding rooms; women, less ethnically segregated, were compressed into a narrow range of middle-level jobs (Lamphere 1987). Canneries have hired immigrant Mexican women for some jobs and Mexican-American women for others (Zavella 1987). Blacks are often recruited to service and clerical work in hospitals, while nursing remains chiefly a white female occupation (Sacks 1988).

In the industries locating in Albuquerque in the 1970s and 1980s, however, women of Mexican-American, Anglo, black and Asian backgrounds were in mixed departments and teams and experienced much the same working conditions. Furthermore, in a primarily English-speaking labor force, language was not a barrier to informal relations between workers. In plants where Mexican Americans predominated (for example, Leslie Pants was 60 percent Mexican American and 20 percent Anglo), many lunch or break groups were dominantly Mexican American. Several of the Anglo women we interviewed were, similarly, part of an all Anglo group. But in other plants these groups were more varied and mixed. In either case, when we examined workers' response to management control, ethnic difference faded into the background. Women's practice in dealing with management policy and the dialectical relationship between management and women workers as it evolved in each plant was much more an outcome of women's relationship to the labor process, wage system, and plant culture than to their own cultural or ethnic background.

We interviewed working mothers in three plants where the production process was embedded in a traditional hierarchical system of control (see Table 15). Each plant was organized into large sections (of at least thirty workers) managed by supervisors or foremen who reported to a line or area supervisor, who in turn reported to the a production manager or plant manager. Each firm used a slightly

Table 15. Characteristics of hierarchical plants

Firm	Size	Production process	Pay system	Management policies	Work culture
Leslie Pants	600 (450 female)	batch process	piece rate	3 line managers, 4–5 supervisors; clocking out	piped-in music; President's Club, Entertainment Committee, Community Involvement Team
Southwest Electronics	1,006 (586 female)	assembly line batch process	piece rate quotas	large depts.; 10 supervisors, 80 foremen; 8 grades	union election; picnic, Entertainment Club
Aerospace, Inc.	1,678 (320 female)	batch process	quotas (not enforced)	large depts.; area manager, area supervisors, foremen; 24 grades	union; little management-sponsored activity but active union celebrations

different combination of techniques (some technical, some bureaucratic, some simple) for exerting control. Given our emphasis on the
extraction of labor through control systems, we view each plant in
terms of a dialectical relationship between management policies and
women's responses. We characterize these responses in terms of
"work practice," including the development of both individual and
group-level tactics and strategies for either coping or resisting.

We interviewed thirteen women who worked at Leslie Pants and
three at other apparel plants, ten at Southwest Electronics, and six at
Aerospace. This chapter focuses on three or four women at each
plant to illustrate the dialectal relationship between the management
control system and resistance in each one. We have selected both
Hispano and Anglo examples in order to demonstrate that the labor
process, wage systems, and management policies, (rather than ethnic
identity or cultural background) shape women's responses to their
work.

Women's Work in a Hierarchical Apparel Plant

At Leslie Pants the organization of the labor process around batch
processing, the piece-rate system with an attendant training program, and the important role of supervisor was similar to that of
other large garment factories in the United States (see Lamphere
1979). In the apparel industry the sewing machine is still the center-
piece of the production process. Most stitchers (90 percent) are
women. Each one works at her own machine and has control over it.
Like most modern apparel manufacturers, Leslie Pants used the
progressive bundle system, a form of batch processing. The garment
pieces were cut in the cutting department by men whose jobs were
more highly skilled and better paid than those of stitchers. Then the
pieces were tied in bundles and sent through a progressive series of
operations. At Leslie Pants, "parts" such as pockets and zippers were
attached in the early stages of the process; the back and front panels
were assembled in the next set of operations; next the two halves
were sewn together; and, finally, the labels were sewn in and the
pants inspected. There were three production lines, each with a line
manager and four or five section supervisors. The line managers reported to the assistant manager and the plant manager.

Control was exerted both by the piece-rate system and the supervisor. A third important aspect of control was the training program with instructors, a "blue book" of instructions on how each sewing operation was to be done, and a learning curve that prescribed how many pieces should be completed each day during every week of training. Supervisors exercised some simple control: that is, they could make some decisions on their own "gut feelings." The supervisor's job and the piece-rate system, however, were highly bureaucratized and "rule bound." Wages were supplemented by a benefit package and a profit-sharing system. A host of activities buttressed the piece-rate system itself, including rewards for reaching higher and higher levels of efficiency, bonuses, plant-sponsored events, and informal women's celebrations. Those activities outside the production process, were thought to build worker morale and a loyal work force.

The essence of the piece-rate system is that a worker's wages depend on the level of efficiency she reaches. "Efficiency" is defined as the number of, say, hip pockets or belt loops that must be sewn in a day to reach a base rate, or 100 percent efficiency, which in 1982 was $4.25 an hour. In the system used at Leslie Pants, the hour was divided into 100 parts, and rates were calculated by standard average hours (SAH). Each operation therefore had an SAH number representing the units per hour a worker needed to complete in order to earn the base rate.[2] Since workers were paid incrementally for work over the minimum wage, women often calculated how many bundles a day they had to do in order to reach a particular "efficiency rate" 110 percent efficiency or even 130 percent or 140 percent.

Jeans were cut in bundles, with sixty pairs to a bundle for designer pants and fifty-four for "basics." There were forty bundles to a cut, and work orders were processed by the cut. Each bundle was placed in a buggy and had a ticket composed of control stickers with operation and SAH numbers. A worker took the control sticker for her operation off the larger sheet and stuck it on the "gum sheet" that she turned in at the end of the day; it contained the cut number and bundle number for each bundle she did, plus the operation number, the size, and the SAH (the number that determined how much she got paid per bundle for an operation). Jobs were divided by class: belt loops were class 3, sides seams were class 5, banding was class 6.

---

[2] A worker could calculate her hourly pay by the following formula: SAH times units (in dozens completed per day) times base rate, divided by the number of hours worked. Alternatively, dozens times SAH times base rate equaled the pay per day.

Since the base rate was multiplied by the SAH, which was different for each job class a higher class meant a higher rate of pay: the 100 percent efficiency level of class 5 jobs paid $4.00 to $5.00 an hour; a class 3 job, $3.00 to $4.00.

At the plant level, the manager's monthly budget was calculated on cost translated into standard average hours. For example, one pair of fashion jeans was .22 SAH—that is, it took about one-fifth of an hour to produce one pair of pants—and only .18 SAH for a pair of "basic jeans." About 40 percent of the monthly budget was spent on sewing wages. One-third went into overhead (including training, benefits, and time lost when machines were being repaired or workers waiting for bundles). The remainder was spent on materials and supervisory and clerical wages. The plant manager was allowed 30–40 percent overhead but tried to keep those expenses down to 25 percent of his monthly expenditures. Thus, supervisors were always under pressure to reduce sewing overhead, especially "off-standard time" due to machine delays or a shortage of work.

During the recession of 1982 and 1983, Leslie Pants often operated on reduced hours. Workers would sometimes arrive at 7:00 A.M. and be dismissed at 11:00, or come in from 11:00 to 3:00 P.M. (Those who came in were guaranteed at least four hours of work). Each line had a quota to get out for the day—perhaps ninety bundles. The supervisor had to see that the work moved through the line and that there were enough women on each operation to complete the quota— or cut back on the number of workers to adjust to a lag in orders.

The Labor Process in Sewing

Although Leslie Pants was part of a large, multinational firm, relatively little automated equipment was being used in the Albuquerque plant. For example, cutters were not using the new computer-guided laser systems which can cut fifty layers of cloth at a time. In addition, there were relatively few numerically controlled devices on the sewing machines (Lamphere 1979; U.S. Bureau of Labor Statistics 1977). Cutting-room innovations had taken place in the men's shirt and suit industry but were not common in work and leisure clothes; neither had stitchers been transformed into machine loaders. The women we interviewed used standard industrial one- or two-needle machines and were working on learning curves with an attendant piece rate. The labor process was similar to that of the Rhode Island apparel factory described by Lamphere (1987), although neither the number of styles produced by the Albuquerque plant nor the number of style changes per year were as great as in a plant that made children's clothes.

Their own descriptions of their work give a sense of how women learn to do an operation as fast as possible without making mistakes. This takes a great deal of hand-eye coordination and an ability to pace oneself throughout the day, always being aware of how many bundles must be done in order to keep up one's production. A weekly paycheck was based on the work done throughout the whole week; thus slow days were averaged in with ones that went well. In addition, workers were able to "clock out" (go on nonstandard time) if there was no work or if they were having machine trouble; they were then paid the average hourly wage they had earned over the previous quarter of a year. The decision to let a worker clock out was made by the supervisor and was part of the way she controlled work flow and the actual work of her subordinates. As noted, she was always under pressure to keep clock-outs low in order to reduce overhead.

We focus here on four workers, two Anglos and two Hispanas. Carrie Adams, an Anglo and a highly successful stitcher of hip pockets, had been employed at Leslie Pants for six years when we interviewed her in 1982; she was making $6.50 an hour at 130 percent efficiency. Delores Baca, a Hispana (one of the coproviders described in Chapter 3), had worked at the plant for eight years. In 1982 she was working on belt loops but had been trained to hem pants as well. She was making $5.37 an hour, had recently reached 110 percent efficiency, and was working toward 120 percent. In contrast, Mary Pike, an Anglo and a mainstay provider (see Chapter 3) had been employed for only one year; she made $5.11 an hour and had been struggling to keep her piece-rate average up to 78 percent on the new job (elastic waistbands) she had been assigned after she returned from her pregnancy leave. Toni Sena (also in Chapter 3) had worked for Leslie Pants for five years and was retraining on front pockets. She had reached 100 percent after two and a half weeks of retraining and was attempting to achieve 110 percent when we interviewed her. She was earning only $5.04 an hour, however, because her job was only a class 3 operation.

Each worker developed tactics or individual coping strategies to

[99]

deal with the piece-rate system, which pushes workers to produce as quickly as possible but also accurately, or the work will be returned for repairs, resulting in lost time and wages. Individual response begins during training or retraining, which introduces workers to "the method" or routine for doing a job, as written up in a "blue book." As Delores Baca explained:

> They do expect for you to go by the method, that's what the instructor is for. To show you the method and how to do it in order to be faster. But sometimes . . . you think, but I can do it this other way, and it'll be faster for me. But they do come around and check you to see if you're on your method. . . . Once I see her coming I right away go back to my method, you know. But to me doing it the way where I feel more comfortable and faster at it . . . I do it that way. But when I do see them, I right away go back to my method.[3]

Carrie Adams, who sewed hip pockets on line 3, was particularly articulate about the strategies she developed to gain some control over her work. Carrie was able to sew seventeen bundles a day, an efficiency rate of 130 percent. She and a close friend who could complete eighteen bundles were the highest producers of the eight workers on their operation: the workers who helped make it possible for their group to put out eighty bundles each day. Carrie explained at length how she did backtacking without actually changing needle direction. It was tricky, and she was one of the few who could do it. "I lift up the presser foot . . . just a little bit, not much, while I'm still going with the pedal," and would pull the material forward so that the machine stitched backward. Then she would let the presser foot down and continue to sew her seam. The process outlined in the blue book involved putting the presser foot down, sewing backward, picking it up, adjusting the material, and then putting it down and sewing forward. Carrie, who learned this trick by watching a co-worker, explained that it saved "just a second, but every second counts when you are putting out that mass." That Carrie had been able to master a faster way of backtacking accounted for her success at the job.

[3] Jennie Garcia, an interviewee who had been an instructor for four years, noted that not all instructors insist that their trainees follow the blue book: "If you see that somebody's making their goal and is producing more . . . why do anything?"

[100]

In addition to the "tricks" associated with performing an operation as quickly as possible without making mistakes, workers must learn to keep their production up during the day. Lucy Benavidez, an inspector, described how she paced her work: "It requires ten bundles a day. . . . I have to have six and be starting my seventh by lunch time. [By the second break] I have to have eight . . . and ten by the end of the day. I usually start my eleventh and leave it for the next day." Other workers, including Linda Bennett, whose operation was called Hang Pockets, described much the same system of pacing their work.

Struggling with Work Difficulties

The tactics or coping strategies discussed thus far give a worker a measure of control over her work so that she is less at the mercy of the piece-rate system. These tactics are acquired with continual work experience and assume that work progresses smoothly. Others evolve because of difficulties that arise in the labor process itself: errors made in the cutting room or by previous stitchers; machine problems that can slow production and mean a loss in take-home pay. Some of the more seasoned workers were able to obtain clock-outs from their supervisors or have faulty material replaced; others were less successful in developing individual tactics to deal with work difficulties.

Delores Baca explained one difficulty: "Like now we've been having problems with our [belt] loops. They've been like over-lapped. . . . And we've been having trouble with that because they're too fat on the bottom and we can't fold them and they don't look right like that, you know . . . [so we] throw them away. So we've been having problems with that, but we do go straight to our supervisor or line manager." In this case the supervisor was crucial in getting new loops, so that workers would not lose pay.

Mary Pike was less successful in coping with problems from the cutting room. She was being retrained on elastic waistbands and was sewing only five bundles a day, or 78 percent efficiency—below what she should have been doing in her fourth week. She had difficulties with uneven edges and skipped stitches, but she also often had problems with shaded parts, a difficulty that emanated from the cutting process. Mary apparently absorbed the mistakes herself, doing repairs when garments were returned to her. "If they're shaded [from fabric dyed in a different batch] like say the bands are dark brown and the pants are a little beige or something . . . if you sew it on you get it back. . . . You get pretty quick at ripping out too. But it does take a long time to make repairs on the operation."

Others had difficulties with their machines. Workers often felt that each machine had its own idiosyncrasies, which one learned to handle. But if a machine was down for a good part of a day, a worker's production for the week would be lower, and it was the weekly average production on which pay was based. Some women struggled with machine difficulties but were never able to overcome them and began to lose pay. Maria Apodaca had so many machine problems when she was being retrained on a new, higher-class job that she began to experience difficulty with her eyes. Her percentage dropped, and when we interviewed her she had just been suspended for three days for a low efficiency rate.

Carmen Archuleta, a relatively new worker like Mary Pike, was also having machine difficulties: "You try so hard all week and then one day you mess up, or something happens. That's it. . . . Your whole effort . . . and everything that you've done that week just goes down the drain." Because Carmen was having machine troubles in addition to problems in learning a new task, her weekly pay had dropped from $250 to $80. As a single parent she could not keep her apartment on those wages and was forced to move in with her parents (see Chapter 7).

Carmen, Mary, and Maria were all relatively new workers who were also being retrained on a new job and simultaneously experiencing machine difficulties or trouble with cutting-room mistakes. Carrie, Toni, and Delores, who had been at Leslie Pants for three to nine years, were in jobs they knew well and were not struggling with work difficulties. Carrie was earning $6.50 an hour; Toni and Delores were making less but still operating at better than 100 percent and were not being sanctioned by the management for poor production. These more experienced workers felt less ambivalent about the piece-rate system.

Attitudes toward the Piece Rate

Piece-rate pay often divides workers and creates competition. Some fast workers are labeled "rate busters" because their productivity is often used as the standard for a new piece rate on a particular operation (see Lamphere 1979). Leslie Pants, however, produced men's pants which involved a limited number of operations and few drastic style changes (compared with plants that specialize in women's or children's wear). Operators did get shifted from one job to another, depending on production needs and new styles, but a large number of operations (side seam, left fly, right fly, hip pockets) kept the same rate over a number of styles of pants. Thus many women had a steady chance to master an operation, and we found little sense that the piece-rate system produced competition or individualized behavior—perhaps because we interviewed chiefly women who were high producers and had little to complain about. Many expressed the view that "you are working for yourself" and "how much you earn is really up to you." Some women understand that piece rates could be used against them but felt that management operated the system fairly. As Toni Sena said: "When a new job comes out, they come out and study you . . . but they study a couple of girls; they watch and make sure that they're doing it by the method. And they time them, and that's how they come out with the base rate. . . . So that's pretty fair, I think." Other workers, such as Mary Pike did not emphasize competition but did acknowledge that there were problems working under a piece-rate system when cutting mistakes or machine problems got in the way of production. One or two workers even took a management perspective, arguing that any competition was friendly and helped them to produce more, or that the piece-rate system kept workers from slowing down their production.

The operation of the piece-rate system at Leslie Pants contrasted with that of the apparel plant studied by Lamphere in Rhode Island in 1977. There the plant was unionized and characterized by a women's work culture in resistance (1985:529). Workers protested rates that seemed arbitrarily high through the union grievance structure. Workers in the same department constructed a set of informal work rules to even out the work and keep competition and rate busting from developing, especially among new immigrant Portuguese workers. At Leslie Pants, perhaps because of fewer style changes and less complex operations, management of the piece-rate system seemed less arbitrary and divisive. Hence, tactics for coping with it remained at an individual rather than a group level. Overall management strategy in the past (which may have organized the piece-rate system so that women could reach high efficiency levels) had kept

[103]

out a union, leaving the role of the supervisor important to the overall control system.

The Role of the Supervisor

Supervisors allocated work to keep it moving evenly through their sections, laid off workers for the remainder of the day when their production quota was completed early, and periodically checked the production of workers in order to keep track of how things were progressing: "If we're falling behind, she reminds us of it." One of the ways a supervisor exercised control was by dispensing or restricting clock-outs. "If we run out of work or something, she has to realize that before we clock out, I mean we're out of work, you know. Cause they're real strict on clock-outs over there. . . . [But]if you're out of work . . . that's time moving on you, so she has to be around to find us work or clock us out."

Supervisors were also instrumental in a decision to suspend a worker for low production or even insubordination. These situations often led to the exercise of simple control, to supervisory discretion rather than "company policy." At least one woman felt that supervisors had their favorites. Maria Apodaca, a monolingual Spanish speaker, believed that "women who have friends there" could get what they wanted, and that had she been able to speak English she would have been better able to "defend herself."

For each woman, then, her relationship to her supervisor was crucial. A supervisor's intervention in giving a clock-out could help a worker keep her quarterly average up, but supervisors were not always generous with clock-outs, since they counted against the department. Many women were satisfied with their supervisors, but clearly there was room for favoritism and other problematic elements of simple control. Women needed individual tactics to keep on good terms with supervisors, so that they would not be at the mercy of machine difficulties and cutting-room mistakes.

Incentives and Benefits

The piece-rate system acts almost automatically to extract labor from workers as they push each day to increase their pay. At Leslie Pants, management's major intervention was to buttress the piece rate with a system of rewards, incentives, and benefits. Yet the piece-rate system and supervisory control could also create worker competition or disgruntlement with supervisors. Efforts to prevent this divisiveness and keep up morale led to a second strategy on management's part: the creation of a strong plantwide work culture. This included sponsorship of nonwork activities ranging from picnics to raffles, and included contests at Halloween and Christmas. By co-opting workers' organizational skills and cultivating their participation in plant activities, the firm prevented the formation of a strong women's culture of resistance. The plant manager was quite clear about this: "If a manager takes care of his people, then there are no problems"; if not, he might "tap out" the available labor pool or encourage unionization.

Awards were given for higher and higher levels of productivity, culminating in membership in the "President's Club" for workers who produced at 130 percent efficiency. Each worker graduated from the training program when she reached 100 percent efficiency, but further recognition was given to those who reached 110 and 120 percent. Graduations were held on Thursdays, and those being recognized were presented with a diploma and given soft drinks or coffee and brownies during the morning break. As Delores Baca described the system, "First they give you little flags, and then with 100 percent you get a pin that says [Leslie Pants] and then you get a flag that says 100 percent [which goes above the worker's machine]. And then your 110, you get another pin and your flag for 110." Delores, who had received her pin for reaching 110 percent on belt loops, said that the recognition made her feel "proud, happy . . . because you're working so hard, cause you know you want to make money see. And . . . you feel happy that you have already made it and you know you can make it everyday and you can make some money, you know."

Once a worker had maintained 130 percent for seven weeks, she joined the President's Club, and her color photo was posted on the wall in the front entryway. Members were taken out to lunch yearly by the plant manager and thanked for their effort on behalf of the plant. Delores and others were very positive about the President's Club: "I like it but you got to work, you got to work hard to get into it." Toni Sena emphasized how difficult it was to maintain high levels of production because of daily layoffs during the recession or disruptions in the production process. Toni was trying to achieve 110 percent on front pockets but was having difficulty accruing the thirty-two hours per week for two weeks necessary to get the award, because reduced production had sent women home early several days a week. Nevertheless, reactions to the reward system were positive, and some women showed us their certificates and pins. There was no sense that the system was an unnecessary embarrassment, at odds with actual production. Instead, workers felt that the plant really depended on the 130 percent workers to keep production up.

As part of the incentive system, the plant manager also tried to promote from within. "This is one of my weapons against the union," he admitted. Another policy he instituted was a grievance committee. A representative from each section met monthly with the manager, who listened to complaints and later went out on the shop floor and looked into them. Carrie Adams, in particular, had found the current manager very sympathetic and innovative: "He's trying to bring in a lot of new things."

Wages at Leslie Pants were supplemented with a range of benefits that included medical insurance, ten paid holidays, two weeks' paid vacation for employees with three years of experience and three weeks for those with five years. There was no dental insurance and a large deductible on the medical insurance, but the benefits package was important to the women we interviewed. Several, including Carrie Adams, had taken advantage of the maternity leave policy, which paid $80 a week ($69 take-home pay) for six weeks after the baby was born. With a doctor's excuse she was able to take two weeks off in April before the baby arrived; adding to her six weeks' leave a two-week shutdown and her accrued vacation time gave her a three-month break.

Mary Pike had not worked at the company long enough to be eligible for the maternity benefit. She came back to work at six weeks because she needed the money. Nevertheless, Mary felt positive about the benefits: "That's one reason I've stayed with the company as long as I have. I do like the benefits. The insurance . . . we get life insurance on us." Carrie, on the other hand, thought the benefits should be improved to include sick leave for production workers, dental insurance, and help in paying for added medical expenses such as birth control pills.

Finally, Leslie Pants had a profit-sharing plan whereby workers were awarded points for each year of service and for the wages they made over $4.50 an hour under the piece rate. A large sign at the front of the plant showed how many points were possible for each worker, depending on length of service and productivity. Slowed production during the 1982 recession, however, meant that the company had not paid on the profit-sharing plan for several quarters. Mary Pike, as a newer worker, had never benefited from the program: "As long as I've worked there they never had any profits to share."

A Plantwide Work Culture

The celebration of life-cycle events such as a wedding, the birth of a child, or a birthday is often an occasion for creating a women's culture on the shop floor (see Lamphere 1985). At Leslie Pants, however, a nonunion shop, these celebrations dovetailed with management's more traditional means—incentives and rewards—of building a loyal work force. Workroom celebrations were sometimes even organized by the supervisor or someone she appointed, though in other cases a woman's co-worker or friend took on the responsibility.

The bundle handler had taken the initiative to arrange a baby shower for Mary Pike when her child was three months old, a week before we interviewed her.

> It was a real surprise because you know I kind of expected it before I had her, but then I went to the hospital early. And then when I went back, they didn't throw one for me right away, so I kind of just thought, well, I guess they're not gonna. You know, because I already had the baby. And they surprised me. . . . I got gifts from people that don't even speak English, or some people I never talk to. . . . They made a cake that said, "Welcome Tracy—You Were Early—We Were Late."

The short hours during the recession of 1982 curtailed work-room celebrations because, as one worker suggested, "nobody had the money to pitch in. They're starting up now again though [July 1983]. . . . They're still throwing baby showers, you know they kept up the baby showers. But [they quit doing] the birthdays."

Larger celebrations and plantwide activities, more clearly tied to the manager's efforts to build a strong work culture and a loyal labor force, were organized by management-sponsored committees. The most important of these was the Entertainment Committee. "We try and keep the morale up," explained Carrie Adams, who was a member.

[107]

At first we had a lot of money, but then they cut us back. What we were trying to do was give them something every month . . . to keep the morale going . . . keep everybody happy. We've been cut back a lot. So we do that when we can. Usually, we do the picnic which is in August. We try to have a lot of things going on there. . . . We do have a Christmas dance. We try and give them activities at the plant. Like a Halloween Extravaganza.

The yearly picnic was one of the biggest events planned by the Entertainment Committee:

The picnic has a lot of other things mixed up in it. They do have a softball game. They give you trophies. . . . And they have volleyball tournaments. We have a tug-of-war. And this year we are going to have a sponge-throwing contest, where we get all the managers in. It's going to make a big hit. . . . This is going to be the first year they are going to charge for anything at the picnic. Because we have to pay for that stuff. Usually it costs $1,000 for that picnic, and we don't have it.

The Entertainment Committee has also sponsored a Christmas decoration contest. In 1981, as Linda Bennett described it, "In line l, we just had Christmas balls and paper, crepe paper and tinsel, and the other section had a Nativity scene. Real Nativity scene, the real donkey, the real baby. And one had a toyland, with just nothing but stuffed animals everywhere you looked." Other plantwide leisure-time activities included a bowling league and free tickets to the local baseball games (bought with Entertainment Committee funds). The company gave gifts at Christmas, such as windbreakers or ice buckets, and often provided turkeys to employees at Thanksgiving.

Another important committee was the Community Involvement Team. "They raise money for things like the Ronald McDonald House," Mary Pike explained. "They plan all the fund-raising things. That's what all the raffle money and stuff goes to. Except for a part that you get as a prize . . . you can get $20 or $50. Last year in [the other plant where I worked] they had a cake-baking contest for the men in the company. My husband baked German chocolate cake and got second place . . . and he brought home $25 and a turquoise ring. Just for making a German chocolate cake. Plus we got to eat it."

Despite cutbacks in these events, the plant still had a lively work culture meant to create a congenial atmosphere on the job. The plant manager was quite clear that this atmosphere was an important anti-

[108]

union strategy, along with the policy of filling good jobs internally and rewarding workers for high production. This particular manager had been brought to Albuquerque in June 1981 when there had been a union drive. The previous manager, considered responsible for the mounting of this drive, was "no longer with the company." "If you come to a non-union plant and it becomes union, you don't have a job."

A Successful Management Policy

Leslie Pants had been very successful in creating a labor force that contained a number of high producers (members of the President's Club). Equally important, most of the thirteen women we interviewed there were reasonably satisfied with their jobs, rating aspects of them as "2" on a scale of 1 to 4 with '1' representing the best evaluation. Delores Baca and Toni Sena rated the three most important aspects of their job closer to 1 (very good); Carrie Adams gave the same three aspects an average of 2.7 (a negative ranking); our data indicate that in general, working mothers at Leslie Pants saw their jobs as "good but not great." Negative feelings were focused primarily on the shortened hours and curtailment of income suffered during the 1982 recession, rather than on management policies per se.

We have described Leslie Pants first in this chapter because the plant clearly illustrated the dialectical relationship that emerges between management and women workers as women respond to management's effort to extract increased levels of production from them. Leslie Pants had preserved unchanged the hierarchical relationship between plant manager, line manager, section supervisor, and woman worker. The manager at another plant of the same company indicated that the corporation had once been more receptive to aspects of participative management (particularly flextime), had tried them only for a few years, and, on the whole, preferred a more hierarchical arrangement.

Much of the control system was embedded in the piece-rate pay system—which pushes each worker to higher levels of production through her own effort—and in the simple control exercised by supervisors. Tactics or strategies remained at an individual level, between a woman, her work, and her machine, and between a woman

[109]

and her supervisor. The absence of a strong set of resistance strategies at a collective level was due to management's ability to make the piece-rate system more palatable through nonmonetary rewards (membership in the President's Club) and monetary incentives (good benefits and a profit-sharing plan), to encourage morale and loyalty through a wide range of company-sponsored events. Resistance thus did not go very far; co-optation was more characteristic as women came to consider their goals consonant with those of the company.

Women's Work in Digital Phone Equipment

Southwest Electronics is a second example of a hierarchical plant structure. Southwest, an electronics plant that made digital phone equipment, had a work force of over 1,000 in 1982. Among Anglo and Hispano production workers, 66 percent were female and 34 percent male. Typical of the electronics industry where both men and women are employed in assembly and testing facilities, this plant illustrates the way gender rather than ethnicity becomes the major source of difference in the workplace. Women were employed largely in the lower-ranking jobs and confronted control systems ranging from jobs paid on an individual piece rate to work on a "progressive" assembly line with a group piece rate. In the former case, control was exerted through the pay system, and women's work practice and tactics resembled those of workers at Leslie Pants. In the latter, the assembly line (a technical form of control) and the piece rate (control embedded in a pay system) created a double means of extracting labor from employees and resulted in more collective response.

Management-worker relations and the plant's work culture were shaped by two factors: the hierarchical structure of management, and the fact that the plant was unionized. At the lowest level of the hierarchy on the management side were eighty supervisors, usually promoted from within, each overseeing eight to ten workers. Above the supervisors were ten foremen, who in turn reported to the plant manager. Within the work force there was an elaborate set of job categories ranging from grade 1 (GR-1) to grade 8 (GR-8). The plant operated on two shifts in a modern facility, built in 1972, with a large open production space beyond the office section of the building.

The central part of the labor process involved making printed circuit boards and "stuffing" them with components. Stuffing was done on a progressive assembly line by women (and a few men) who were GR-1; women were also among the materials handlers who supplied components to the board stuffers (GR-2). The assembled boards were then run through a wave solder, tested, and inspected. Boards that failed a test or inspection were sent to repair. Women were hired for repair work (GR-2) and as inspectors (GR-3), testers (GR-4), and quality control workers (GR-4). The higher grades were paid more, had more autonomy on the job, and were less subject to various forms of control (through pay systems, the assembly line, or supervisors) than were women on the assembly line or those who made the components.

Table 16 shows how management's hiring policy created differences based on gender in the workplace but did not segregate females of differing ethnic background in contrasting work situations. Of the 586 women, 321 (55 percent) were Mexican American, and

Table 16. Wages, gender, and ethnicity at Southwest Electronics

Grade[a]	Wage[b]	Female		Male	
		Mexican American	Anglo	Mexican American	Anglo
GR-1	$4.80 5.92	172 (53.5%)	118 (44.5%)	62 (39.0%)	45 (31.4%)
GR-2	$5.04 6.22	78 (24.3%)	72 (27.2%)	16 (10.1%)	9 (6.3%)
GR-3	$5.27 6.51	48 (15.0%)	5 (18.9%)	14 (8.8%)	4 (2.8%)
GR-4	$5.57 6.89	14 (4.4%)	8 (3.0%)	18 (11.3%)	18 (11.6%)
GR-5	$5.85 7.24	7 (2.2%)	11 (4.2%)	9 (5.6%)	4 (2.8%)
GR-6	$6.27 7.01	0 (0.0%)	2 (0.7%)	3 (1.9%)	4 (2.8%)
GR-8	$6.76 7.56 8.37	2 (0.6%)	4 (1.5%)	37 (23.2%)	59 (41.3%)
TOTAL		321 (100.0%)	265 (100.0%)	159 (100.0%)	143 (100.0%)

Source: Union data on 888 of 1,006 employees.
[a]There were no GR-7 employees.
[b]The first number is the starting pay; the second is the hourly wage after 120 days; the third (if any) is the hourly wage after one year.

265 (45 percent) were Anglo. About the same proportion of Mexican-American and Anglo women held GR-1 jobs, and the proportions in Grades 2 through 5 were not significantly different. Of the males, 159 (53 percent) were Mexican American and 143 (47 percent) were Anglo. Men were concentrated in the higher paying jobs. Many were printers (GR-3), plating operators (GR-4), machine setters or transport operators (GR-5), and technicians (GR-8). Technicians, who included many Anglo men, were required to have either an electronics certificate from the local technical-vocational institute or extensive on-the-job training. Women and Mexican-American men apparently had little access to these opportunities. Hence, 41.3 percent of the Anglo men were GR-8s, while only 23.2 percent of the Mexican American men and 2 percent of all women had these top jobs, often paying about $7.00 to $8.00 an hour.

The practical relations that developed between management and women workers over the first ten years of the plant's operation were a product of management's policy and the history of unionization. Southwest had fought a bitter struggle to keep the plant from being unionized. During the union campaign in 1972 the company was found in violation of the National Labor Relations Act and was ordered to rehire fifteen workers who had been fired for taking part in union activity. Although the union won an election in 1973, the vote was not certified until December 1974 and a three-year contract not signed until January 1976. Four workers were suspended in 1978 for following a supervisor home from work; protests over the suspensions led to workers being forced to leave the plant and 550 employees being suspended. Eventually, twenty-four workers were fired, but the remaining workers were reinstated (see *Albuquerque Journal*, May 6 and 21, 1978).

In February 1979 there was a two-week strike over the new contract. The terms of the settlement were not much different from those of the original offer, but the union was able to get the proposals in writing and to have a number of jobs restructured and upgraded. Negotiations for the 1982 contract went much more smoothly, and the new contract was in place at the time we interviewed working mothers. During the recession years there had been several layoffs. In early 1982 the plant began hiring assembly line workers and testers again, but by July they had begun to lay off some of these new workers. Between 1980 and mid-1982 the work force had been reduced from a high of 1,850 to 1,006.

At the time of our study, most employees had worked for Southwest since 1979, surviving the multiple rounds of layoffs. Many women had moved up from assembly line work to better-paying jobs as materials handlers, quality control personnel, and testers. Having been through the bitter union-management struggles, they had seen some of the benefits of collective resistance; though they had little opportunity for mobility in a contracting labor force, workers did engage in group-level as well as individual strategies of resistance.

We interviewed ten women and two husbands about their jobs in Southwest Electronics. Eight of the women were Hispanas, including three single parents, and two were Anglo (one of Irish descent and one a Greek immigrant). Both husbands were Hispano, including one married to one of the Anglo women. Our interviews overrepresent the situation of Hispanas, since the female work force was more evenly divided between Mexican-American and non-Mexican-American female workers. The ten women, however, did represent the wide range of jobs held by females in the plant's production process. Three women worked on the progressive line; Rosa Gomez and Susan Anaya, both single parents, will serve as examples. Two were materials handlers; one repaired hybrids, one worked as a payroll clerk on the shop floor, and two worked in the components department (we focus on Vera Chandler, a winder). The tenth, and highest in rank was Deborah Rivera, a tester and trouble shooter. She had had previous electronics experience in the armed services but had worked her way up through the plant hierarchy to GR-8, a level attained by only six women at the time of our interviews. Her husband was also a GR-8 but had reached that rank more quickly. The other husband was a GR-5 (machine setter). These two men held the higher-paying jobs typical for male employees.

The Individual Piece Rate in Components

Vera Chandler, like the stitchers at Leslie Pants, worked at her own machine and was paid on a piece rate, her production measured against an efficiency goal of 100 percent. She had worked for Southwest Electronics off and on since 1973, and she described her job as a winder in the components department as follows:

> We take a core that's called a bobbin, put it in a machine. It has a little
> metal thing that sticks out, and you put it in. . . . right now we are

making transformers. So we put them, it's like threading. You turn on the machine and you have to guide the wire. We have spools . . . the wire coming down. We thread it into the machine, and then you have to guide the wire with your hand as it winds and make sure that it goes on smooth. . . . It's like working on a sewing machine . . . winding the bobbin you put underneath the sewing machine.

Like sewing, the operation Vera performed required manual dexterity, hand-eye coordination, and fast work to attain 100 percent efficiency. For the order she was working on at the time, there were 600 bobbins to be wound, and she had to put four winds on each. The whole order took forty-eight hours—six working days—to process.

Vera Chandler's work practice, evolved from confronting the piece rate, shared many similarities with that of apparel workers. Like them, she often had difficulty with her materials or with the machine, and since she had not worked in winding for a number of years, she had experienced problems in achieving the rate. When she started the job three months earlier, she was making only 46 percent, but on the day before the interview she had made 107 percent. Doing rework (such as replacing tape that came loose from some components if there was not enough glue inside) lowered her rate to about 77 percent, however—just as making repairs cut into the garment worker's production for the week.

In describing individual tactics for doing the work more quickly, Vera said, "Ya, people take short cuts . . . everybody does it differently. . . . I really don't have that many because I'm really not that experienced." Other workers, she explained, performed the process of "snagging" the wires and taping them by using a clip to separate the red and green wires: "Now I can't do it that way. I take both wires and I mount them around to the clip, because I think it's faster for me."

Under a piece-rate system, especially if there is a variety of jobs, those who allocate the work can significantly affect the take-home pay of different workers. This is less likely to happen in an apparel plant, where a modified production line and large production runs even out the work automatically, than in plants with batch processing and a variety of operations (see Shapiro-Perl's account of work in a jewelry factory, 1979, 1984). Vera complained that the materials handler gave the "better orders" to her friends. Vera had been getting the same orders time after time, while others were getting different orders. Also, the day shift sometimes got the better orders, and Vera's evening shift had to process the "bad" orders.

One of management's practices had been to keep the rates on winding high. Women protested (a collective strategy of resistance), and Vera reported that they had a meeting with the foreman. "She told us they were going to lower the rates . . . because a lot of people have been complaining. You know, you can work like a dog all day and you still can't do it. Very few can make it."

Group Incentive on the Progressive Line

An assembly line (an example of technical control) creates a different kind of work practice, since the speed of the line regulates the work for all: it pushes workers toward more collective responses because all are facing the same work conditions. Rosa Gomez described the job:

> We sit on a progressive line stuffing P.C. [printed circuit] boards, putting on components and inductors, transformers, all kinds of parts that they have. . . . We just sit on a line, the boards just come down, and we all have our parts on each station. We have up to maybe about twenty parts to put in, at different times we have like maybe five. It all depends on the board, if it's a big board or a small board.

Workers had diagrams tacked up in front of their stations to tell them what parts to place in what section of the board. Their work was checked by two women at the end of the line who had a picture of all the parts for a particular board.

Women responded to the demanding pace of the line by helping each other out, a tactic that kept the work process flowing and cut down on potential work stoppages. Susan Anaya explained:

> Let's say like I have one part that I can't put in sometimes, it's easier for somebody else to put in. Sometimes the engineers, by the time they get around to doing all that paperwork—we just fix it if we can by ourselves. Or let's say the lady beside me, there's one board that she does, that I put in two parts for her because it's harder for that one lady because she's got this one part that has got a lot of legs and it's kind of hard.

[115]

Materials handlers were crucial to the efficient operation of the line and also kept it running smoothly by substituting for absent workers. Irene Tafoya, materials handler for one of the progressive lines, explained how she set up the parts for each new board, placing the components in trays arranged at each of the ten stations. After an order (called a PA) is finished, "you just turn the complete station around" to make the new parts available. Irene was responsible for checking each station while the line was running and providing replacement parts. If a worker had to go to the bathroom, Irene sat in for her. "Let's say they have about three or four absent and they don't have enough people to sit in on the line, then they'll call one of the materials handler specialists to be the materials handler, and they'll put me in to stuff on the line."

Despite workers' efforts to help one another, the kind of technical control exerted by an assembly line creates a difficult work situation. Workers thus are quite conscious of management's efforts to extract production from them. "It's a hard job, working on the progressive line," Rosa commented.

> There's a lot of women I have know who have quit maybe their third night cause they just can't handle it. They even leave crying and stuff. It's hard. And then the supervisor when I went on days, she was mean. . . . She'd sit there and watch you. . . . I had to take it because I needed the job. . . . [Q: There's a lot of pressure?] It is constantly. And then we get a piece of paper and it tells us how many boards we got to put out an hour. We've got a little diode at the end of the line that tells us what number we got to put it on in order to make our rate. . . . we used to have to run 210 boards an hour. Those were fast boards, and those just speed right by us.

For several years, Southwest Electronics paid group incentive on the progressive line, adding a second but contradictory control mechanism to the technical control of an assembly line. Several workers commented that the initial incentive pay had been high until the company raised the piece rates. Susan Anaya summed up her view of what had happened:

> The disadvantage is that sometimes once you start making and you make pretty good, sometimes they'll higher up the rate so that you have to try a little bit harder. That's what happened with ours, you know. It was pretty good at first, but then . . . a couple of months went by, and all of a sudden . . . you just couldn't hack it, you know. You

just couldn't make the rates and then you'd realize. Let's say that the engineers would come down, one certain one that was taking care of the timing involved. He would raise it, says well, no, they have too much time. Where it got to a point where we couldn't even make the rate, much less extra.

Both Susan Anaya and Irene Tafoya felt that the group incentive system created pressure and conflict among workers. "You just find a lot of conflicts between people that want to make incentive and people who just think that 100 percent is good enough," Irene commented. "When it comes to incentive and especially group incentive, that's bad, because it's got to go by group. And if the group doesn't work well together, you can kiss that goodbye." While the technical control of the line created an atmosphere of "we are all in the same boat" and brought workers together to help each other out, management's additional strategy to extract production through the wage system brought individual competition and conflict.

Again, as in the components department, there was collective resistance, not just in complaints to the foreman but at the union level. During the 1982 contract negotiations the union bargained to discontinue the practice; in compensation for the loss of incentive pay, workers received a one-time payment of $1,000. Workers did not attempt to change the nature of the assembly line itself, but they were able to get rid of the group incentive through collective action.

The Minimal Role of Supervisors and Training

Unlike Leslie Pants, Southwest Electronics had not buttressed the labor process with a range of incentives. The technical control of the progressive line set the workers' pace more consistently than the progressive bundle system in an apparel plant; this, in combination (for a time) with a group incentive pay system meant that supervisors were less needed to control productive output. Thus there was no elaborate system of clock-outs, and less attention was paid to moving the work through the production process, since this was done by the line itself. Supervisors still had an important role in work allocation, however. For example, Rosa Gomez's supervisor on the progressive line "passes out this form to our checkers and to the materials handler and tells her what jobs we're going to run for the day."

Also, unlike Leslie Pants, Southwest Electronics put little effort into training. Workers had to teach each other (though sometimes the person who setup the machines would take on the role of a trainer). When Nina Griego went to second assembly, her second job in the plant, "they gave me a board and said 'do it.' [It was] very hard." It took Nina a couple of weeks to figure out how to do the work.

Finally, there were often difficulties in getting the line to run smoothly, as Vera complained when she described her previous job on the progressive line: "That plant isn't organized at all. . . . Like they'll bring out a job to us and they'll say . . . they checked everything out right and they know that there's enough, you know, for 100 boards . . . and we find out that they're not even all there. . . . Then . . . the supervisor gets all mad, or the foreman gets all mad because those boards are hot boards; they have to be out by today, and all this time we're waiting."

A "Halfhearted" Work Culture

Since Southwest Electronics was unionized and had a long history of management-worker conflict, there was less interest in building a loyal work force through extracurricular activities than at Leslie Pants. The firm did sponsor several events for workers, however, mainly organized through a committee called the Entertainment Club. In addition to a company picnic, the Entertainment Club had organized a Christmas dance and a children's Christmas party. Rosa Gomez, a single parent, took her daughter and her nephew to the party.

> This last year it was really neat. They really had it well organized for the first time, of all the times I've gone. They had characters like Scooby-Doo and Shaggy . . . and Pebbles and Barney and Fred. . . . They dressed up and they start dancing and doing all this and do a little play and things like that. And then they've got Santa Claus, and he hands out stockings. And then they give out free balloons.

Among our interviewees in general, however, there seemed to be less enthusiasm and involvement in these company-sponsored activities than at Leslie Pants.

Informal celebrations were organized within sections in each department. Each section put up a Christmas tree and decorations as part of a plantwide contest. Birthdays were often handled by the supervisor or the materials handler. In Rosa's section,

> we just had cake for two guys that had their birthdays on July 4th, Sunday. We had cake for them. We usually all pitch in a dollar. . . . The supervisor has our birthdays written down. This girl just quit and went to [Howard Electrical], and we all bought her a cake and we pitched in for a gift. We usually have things like that. For Christmas we all draw names. And we get together and buy the supervisor one gift from all of us . . . like this last Christmas we got her a little holder for pens and pencils.

In 1982 Southwest's management was just beginning to use "quality circles"—volunteer committees organized to work on production issues—but did not have well-developed reasons for putting them in place. As Sandra Abeyta explained:

> So you go and you talk about your problems or your disadvantages. Let's say like I tell them—well I really think we should have another person just to sit in, period, and that's all her job is. Well, they'll discuss it and see whether it's a good idea or if it's just too much. . . . A lot of people don't care either way and some people think—hey that's a good idea, we might solve a lot of these problems that we have that are just there, that we can get rid of.

Quality circles not withstanding, there was little effort to apply participative management policies to the transformation of the labor process or the creation of a new climate of worker-management relations. One company spokesperson, possibly as a result of previous labor disputes, had a very negative view of the labor force. She felt that recent migrants to Albuquerque from "back East" were much more appreciative of work conditions and benefits than were locals. Locals, she maintained, "think Southwest Electronics is a sweatshop, whereas people who have worked in factories back east have worked at 85 degrees in 80 percent humidity with heaters turned on to dry out the air and with no air conditioning. A first-generation industrial labor force that doesn't appreciate the good conditions is one of the problems with Albuquerque."

Women's assessment of their jobs reflected their pay level, the relative autonomy and skill inherent in their work, and the plant's

[119]

history of layoffs and union-management conflict. Of the ten women we interviewed, most rated various aspects of their jobs between 1.8 and 2.3 on a scale of 1 (high) to 4 (low). Vera Chandler and Rosa Gomez were in this group. But Susan Anaya and Marta Ortiz (in second assembly) rated their jobs near a 3. Susan, for example, gave her pay a 4; further, she said, the work was not challenging, and there were few opportunities for promotion. In a plant with a history of layoffs, workers were insecure: "There's no place for advancement right now because everything's kind of like in a standstill. There's some people that worry if they are going to be here next month, you know." On the other hand, Irene Tafoya, a materials handler (GR-2) and Deborah Rivera (GR-8) were much more positive about their jobs, rating various aspects between 1 and 2.

Our interviews revealed a complex set of responses to management control. Women like Vera, who worked at a machine on piece rate, developed individual tactics and "tricks of the trade"—a work practice very similar to that of the women at Leslie Pants. Group-level resistance was evident when women in Vera's department complained to the foreman about management's manipulation of the piece-rate system. The assembly line also forged group-level strategies ranging from workers helping one another to the resistance that resulted in the termination of the group incentive rate through union negotiation. Given the antagonistic relationships that had developed between management and union, many women—although satisfied with their pay—were critical of the content of their jobs, the lack of job stability within the plant, and the lack of attention to good management practice. In other words, women felt that they had good jobs but were unenthusiastic about the company they worked for.

Women's Work in a Jet Engine Plant

Our third "traditional" plant, Aerospace, Inc., resembled Southwest Electronics in several ways. Wages were seen as the major benefit of the job; management put little effort into training, management-worker relations, or creating a positively valued work culture; informal activities were left to the union (which was stronger and better organized than that at Southwest); and workers grumbled about the quality of management but felt they had good jobs.

Aerospace produced jet engine parts and employed 1,678 workers at the end of 1981, of whom 320 (28 percent) were women; 1,350 employees were union members. The creation of difference around a gender division of labor in the workplace was even more marked than at Southwest Electronics. Most of the men were machinists and commanded the highest-paying jobs. Women, according to the community relations representative, were employed in jobs that called for "repetitive hand motions" and dexterity. Still, in this plant the women had benefited from the high level of male wages, because union negotiation had created a very narrow range of wage levels, bringing women in the lower ranks much higher pay than they could have earned at Leslie Pants or Southwest Electronics. The 1982 union contract specified that toolmakers (the top job) were to be paid $11.45 an hour; janitors at the bottom of the pay scale made $8.51; and the average pay was $9.00. The women we interviewed were making between $9.00 and $11.00 an hour, almost twice what the women were making in some jobs at other plants we studied. These were clearly "men's wages," and for three single mothers they not only provided the sole support for the family but allowed one to buy a house and another to put her children in a Catholic private school. Aerospace, Inc., was clearly the best-paying manufacturing plant for women in Albuquerque.

Overall, 52 percent of the plant's employees were minority workers: 5 percent (75 workers) were black and 47 percent Mexican American—not very different from Southwest's 55 percent Mexican American work force. Anglo and Mexican-American women were in similar jobs, however, and did not experience the Aerospace management control system differently. Again, gender rather than ethnicity was the basis for difference in the work-place.

In 1982 the plant used four technologies or methods in four departments to produce aircraft engine parts: castings, shrouds, plastics, and metal shop. Men were employed in the metal shop, where machinists made the turbine casings for the engine. Women, as well as significant numbers of men, were employed in castings, shrouds, and plastics. Through contacts with the union we interviewed one worker in the shroud area, one worker who handled the tool crib for plant maintenance, and four women who worked in the plastics department.

In plastics, the parts produced were primarily for sound suppression and generally used in the front or cooler end of the engine. The production method was similar to that of making plastic auto bodies and boat hulls. Women workers started with a sheet of mate-

[121]

rial and bent or compressed it into the shapes needed. The plastic parts were cured in huge autoclaves, where the parts were wheeled in and kept under heavy pressure (*Albuquerque Journal*, December 23, 1979).

Management was hierarchically organized in all four departments. In the shroud area, for example, the employees were supervised by a foreman who reported to an area supervisor and then to an area manager. The plant manager was at the top. As at Southwest Electronics, union negotiation had created an elaborate hierarchy of workers as well. Production jobs within the plant were ranked from Grade 1 to Grade 24; most women were concentrated in jobs ranked from Grades 9 to 15. In 1982 the wages in these grades ranged from $8.67 to $9.40. Since the wage scale was so compressed, there was little difference in wages, yet women experienced job mobility and periodic wage raises because of the union contract. The union contract and elaborate system of job classification had bureaucratized the process of control, making seniority an important criterion in job mobility. Also, since the plant operated on a "bump and roll" system, layoffs meant that the least senior employees lost their jobs and more senior ones were often demoted to employment in lower grades, sometimes in different departments. There was still room in this system for considerable "simple" control on the part of foremen, who watched over the work process and disciplined workers, but employees could use the union grievance system to defend themselves.

The Labor Process and Wages

The labor process in each department was organized through batch processing: each person worked individually on a part or group of parts, and then a whole "batch" was moved on to the next step. There were no assembly lines. Jobs in each department were done "by the process," a form of bureaucratic control: engineers wrote specifications for each operation, and workers were supposed to follow the steps of the labor process without taking shortcuts. Foremen seemed to know little about the technical side of the labor process but generally oversaw the allocation of work and handled discipline. Workers were paid hourly wages and each job was estimated in terms of how long it should take to complete it. There was a reluctance to push workers to meet production quotas; in some cases women reported that they could do more work in a day than they

[122]

were expected to do.

Because of the batch-processing system, women worked on isolated operations. Their work was not coordinated or dependent on others within the department. Compared with Leslie Pants and Southwest Electronics, Aerospace utilized a labor process (based on batch processing) and wage policy (hourly wages and unenforced quotas) that created a relatively weak system of control and that focused more on quality than on the extraction of production from workers.

As at Southwest Electronics, relatively little attention was given to training. Workers were told to read the process, and workers trained each other and gave new employees tips. Inspectors also had a role in getting workers to do their work well by giving advice on whether the part would pass quality control.

Thelma Barela, a second-shift plastics fabricator, made parts out of dry fiberglass. She did all her work by hand, not machine, using an instrument called a "bone" to press the sheet of fiberglass to the shape of a mold. Since the fiberglass was paper thin and could be stretched, she would get it in the "groove" by pressing it down with the bone. Thelma put on four layers of fiber glass, then teflon, and then "ossenburg" (a fabric) and glue: "You have to bone that down too." Next she put a thick plastic bag over the part, put a vacuum on it, and sucked the bag down so that there was no air at all inside. "If there's air in there, it'll cause 'onbonds' on the fiberglass itself . . . the glass won't bond, and it will fall apart." Next, the part went to "autoclave" to be baked or cured, then traveled to "off mold," where the fiberglass was "popped out" and the form returned to be used again.

Christina Espinosa worked the first shift in plastics, in a section called "routing." After the parts had gone through Thelma's section, "plastics assembly," "they went to" bond assembly," where three or four pieces were put together to make a larger part. Then that part went to routing, where, Christina explained,

> you have to drill the holes in them; we have to cut them into the formations they're supposed to be . . . sand them and put them together. . . . Potting is located where the holes are, you know, like just about everything you have that has holes that screws go into, they need bushings, or things like that, so inside the holes we have to put inserts. . . . If you're drilling, it's usually twenty minutes a part. If you're potting, it's a half-hour a part.

On one shift, Christina worked on eighteen different pieces; it took her twenty minutes to a half-hour to do each piece. Christina earned $9.75 an hour on first shift; her job was a Grade 15, as were the jobs of most workers in her area. She was the only woman in a section of twenty workers, except for four "grit blasters," and they did not work near her. Most of the men were Hispanos or Spanish. "In my opinion, it's mainly a Spanish-dominated plant. There are more Spanish people than anything else."

Karen Smith was an inspector in plastics. Both she and Betty Thompson, also an inspector, worked on second shift and were Grade 15. Karen had also been secretary-treasurer of the union. At the time of the interview she was at home because of a foot operation, and Betty was working with Charley, Karen's usual partner, in a "white room." Betty's usual job was to inspect "piece parts," but at that time she was inspecting assembled parts as well.

For each inspection too there was a "process," a step-by-step description of the part and all the points Betty or Karen needed to examine in a visual inspection or measure with gauges. If the part did not meet the specifications, it was rejected and sent to "rework," where employees often came to Betty to ask her advice on fixing it. Betty felt that inspectors had to know a number of different jobs (how to rout, how to assemble), and they often did some of the work of the foreman (handing out materials). But most important they evaluated and approved the work that was done.

The final woman we interviewed at Aerospace was Laura Davidson, who worked in "stock and process" on first shift. As a crib attendant in the maintenance department, she was Grade 12 and earned $9.40 an hour.

> I issue tools—machine tools—coveralls, you know, anything they need on the job. Currently they are expanding the crib—which by the way, I'm proud to say, I began four years ago. It's my baby and its great. . . . We've expanded from a couple hundred items. Now we are building up to 4,000 items in our crib. . . . We do stocking and ordering . . . we put away stock and the whole shooting match.

The Role of the Supervisor

All the women we interviewed, especially the inspectors, had considerable autonomy on the job. On the negative side, this meant that most had learned their jobs from co-workers or by themselves. On the positive side, it meant that they could exercise a great deal of decision-making and responsibility in carrying out specific tasks. Their relationships with foremen and supervisors in some cases reflected the company's laissez-faire philosophy and in other cases the possibilities for personal (simple) control inherent in the situation.

There was a straight hierarchy of command at Aerospace, Inc. Foremen and area supervisors reported to area managers who reported to the shift manager and on up to the plant manager, who had a fair amount of control over the work force. At the time of our interviews, a new plant manager was rumored to be planning major changes. Betty said, "Whenever you get a new manager, you got a lot of turmoil. . . . The rumor I heard—like I say, it is a rumor— they said that [the new plant manager] wants to bring the work force down 30 percent [from] what we had come January 1st, when he moved in there. And he wants to function that plant 100 percent efficiently with . . . 30 percent less workers."

At Aerospace as at Southwest Electronics, foremen were responsible for the allocation of work, though they often posted what needed to be done for the day rather than directing workers individually. The women we interviewed had had very different experiences with various foremen. Some seemed efficient and well versed in technical matters, leaving their workers alone. Others exercised more control, used their authority arbitrarily, and even harassed women and union members.

Christina Espinosa, who had been vice-president of the union, had had difficulties with foremen. For three and a half years, she said, "every foreman I had tried to write me up, get me suspended . . . but I never did nothing wrong, so nothing ever stuck." She got a new foreman early in 1982, and "right away, he had me written up." She went to the National Labor Relations Board (NLRB) and Equal Employment Opportunity Commission (EEOC), but "nobody would help." Then, the Thursday before our interview, "I told him off, and they suspended me." Christina felt that it was very difficult for a woman to work at Aerospace because it was such a male-dominated shop: "You know, it's really . . . hard working there, because they don't care if the men are yelling dirty words and if they have their dirty pictures and everything like that. I mean, people stand there and yell things that are horrible all the time. They have names for you that you wouldn't believe."

In contrast, others experienced relatively little control of their work by foremen. Supervision on the evening shift especially seemed lax. Thelma said that if she finished the work assigned for eight hours in less time, she could relax for the rest of the shift: "You just look busy . . . the boss says, just look busy in case some big shot comes along. In the daytime, they have that problem, but we really don't have that problem. There's nobody around."

A Union-Based Work Culture

Aerospace was perhaps unusual among Albuquerque plants in not buttressing its production process with extra incentives and entertainment. The acceptance of a hierarchical management philosophy was perhaps best indicated by the limited way in which Aerospace, like Southwest Electronics, had used quality circles. The union's reaction was critical to the success or failure of the program.

The plant introduced quality circles in August of 1981, through a "Can Do Committee." One interviewee commented:

> It was something that originated in Japan. They are called the Quality Quibblers. There are seven of us. . . . Well, what it is, is to make the job easier in the area. . . . The original purpose of me getting on the Can Do team is that the Union was against it, because we are doing engineers' work. And so we couldn't fight it, but [the union president] said, "Well, let's get some of our people on it." So that's originally why I got on it, because they were violating the contract.

Workers had the right to put ideas into a suggestion box and get paid for them, and the union preferred to support the suggestion box rather than the Can Do teams or Quality Circles. In the beginning, every department had one team or possibly one for first and one for second shift. By July 1983 Christina thought the Can Do teams were on the way out: "Well, to me they're sort of dying out. I haven't seen them really do anything worthwhile, to me. I was in one. And I quit. . . . We did something that saved them . . . could be $10,000 a year just for our plant. . . . They turned around and gave us each $25 and said, 'Be glad you got that.' You know, I mean, now who wants to give me any good ideas after that? It's just bullshit now."

Aerospace management did not feel that it was "worth it" to put funds and energy into creating loyalty, since doing so would not substantially lower the wage bill or keep an organized work force from going out on strike. The major event sponsored by the company was an open house held every five years; one was being planned several months after we did our interviewing. The management also sponsored sports teams, but several workers commented on the separation of teams for salaried employees from union-sponsored teams for the hourly workers. "I know we have bowling leagues," Betty said. "I think those are for salaried people, only . . . they aren't allowed to associate with hourly people."

Christina Espinosa had the clearest statement of the connection between the union and the company's lack of interest in sponsored events. "The company doesn't do nothing for the people. The only thing that goes on there is what the people get together on their own. The people want to have and share gifts at Christmas-time . . . they get together and they do it. . . . But as far as the company, they don't do nothing. They figure they pay us enough. You know companies that don't have a union do that kind of thing. But companies that have a union won't do nothing for your people, because they pay them better."

It is not surprising, therefore, that even informal celebrations at Aerospace were organized by a network of union supporters in one department or area. One enthusiastic union supporter reported an active set of celebrations in her department:

> I'm getting ready to have a baby shower now. Every time . . . there's an illness in the family or say one of our people goes out on sick leave, or there's going to be a baby born . . . even if it's a guy, we throw them a shower. . . . Usually a couple of the women [organize it]. We have potlucks at Christmas, every Christmas we exchange presents. We have potlucks for Thanksgiving. Sometimes we have potlucks for the heck of it all.

Laura Davidson, the only woman in her department, described her role in organizing men for dinners and holiday festivities (even though they had had potlucks at Christmas and Thanksgiving before she came into the area): "I've got a little ceramic Christmas tree . . . and I usually take it in. . . . I take my nativity scene in and we always have a potluck dinner." Most of the men "have their wives make up a warm dish. A lot of them even have their wives drop it off, you know, which to me seems like it's a lot of trouble for the wives, but I guess they're agreeable or they wouldn't do it." Two women mentioned that their foremen had been opposed to potlucks because they took workers away from the job, but this seemed atypical. Other interviewees reported a lively informal work culture, but one organized mostly by women and definitely part of union rather than management activities.

Workers' Response to the Control System

Women at Aerospace were especially aware that the high wages they earned were an important advantage of the job, overriding such considerations as dirty shop floor conditions, disorganized management, potential layoffs, and the male-dominated nature of the plant. In addition, several women found their jobs complex, interesting, and full of variety. Unlike some workers at Southwest Electronics and Leslie Pants, no one found her job boring or full of tension and pressure.

Furthermore, the benefit package was much better than at Leslie Pants: it included better health insurance, two days sick leave a year, ten paid holidays, two weeks' vacation even for new employees, and sickness and accident insurance that paid 80 percent of an employee's wages up to $225 a week.

Women's comments on their jobs almost always mentioned pay and benefits as important positive aspects of their employment at Aerospace. For example, Christina Espinosa stressed that her pay had allowed her to put her children through Catholic school. Because of the harassment she had experienced in a male-dominated workplace, she had often thought of looking for another job but realized, that "there's not too many jobs with that kind of income." Likewise, Betty Thompson commented: "I like the pay. We always want more, but I have to stop and think, I know for a fact there's a lot of people working for less."

In other words, high pay, benefits, and the autonomy that comes with batch processing in a plant where the labor process is very complex and involves the completion of a number of steps by each worker meant that women workers rated their jobs highly. Unlike Leslie Pants and Southwest Electronics, Aerospace exercised little control through either a pay system (such as piece rates) or the labor process (as in an assembly line). On the other hand, these women regarded management as anti-union, not careful about quality control, and not well organized. Impending layoffs also led to a sense of insecurity, as they had at Southwest Electronics, mainly among workers who did not have high seniority. Furthermore, the Aerospace management seemed relatively unconcerned with creating a plantwide work culture.

These three plants illustrate important variations in the dialectical relationships that develop as women workers confront control systems in hierarchical plants. Work practice evolved in the particular mosaic of labor process, wage structure, management-worker relations, and work culture in each plant. Workers could clearly "see" the major contradictions in hierarchical plants, including the role of an assembly line or piece-rate system in extracting labor. Women were also clear about the kinds of simple control systems used at their workplaces. Management, in turn, sought to co-opt work practice or to channel worker tactics and strategies in the direction of coping rather than in the direction of resistance and confrontation. Leslie Pants had been much more successful in this regard than had either Southwest Electronics or Aerospace, Inc.

Leslie Pants relied on the modified bundle system, the piece rate, the simple control of the supervisor, and a panoply of rewards designed to build "morale." Women's tactics and strategies remained at an individual level.

Southwest Electronics used both an assembly line and batch processing in combination with straight-time pay and piece rates (individual and group). Women's work practice varied with the job: those working at individual machines developed tactics and strategies very similar to those of the women at Leslie Pants; for those subject to the technical control of an assembly line, group strategies included attempts to help one another out and resistance to the group incentive, which was abandoned in the next union contract.

At Aerospace, Inc., there was no attempt to use technical control or control through a wage system. Batch processing and the "process" system left workers chiefly on their own. Supervisors exerted some simple control, but supervision seemed somewhat sporadic, and training was not systematized. The management relied on high hourly wages and benefits to keep workers motivated.

At the level of plant work culture, there were important differences between union and non-union plants. The management at Leslie Pants was very active in buttressing the piece-rate system with monetary rewards and in sponsoring entertainment events to build a loyal work force. Management at the two union plants was much less interested in these tactics, keeping such activities to a minimum at Southwest and actually leaving them to the union at Aerospace.

[129]

Difference at these plants was created along gender rather than ethnic lines. Each plant had a gender division of labor typical of its particular industry; men and women generally had different jobs and experienced different control systems. Women were paid less than men, but their jobs were still highly paid relative to the general female labor market in Albuquerque. The gender division of labor at each plant had a different impact. At Leslie Pants, a female-dominated plant, a top woman stitcher who worked at 130 percent efficiency made $6.50 an hour, while men who repaired the sewing machines made only around $6.00 an hour and men who worked in the stock room made less than many stichers. At Southwest Electronics, Anglo men were concentrated at the top of the job structure, making between $6.75 and $8.37 an hour, while women were in jobs that paid between $4.80 and $6.50 an hour. At Aerospace, women actually benefited from male wages because the plant was unionized. Women made $9.00 to $11.00 an hour, not much less than the top male job in the plant, which commanded $11.45 an hour.

More important, women of different ethnic and cultural backgrounds were not segregated within female jobs. Thus Hispanic and Anglo women who confronted the same system of control did not differ in their tactics and strategies. A woman's position in the production process, the kind of pay system she worked under, and the structure of management-worker relations in a plant—rather than cultural values or background—shaped her work practice.

The women we interviewed in hierarchical plants were quite conscious of the contradiction between the pressures to extract more labor from them and their own efforts to control their work. They did appreciate their jobs, however, and often rated them highly, variously emphasizing job stability, high pay, good benefits, and a good supervisor. This appreciation followed from their own family situations and job histories. For most, even though they may have felt their jobs were "good, but not great," their work was relatively high paying, and often placed them in a position of mainstay or coprovider in their own families. In our sample there were similar proportions of Hispanas and Anglos in these categories. Since Hispanas are a larger proportion of these labor forces in Albuquerque, we suspect that the absolute number of coprovider and mainstay Hispanas is larger than that of Anglos. Women's assessment of their jobs emerges as even more important when we turn to participative plants.

[130]

1. The shop floor in an apparel plant. Patterns for men's pants dominate the foreground; rows of machines where women stitchers perform individual operations are shown in the background. Bundles of cut garments move through one of several "lines." Small operations on pockets, belt loops, and other parts are completed first, and the zipper, side seams, and waistbands are sewn later in the process. Photo by Jim Fisher, by permission of the *Albuquerque Journal*.

2. Stuffing boards on an assembly line. Each woman places a number of parts on a printed circuit board. In a traditional plant like Southwest Electronics, workers are not allowed to let boards pile up, but must learn to keep pace with the line. Workers were for a time paid on a group piece rate, which created conflict and competition, leading the union to bargain for its elimination. Photo by Brian Walski, by permission of the *Albuquerque Journal.*

3. A Hispana employee working on a stage-2 fan stator for the TF-39 jet engine. In this complex production process, batch processing (rather than an assembly line) is used, and women work on individual parts. In a unionized plant like Aerospace, Inc., women earn "male" wages, often as high as $9.00 or $10.00 an hour. Photo by Dean Hanson, by permission of the *Albuquerque Journal*.

4. Assembly lines in participative plants have been modified. Here a Hispana works on a video terminal. Management stresses an open-door policy and supports a lively plantwide work culture. Photo by Richard Pipes, by permission of the *Albuquerque Journal*.

5. Putting the housing on a video terminal, this Hispana works on a line, but units are allowed to pile up, so that she is not pushed by the speed of a moving belt. Photo by Richard Pipes, by permission of the *Albuquerque Journal*.

6. Testing the components on a printed circuit board. At a plant like Computex, workers appreciate flextime, which allows them to come in to work and leave at times that fit with family schedules. Photo by Richard Pipes, by permission of the *Albuquerque Journal*.

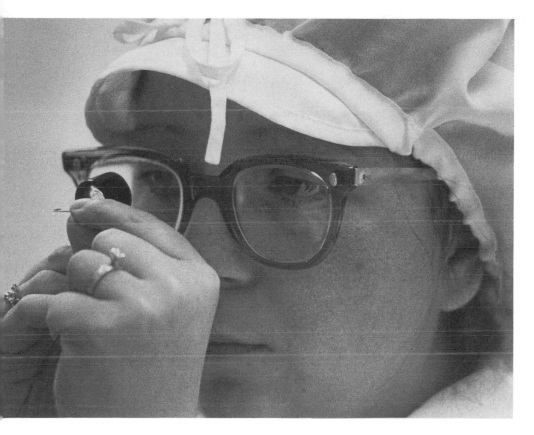

7. Specially garbed employees assemble surgical sutures and other health products at a plant like HealthTech. Team meetings stress quantity, quality, attendance, and group involvement. Photo by Richard Pipes, by permission of the *Albuquerque Journal*.

[5]

Management Ideology and
Practice in Participative Plants

During the early 1980s, as many American firms were enthusi-
astically adopting new forms of management derived from Japan,
several new plants in Albuquerque—including four where our interviewees worked—were experimenting with "participative management." Moving away from a hierarchical structure with assembly
lines and piece-rate pay systems, they were becoming what Perkins,
Neiva, and Lawler (1983:5–15) describe as "high involvement plants."
Such firms have with a flat organizational structure with few levels
between plant manager and shop floor workers, a mini-enterprise or
team work structure, and a strong emphasis on egalitarianism in the
way work and leisure areas are designed. There is usually a high
commitment to employee stability, heavy emphasis on training, pay
based on the attainment of "skill levels," and job enrichment whereby workers have some control over the organization of work.

The actual mosaic of policies varied with each of the four firms we
studied: Computex, Howard Electronics, SystemsPlus, and Health-
Tech (see Table 17). These ranged from flextime for employees,
equal benefits for clerical and blue-collar personnel, and worker selection of the vacation schedule to more direct participation in hiring and firing decisions. Managers fostered an "open door" policy
emphasizing that workers could talk over problems with top management and have a say in policy. In all four plants there was a clear
ideology of egalitarianism and participation. Management took steps
to alter the labor process, the wage system, or (particularly) management-worker relations so that there would be less focus on the ex-

Table 17. Characteristics of participative plants

Firm	Production Process	Pay System	Management Policies	Work Culture
Computex (1982) 1,000 employees (425 female on direct line)	modified assembly line (hand assembly, final assembly and test); batch process (hand assembly, cables); job rotation (machine insert)	hourly wages; quotas but not enforced	flextime; weekly meetings; open door	dance and luau, sports teams, open house, showers, potlucks
Howard Electronics (1982) 200 employees (120 female)	assembly; job rotation (line/machine insert)	hourly wages; quotas, but not enforced; good benefits	plantwide meetings; open door; few clerical/production distinctions	Christmas tree contest, Winning Edge Committee, showers, potlucks
SystemsPlus (1987) 599 employees (258 female)	continuous process; job rotation; "clean rooms"	hourly wages plus overtime; quotas; learning curves	3½ day shifts; teams; daily meetings; team schedule	Christmas dance, picnic
HealthTech (1982) 219 assemblers (174 female)	batch process; machine tending; "clean rooms"	hourly wages; learning curves	rotating day/evening shifts; teams with facilitators; team meetings; team schedule; team support in hiring/firing	union drive

traction of labor from workers. Such alterations dovetailed with the creation of a work culture that emphasized "high involvement." Thus workers did not confront a control system in the same way as workers in hierarchical plants.

Control over workers' productivity was still present, however; the new participative ideology and the concomitant shop-floor policies often masked more subtle forms of management control. Women faced a new set of contradictions between the explicitly participative ideology and reformed labor process on the one hand, and actual management practice—considerably more authoritarian—on the other. This was best seen in HealthTech's use of its production teams to thwart a union drive during 1982–83. In three of these four plants, women experienced a "new atmosphere" that brought tangible benefits and satisfaction, but the HealthTech example exposes the darker side of participative management.

Difference and Participative Management

Participative plants retained a gender division of labor despite their rearrangement of the labor process and management-worker relations. At Computex, for example, 600 of the 1,000 plant employees were in "direct line" jobs. About 570 were assemblers, and 75 percent of these were women.[1] There were only thirty technician positions, and 90 percent of these were held by men. At Howard Electronics, the plant was 60 percent female and 90 percent of the assemblers were women. SystemsPlus was a more male-dominated plant because the labor process involved a large number of engineers and technicians, jobs held usually by men. In 1987 the plant had 599 employees, only 43.1 percent of whom were women. Finally, of the 219 production and maintenance workers at HealthTech, 79.5 percent were female and 20.5 percent were male. HealthTech's labor force was the most female-dominated and the most like Leslie Pants, the apparel plant described in Chapter 4.

Only at SystemsPlus, which was structured around teams of manual workers, technicians, and engineers, did women routinely work to-

[1] These 425 women would be only 43% of the entire plant labor force, but since there were undoubtedly women in clerical and some managerial positions and in sales and service, the total proportion of women in the plant was probably between 60 and 70 percent.

[140]

gether with men. Here jobs were probably gender segregated but work groups integrated. In the other three plants, women worked together in the same departments, though men holding other jobs might interact with them frequently.

Three of these plants had a high proportion of Mexican-American workers: 58 percent at Computex, 64.8 percent at HealthTech, and 70 percent at Howard. As a whole these three had slightly higher averages than did Leslie Pants (60 percent) Southwest (54 percent), and Aerospace (47 percent). SystemsPlus, with its high numbers of engineers and technicians, was only 33 percent Mexican American, though the proportions of Mexican-American and non-Spanish-surnamed females were similar: 18.4 and 24.7 percent respectively.

Hispano and Anglo women worked side by side in departments and on teams where we interviewed working mothers. The position of women in the labor process had an important impact on their experience of participative management, but their family situation was also a relevant variable. Both Anglo and Hispano women came to appreciate management policies such as flextime and good benefits that had a direct impact on their family situation. At the same time, both Hispano and Anglo women engaged in collective strategies of resistance during the HealthTech union campaign. A greater proportion of Mexican-American women voted against the union, however. Our account shows how both the more economically vulnerable situation of Mexican-American women in relation to their family economies and their position on particular teams contributed to their cooptation by management.

Assembling Computer Terminals

On the surface, the labor process at Computex had a great deal in common with that of Southwest Electronics. In manufacturing video terminals, Computex followed one of the key sequences found at Southwest: stuffing printed circuit boards, running them through a wave solder machine, and then testing and inspecting them. Southwest, however, used an assembly line and piece rates to keep production levels high, whereas Computex did not focus so explicitly on either technical control or control through a wage system. It modified the assembly line, did not enforce quotas, and had informally restructured worker-supervisor relations. At the plant level, manage-

[141]

ment established an "open" form of work culture, emphasizing plant meetings, freer communication with top management, and worker participation.

We interviewed nine women (all Hispanas) and two husbands (one Anglo and one Hispano) who worked at Computex.[2] In 1982 the plant employed 1,000 workers; it was operating at only 50 percent capacity because orders had slowed during the recession that year. Unlike Southwest Electronics, Computex did not lay employees off during a slow period, and so workers had much more stable job histories than at Southwest. There was a job hierarchy in this plant, but it was much "flatter" than at Southwest Electronics (where there were eight grades and a pay differential of about $4.00 between GR-1 and GR-8). Of the 570 assemblers at the plant, most women were in either the Assembler 1 or Assembler 2 category and were earning between $4.60 and $6.40 an hour.[3]

We interviewed four assemblers, one machine operator, and four inspectors. We focus on five of these women, representing different production situations. Josephine Perez, in "hand assembly," stuffed boards on a modified assembly line. Jeanette Garcia, in "machine insertion," operated a machine that automatically stuffed the board. Her work was regulated by the speed of the machine, a form of technical control, but workers in her department rotated their jobs among different machines. Patricia Torres and Lucy Valdez held Assembler 2 jobs in the cable department; their operations were handled by batch processing and production quotas. Since the quotas were not enforced, however, they were not pressed into coping strategies like the apparel workers and winders who worked on the piece rate. Finally, Deborah Peña was an inspector in "final assembly and test" and worked on an assembly line where the terminals were put together and inspected. Here again the assembly line was modified, and women were able to rotate jobs.

On Josephine Perez's line in hand assembly, where boards were sent after a number of parts had been automatically inserted, each worker added about twelve components to the board. The line had a

---

[2] A tenth interviewee was a young black single parent, but we have eliminated her from the final sample so that our study focuses only on Mexican-American and white working mothers.

[3] Female assemblers at Southwest earned between $4.80 and $6.89; women at both Southwest and Computex were concentrated in the lower pay grades.

quota of some 300 boards a day, but Josephine's line usually completed about 280. Falling below the quota did not penalize workers in terms of either pay or more informal sanctions.

Josephine emphasized the differences between the Computex line and a regular assembly line.

> It's a progressive line. . . . We put integrated circuits, capacitors, and . . . ECO wires for changes that they make. . . . It's not a conveyor belt. . . . There are different stations for one person. . . . As you come in the morning you sit down in an empty station. And whoever is on the first station, they starting building them and they pass it down. . . . If you're not fast enough, well, they'll rack it up on the racks, and you work as your own speed will allow you to. Then you pass it on to the next person. They each have different parts to put on, and you work from a process sheet. And it goes on down the line to the end.

Josephine explained that some workers preferred a particular station, but others got bored at one station and liked to switch around. Josephine said her group had worked well together for two years. She described the atmosphere: "We don't work too fast at first, we just kind of talk and listen to each other's problems and gripes. That's what I like a lot about that place, because we're close-knit there." With a congenial set of interactions and informal rotation, the work practice of those in hand assembly was quite different from that of women at Southwest, who were pushed by the speed of an assembly line and a group piece rate.

Jeanette Garcia worked under different conditions with more technical control. In machine insertion, she and thirty others operated machines that automatically inserted components into printed circuit boards. Unlike Josephine, who could pace her own work, Jeanette had to keep up with the machine that did the job previously done by hand inserters: "It's computer operated, and it's programmed by computer. And the machine mostly does all the work. You put the tape into the machine. . . . And we have to keep filling the tubes up with the ICs [integrated circuits] and the machine knows where to put them. . . . We just sort of keep the machine going. On and off switches . . . filling up the tubes with ICs and loading the machine." Hand-eye coordination had been replaced by machine tending, but Jeanette and her co-workers had learned to operate each of three machines in the department, and they rotated their jobs in order to create some variety.

[143]

Patricia Torres and Lucy Valdez and other workers in the wire prep and cable department operated several different kinds of machines, including a crimper that took the twenty wires inside the cable and set them into twenty connectors. Lucy described the process of making cables:

> We get them from the stockroom and this is, you know, a long cable. . . . They come in a roll and then one of the guys . . . he'll cut them up for us, and then from there we start prepping them, which is, we start taking the insulation off. And we have to put [on] the rings . . . there's two insulations, and we have to remove the insulation; we solder, we have to solder some black wires with the white wires. . . . And then from there we connect them to the connectors, and we have them tested with a test machine. . . . And they pass and then go . . . to the stock room.

The department used batch processing rather than an assembly line, and workers did their jobs individually. A monthly schedule for the number of cables the department was to produce and send out was broken into weekly quotas, and each worker was assigned her quota by the supervisor—ranging from twelve per day for the largest cables to 200 for the smallest. Patricia was working on large cables with a daily quota of twelve; the day she was interviewed, she finished thirty-five cables. Lucy reported a weekly quota of sixty cables but said she usually finished only fifty. In other words, Patricia was producing beyond the quota, while Lucy was not making it, yet neither reported any punishments or rewards for their productivity. Thus, quotas in this department, as in hand assembly, were production goals, neither tied to wages nor strictly enforced. Workers reported no "tricks" to keep their production up, since they were not being pushed to work faster.

Four of our interviewees worked in the final assembly and test department, the area of the plant where the terminals were "built" or assembled and then tested. Eight workers were involved in "basic build" where each unit was "built from scratch"; then the units traveled on a conveyor to the "burn-in stations," where four people turned on the sets to see if they worked, and on through a series of inspections and tests. Deborah Peña was an inspector on the day shift; Prelinda Duran performed the same job on second shift. Deborah described her job: "You inspect the plastic . . . you make sure they're not dented, scratched, the CR-T, which is a tube, has no burn spots, anything on it. And then you open up the plastic and check the inside for all the hardware, make sure everything's in."

All four of the women we interviewed in this department worked on an assembly line, but since their jobs involved inspection and record keeping, they were rewarded for quality rather than quantity. Prelinda Duran did complain about the pressures of working on a line: "When I get all backed up with units, it gets me nervous. I don't really dislike [the job], however. . . . I like going to work because, you know, I get to talk to different people." On the whole, these women—like Josephine Perez in hand assembly—did not experience the kind of technical control that usually accompanies assembly line work. The pressure to keep pace with the line was mitigated by management's willingness to tolerate slowdowns and pileups in return for accurate, high-quality work.

The lack of strict assembly lines made it possible for the plant to have flextime, perhaps the most innovative aspect of Computex's management policy. Workers could arrive any time between 6:00 and 8:30 A.M. and leave eight and a half hours later (half of all Computex plants in 1982 had flextime). Most of the workers found flextime an advantage, since it allowed them to tailor their working hours to their family schedules. For example, Josephine Perez liked to come in about 6:30 A.M. so that she could leave at 3:00 P.M. and still have time to run errands after work. Jeanette Garcia came in later; as she explained:

> Some people come in earlier, some people come in later. It all depends on what time of the year it is. During the summer time, they'll come in pretty early . . . for the kids, you know, they don't have their kids in school, so you usually want to be home pretty early. . . . I have to get my little one to school, so I usually try and leave by 7:30 and take her to my mom's, and she walks to school from there. And my husband (who also works at Computex) and I ride together.

First- and second-shift workers had to coordinate their schedules among themselves, so that second shift arrived roughly when first shift left; the management left that up to the workers. Sometimes this caused conflict: Prelinda Duran, for example, needed to begin work on second shift at 2:30 p.m. in order to get off work at 11:00 P.M. so that her husband could get to his night job at a dairy. She felt she could not come in later to accommodate the first-shift inspector:

"I told her I couldn't do it. There's no way I can do it, I told her, if I could, I would . . . because of the kids . . . we're going to have a meeting, and discuss it about the overlap." This and other conflicts were usually worked out through negotiation.

Flextime allowed women to mediate an important contradiction between their roles as mother and worker. Each one could adjust her work time to the exigencies of family life, find a daily schedule that fit best with her husband's schedule, and have the freedom to arrive late to work if a family crisis occurred. Of all Computex's policies, this was perhaps the one most appreciated by the women we interviewed.

Computex's open style of management encouraged department supervisors to act in ways that deemphasized their hierarchical relationship to workers. They held weekly meetings to discusss production or quality control, or to give out information about extracurricular activities such as the annual picnic. They cultivated friendly relations with their employees, acting less as "bosses" and more as "just one of us." The women workers we talked to had good relations with their supervisors and generally approved of the plant's open managerial style. For example, Lucy Valdez, who worked in the cable department, said,

> The supervisor's really really nice; she doesn't pressure us or anything, she's real cute about it. She asks somebody else to help us if we're falling behind . . . she goes along with us. . . . She'll join us or she'll sit there with us, on break times, to talk with us or sometimes she'll even go to lunch with us. . . . She's just one of us. She'll joke around with us and everything, you know. She doesn't act like a supervisor, she just acts herself.

These tactics muted the simple control that supervisors held and created a work culture that supported a participative ideology aimed at building a loyal work force. Supervisors played an important role in fostering loyalty at the department level as well.

Departmental and Plantwide Work Culture

Computex had a lively work culture: birthdays and babies were celebrated, and there were numerous occasions for department potlucks. Even male workers received baby showers when a child was born. Marta Olquin's department organized the party for a male co-worker with the cooperation of the wife: "We just called her. Well, it was a surprise for him, really, he didn't know nothing about it, and we happened to call his wife to come down with the baby. . . . We had a potluck and a shower, a cake for them and gifts. . . . We get a list, and we write whoever wants to bring what . . . it really turns out delicious."

In many departments there were also special holiday celebrations, especially at Christmastime. Leona Thomas (one of the supplementary providers introduced in Chapter 3) described her "incoming inspection" department's Christmas celebration: We put up a tree and we exchange. You know, we put names in a hat, we get a gift that could be for a man or a woman. Then we put an M or a W, and then we just picked a number. . . . and that was our gift. We did that for Christmas. Then we bring goodies, you know, brownies, tamales, posole."

Although workers often organized parties and potlucks on their own, supervisors too were important in fostering these events. Each supervisor had a "cost center" and was given money each year for seminars and equipment but could use leftover funds to take workers out to lunch or pay for a cake at a baby shower.

The supervisor's success in creating a less hierarchical relationship with workers was reflected in the fact that sometimes a department would organize a party for its supervisor. Lucy Valdez, told us: "We've done it for our supervisor's birthday; we decorated it and we surprised her. We're always surprising her. For Valentine's or anything, we've always given her [something], and she's really neat. That's why I say I can't ask for a better supervisor."

The participatory nature of department work culture was reinforced by company sponsorship of plantwide events. Computex held a company picnic in August, and each division in the plant had a dance or luau each year. The firm also sponsored softball, volleyball, and track teams. There was a Spanish heritage week and a black heritage week. The Special Events Committee planned the picnic and the luaus, which were paid for out of company funds, but other committees—for example the Christmas Committee, which planned a children's party—raised money for their events. A Recreation Committee organized the athletic teams, using a budget of $15,000 a year. In addition, the company often gave employees free passes to baseball games or for the tramway that ascends the nearby mountains. (Some of these activities were curtailed during 1982 because of the recession, according to one interviewee.)

[147]

The company also rewarded workers for excellent production. These were not individual incentives, like the piece-rate system and profit-sharing plan at Leslie Pants, but plantwide celebrations of good productivity. Patricia Torres reported that once the whole plant put out 100,000 terminals and they gave them a free lunch and sent employees home at noon: "They gave out T-shirts and it said 'Thanks for 100,000' or something like that. They always give us little gifts. I got the windbreaker here that they gave us for reaching a schedule."

Unlike those at Leslie Pants, these company-sponsored events did not buttress a piece-rate pay system. Instead, they complemented the non-hierarchical "open-door" policies of Computex. They made workers feel that the company did things to benefit workers and created a feeling of rapport and good will between management and employees. Workers rated Computex a good place to work, one with a friendly, open atmosphere where supervisors were on good terms with their employees.

Women's Responses: Appreciation or Co-optation?

Policies that altered the labor process and management-worker relations were also successful in creating a loyal work force. Women were particularly appreciative of flextime, a policy that helped them mediate the contradiction between their full-time commitment to both work and motherhood. Other positive comments about their jobs revolved around the good benefit package and the relatively high pay. Some workers had complaints about a specific supervisor, a high turnover of supervisory personnel, or the lack of job mobility within the plant, but these comments usually made for one negative note in a list of positive job characteristics. For example, Josephine Perez emphasized favoritism, which was not an issue for others.

I like the money. What else do I like? Most of the time I like the companionship that the people provide, you know, the conversation. What I dislike, let me think. I dislike the politics that goes on around the plant. If one person wants to get a job and they're qualified for it, another person wants that same job, but she knows somebody, you know, who can help her, and this other person is qualified as much as this other person, doesn't know anybody, more than likely that other person who knows the people will get the job.

[148]

Lucy Valdez, on the other hand, thought that there were good possibilities for promotion: "The advantage is that you can climb. I mean they really, they always put up jobs to bid for, for higher positions. . . . They give everybody a fair chance in that."

Overall, participative management policies made many women believe that a union was unnecessary at Computex. Deborah Peña commented: "Well, I've worked through a union before, and it could have its advantages and disadvantages. I guess it would depend on who came in, you know, and then of course you'd have to have meetings, see what they would promise you, you know, if they were really worth it. Right now, for myself at the moment, I don't think we would need a union."

On the whole, then, the women we interviewed at Computex appreciated their jobs, the plant's benefits, the flextime scheduling, and the overall prticipative policies of the firm. Some felt that there had been too many changes in supervisors or saw other management problems, but even the women who voiced the few complaints regarded their jobs as relatively well paid and worth keeping.

Thermostat Production and People-Oriented Management

Howard Electronics implemented a different mosaic of policies in its "participative philosophy," but there, too, management altered the labor process, did not use piece rates or enforce quotas, and went a long way toward encouraging supervisors to make their relations with workers less hierarchical. Howard invested more effort than Computex, however, in creating a work culture around an ideology of participation.

Howard Electronics opened in October 1980 and by 1982 was employing 200 workers. Even before the building was complete, the firm was inundated with applications: there were lines down the street, and 1,000 people applied for jobs. The firm had no trouble finding experienced people, and the personnel manager told us that there was a good electronics industrial base in Albuquerque with many skilled workers available.

Within the labor process, Howard focused on job rotation. It did not use piece rates; instead, assemblers were paid an hourly wage, and there were quotas on individual jobs. Howard had the relatively flat organizational structure characteristic of high-involvement plants

(Perkins, Neiva, and Lawler 1983:5–15); in addition, it had put policies in place that created fewer distinctions between blue-collar, white-collar, and management positions. There were no reserved parking spaces for management, no time clocks, and no difference in benefits for "nonexempt" (direct production) and "exempt" (salaried) workers. There was one salary structure for the entire nonexempt labor force (clerical, assembly, and technician) with step increases in pay, depending on the time in a job. There was also "merit opportunity" for performing above and beyond what was expected at either a "commendable" or "exceptional" level. Although the company classified workers in eight grades (from A at the bottom to H at the top), there were no A-level employees at this plant. Most women were at level B or C. About 40 percent of the plant's workforce was at B level, including most assemblers, who started at $4.45 and could make as much as $6.30 an hour.

Howard saw itself as having a "people-oriented management." At the quarterly "all employees meeting" the management provided information about financial and employment prospects, production runs, and new products that were being introduced. The plant manager also held "coffee talks," monthly meetings with a dozen employees selected randomly throughout the plant. These lasted one or two hours and provided an open forum for discussion.

Employees were also involved in developing plant-wide policies. For example, they were asked their preferences concerning holidays, so that the resulting list of eleven days off was not the personnel manager's decision but "everybody's holiday schedule." Assemblers, clerical workers, and technicians were also members of the committee that developed "performance appraisals" and later met with fellow workers to communicate the new procedures to them.[4]

Howard, like Computex, emphasized training but stressed the firm's participative philosophy as well as work-related skills. According to the personnel manager, it took three to seven days to "Howard-ize" experienced new workers and two weeks to train inexperienced workers. In 1982 the personnel manager was developing a formal system for moving employees around, designed to introduce variety and to be consistent with productivity needs. Some training

---

[4] Since we interviewed only four workers at Howard and none was a member of any of these committees, it was difficult to know how much input employees really had in these administrative areas.

took place in a "learning center" where two employees created courses, such as one in soldering, which were available to workers who wished to learn new skills so that they could rotate jobs. This attention to skills training and also to indoctrination into the company's good points made Howard quite different from the more hierarchical plants.

The Production Process

At Howard Electronics, as at Southwest and Computex, a central part of the production process involved stuffing boards. Howard made two kinds of electronic thermostats, and on both production lines the workers stuffed printed circuit boards. The boards themselves were manufactured by another company, and then some of the parts were automatically inserted by two machines: a sequencer placed the parts in the correct order, and an inserter put them in place. The production process was very capital-intensive; each inserter machine cost $100,000, part of the $1.5 million worth of equipment in the plant. The major advantage was that the machines saved a great deal of labor by inserting 25,000 components an hour.

We interviewed four women at Howard, three Anglos and one Hispana. Ann Singleton worked at an automatic sequencer and inserter, a job similar to that of Jeanette Garcia at Computex. Linda Henry, like a number of our interviewees at Southwest Electronics and Computex, hand-stuffed boards on an assembly line. Connie Mead touched up completed boards, and Anita Alvarez tested the boards produced on one of the two product lines. All four women had had previous job experience in electronics. Two had friends, already Howard employees, who helped them to get hired at a time when management had the pick of new workers. Connie Mead was pregnant when she finally landed a job at Howard, and she returned to work as soon as her son was six months old in order to retain a job she had worked for a year to get.

At the beginning of the line were the sequencer and inserter machines. The sequencer operator fed parts in prescribed order for each type of board. The machine automatically checked the polarity of the part and stopped the machine if a component was defective. The parts came down through the machine and were attached to a tape which was wound into a reel. Each reel held 500 parts and fit on the back of the inserter. Ann Singleton operated both machines in one of the two production lines.

> The way I can describe the insertion machine is like a big stapler. It's run through a master computer, and Joe, our technician, programs it for the different boards. And it automatically puts the right part into the right hole. And you've got this machine that runs . . . it's constantly running. If you hit override, you've got to pull the boards out, check the boards, put empty boards back in. . . . . If anything fouls up you have to try and fix it. I don't particularly like the machine. It kind of scares me, because like I said, it is like a big stapler, because the parts are going down. . . . I like the sequencer a lot better. . . . It cuts the parts off of reels and puts them in a certain programed order.

At Howard as at Computex, workers were allowed to rotate in jobs that were essentially machine tending and demanded less hand-eye coordination than did board stuffing. When we interviewed Ann, the plant was shifting from running two types of boards to as many as twenty. "It was chaos," Ann commented. They had been running out of parts, and as a result the line was often shut down. A new supervisor was hired to manage this transition, and Ann's work group tried to help him by letting him know how they normally did things. The supervisor gave them a great deal of latitude in organizing their work. Ann and her two co-workers rotated among the machines they operated on a daily basis. "We usually take turns. . . . So what we usually do the first thing in the morning . . . we usually count everything. That's to give us an idea of what's through what stage and what we have to do. Plus it helps [our superisor] out. Then we decide who's going to do what. And we usually just stick with that. . . . It's like a little department within a department." The trio was also responsible for repairs and decided each day how to coordinate the repair work with the machine tending, depending on their work load. This work practice was directed toward organizing the work rather than keeping pace with an assembly line or working against a piece rate, as in hierarchical plants.

Next in the production process was the assembly line where parts that could not be put on automatically were inserted by hand. In discussing what it was like to work on the line, Linda focused on job rotation.

[152]

You almost get to do everything. . . . When we first started work there, they took surveys, and they asked what people thought about rotation. . . . And a lot of us really wanted [it]. We felt that rotation was a lot better way. You didn't get so bored with doing the same thing all day. And so what happened is that our supervisor did a lot of rotating, but . . . she only lasted a year, and now we've got a new one, and no, we don't get as much rotation as we used to before.

Linda and her co-workers felt that their new supervisor was just less familiar with their capabilities and was more focused on meeting his production schedule. They planned to approach him to ask for more rotation.

Linda explained that although she was paid an hourly wage, the standard for her job was forty boards per hour. Management had recently reduced the number of workers on the progressive line from four to three and had changed the rates: "The way we feel is that they figured out the speed of our four people was faster than the speed of the insertion and the terminal. So therefore by taking one person away from us . . . it will give us more parts [to complete in a given amount of time]."

Linda had previously worked on the progressive line at Southwest and thought the piece-rate system there provided a good opportunity to make extra money, but she recognized that "the pressure is a lot higher, and it's hard to get that many people all at the same pace." She believed that in any firm, however, whether it had piece rates or a standard, "once you've reached the speed and once you've made the money . . . then the company usually comes out and reevaluates it and retimes it and changes it purposely. Because they found out that you are making too much money and they want to dissolve it. Or else they raise the rates. Because even like at Howard Electronics, I honestly say that I've been there a year and a half and our rates have gone up four times. And it's not just that we don't make any incentive, but it's just the idea that when we started out, our rates were real low."

Linda did not seem to resent this practice, nor did she report any tactics or resistance strategies evolved by co-workers to deal with it—perhaps because of her anti-union stance. She felt that the union at Southwest had inhibited the possibility of job rotation, since the various jobs were in different grades and at different pay levels under a union. In addition, she had not supported Southwest's 1979 strike

[153]

and felt that union dues could have been better spent "to help the people like their jobs better." She also appreciated a number of Howard's participative policies: "They made it a point to come out and talk to you everyday, and they made it a point to see how you liked it and if you were happy. . . . They didn't segregate you like, say . . . they were the office and you were the factory. Howard is an all-over . . . all-together plant." Although Linda could recognize "speedup," she either did not have difficulty in meeting new quotas or found that other aspects of her job compensated for having to work faster.

The next group of women on the line did touchup. We interviewed Connie Mead who performed this job on the evening shift from 3:00 P.M. to 11:30 P.M. There were seventeen on the evening shift in her department, including twelve Mexican Americans and five Anglos. Among the women, four did touchup, seven or eight workers wired circuit boards, and one tested them. There was one supervisor for the entire shift. Work on the evening shift was "usually to take care of what day shift didn't finish . . . to finish up their quota at the end of the day." Connie described touchup as "just looking for different errors that were made during the assembly. Looking for the good and the bad solder, after it came off the wave solder . . . getting it ready for test and quality control.

Connie usually worked on one type of board each evening; she had completed ten boards the day before our interview. She felt that supervisors were encouraging workers to focus less on quotas and more on quality: "I think the quality keeps coming out more so than the quantity. People are spending more time on it than they did before. Before, it was to get it through as fast as they could, but now it's looking at the quality and making sure that this is going to go through and this is going to pass the test. And not coming back as a reject." Even so, Connie developed a work practice in which she set her own goals, not necessarily the same as the quotas specified by management: "I always have a goal set when I go in there, what I think I'm going to do. But sometimes, there's times I don't meet it either. Because if I run into a certain problem, I don't meet the standard that I set for myself, you know. But I try to set a goal."

After touchup the boards were split in half by a machine to make two smaller boards. Then they were tested. If a board failed a test, it was given to one of three repair girls; the "good" boards were placed on the line where switches and the LCD (liquid crystal display) were put on. This was a smaller assembly line which included several workers. Anita Alvarez tested the LCDs.

> I've got a machine there, and I put it in, and I look at the tester, and it's got to blink from 1 to 12 A.M. . . . And I'm looking for, making sure that it goes forwards, backwards, all the numbers are there, anything on that thing that's bad . . . I'm pressing buttons at the same time. There's different buttons, and I've got to press them so it can tell me what's working and what's not. If the LCD doesn't work, I've got boxes right here, I'll set them down. I'll set the repairs right here, and I'll leave them there, and I'll send the good ones through. These broken ones, I'll try to fix.

Anita's interview also stressed job rotation. She was a "rover," someone who "worked all over" at different jobs. She had been trained to run the sequencer and inserter, and she had worked on the line and on touchup as well. But she found the standard for testing the LCDs unattainable:

> Say like on the LCDs, they have down, well Anita, you've got to put out 200 an hour, okay? There's no way in the world you can put out 200 an hour. But of course, this . . . doesn't come from the supervisors. . . . It comes from a man that doesn't even know what's going on . . . and he just comes and looks at you, he times you and he says, you can do so many an hour. . . . Like I said, you can go to your supervisor: "There is no way I can put out that in an hour." He says, "That's all right, you just do the work, and if you can't put it out, you can't. But if you can, try it."

On the one hand, Anita used the individual-level tactic of complaining to her supervisor about quotas that were too high. On the other hand, supervisors paid little attention to unrealistic quotas and put more effort into building quality relations with their workers. Like supervisors at Computex, they attempted to make their relationship with workers less hierarchical. Three of the four workers we interviewed had the same supervisor and commented on the special efforts he made to create a friendly and egalitarian atmosphere. Anita described his role in bringing the department together: "My supervisor's very nice to get along with. You don't find very many supervisors that come and sit down and eat lunch with you and act like he's not even a supervisor, you know."

Ann Singleton emphasized the extra things that he did: "Our su-

[155]

pervisor brings in stuff all the time. One day his son was ordained a priest, and they threw a big reception for him and everything. And they had cold cuts and bread and all this left over, and he brought it for us. . . . But he's the only one I know of that does anything like that." This supervisor may have been unusual in the plant, but Connie Mead, the fourth interviewee, said that "most of the bosses I've worked under I've liked real well."

Department and Plantwide Work Culture

Supervisors' attempt to create an informal work culture at the department level added to the loyalty generated by policies of job rotation, less hierarchical relations, and little attention to quotas that were difficult to meet. The supervisor mentioned above had been particularly central to creating a sociable atmosphere: Weddings and the birth of babies were marked with a shower and a cake, and birthdays were celebrated with potlucks. These were organized through departmental discussion and voting, which gave workers a feeling of participation. Connie Mead told of the baby shower her department had organized for her during a lunch break: "It was a surprise. . . . I kind of knew, but I didn't know exactly when. . . . They had a nice big cake baked [and] all kinds of gifts."

Howard Electronics had been very successful in putting together a lively plantwide work culture as well. A number of events were paid for by the company. For example, Anita said that at Christmastime the company gave each department a tree: "They give us so much money, and we buy decorations . . . enough to decorate a small tree and put it in our department, and everybody competes over the best tree, and then we all have, we draw names. Everybody fills the Christmas tree with presents and stuff like that. . . . They have a big potluck [or] you can either go out and eat. They'll give you an hour of lunch."

Many plantwide occasions were planned and sponsored by the Winning Edge Committee, as Linda explained: "It's in charge of trying to put on things during the year. . . . It's one representative from each department throughout the plant. They are the ones that's in charge of the annual picnic. And then they also have the open house. . . . They had dancers and singers and they had clowns, and they provided ice cream and drinks. They had like a a smorgasbord."

[156]

Plantwide meetings were another way of building a loyal work force. Anita Alvarez described these occasions:

> Like if they've got something to say, they'll come over and say . . . we're having coffee and doughnuts. We want to discuss something with you. And . . . the whole plant goes into the cafeteria, and you walk in, you get your coffee, you get your doughnuts, cokes, whatever you want, you sit down and eat it. Then he'll come up to the front and say, "Well look, we're getting a new board out, or we did a quota which was really neat. We had to take out so many thousand boards, and we took them out, we want to thank all of you. We really appreciate your work." You know, that makes you feel good. . . . They're nice, they're really nice people.

Other employees too were enthusiastic about participative management policies. Linda Henry mentioned the lack of separation between blue-collar and white-collar workers in appraising her first experiences at Howard: "I liked it especially for the reason that the people in the office were really good to you. And they made it a point to come out and talk to you every day, and they made it a point to see how you liked it, if you were happy. And that's what I really like the most . . . is that the people in the office made you feel really at home."

Still, some saw the lack of work rules as a disadvantage. Ann Singleton, who was on the Safety Committee, thought that the participative management philosophy had gotten in the way of clear rules about health and safety.

> Management I'm not too sure of. The Safety Committee is doing everything they can. We are kind of blocked, sometimes. . . . They don't want a military-type atmosphere. . . . They don't want to say, "You will wear your safety glasses." But they have to, because they are liable for all that. And we try to pound this into their heads, and they're not going to realize it until someday somebody sues them because they lost an eye because they weren't wearing their glasses. . . . It gets sticky sometimes.

Nevertheless the success of Howard's policies was reflected in the high rankings our four interviewees gave their jobs in terms of good pay, a safe place to work, a good supervisor, the ability to talk with

[157]

co-workers, and little conflict with family responsibilities.[5] Job security rated a little lower. But the main negative aspect for these women was the lack of opportunity for promotion, a quality given a 3 by three of the four interviewees. It was here that the flat job hierarchy characteristic of many participative plants had its disadvantages. Even so, taking ten qualities into account, the Howard workers rated their jobs between 1.6 and 2.5 on our four-point scale, higher than the Leslie Pants workers' rating.

Women emphasized the importance of high pay and benefits, particularly since both were important in helping them as providers and in resolving the contradictions between their work and family roles. Linda, a single parent, was quite straight-forward: "I need the job security and good pay. And I mainly need the free benefits which we have. . . . I had gone to dental [technician] school, and I worked in the dental profession for several years, but it didn't give me the benefits I needed, now that I'm by myself." Ann Singleton, a coprovider with her husband, also mentioned benefits: "Up front, if it wasn't for the benefits, we're lost. Because my husband's benefits are down the drain. They're not any good. I think that's one of the main advantages."

Anita emphasized the flexibility of the absence regulations: "I think I like the idea that they pay me sick leave if I've got something personal to do, if I'm sick or our kids are sick. If I'm late, they pay me . . . [They] say, well, her child's sick, or you know, she's got to go to court. . . . They're very considerate on that." But Ann's experience had been just the opposite. She said she would lose out on a raise because her child's illness and her own had affected her attendance. "I keep saying it's not fair to women who have children. Because women that don't have children aren't going to be absent half as much as we are. . . . You just can't send your child to a babysitter, you know, when she's violently ill." Women evaluated their jobs partly on the basis of how well it meshed with their family responsibilities and helped them resolve the important contradictions in their lives.

On the shop floor, the altered labor process and rearrangement of the management-worker hierarchy were important in shaping workers' satisfaction. Linda, for example, emphasized that she enjoyed being

[5] Each of these qualities rated a 1 from two or three of the four interviewees, and a 2 from the remainder, for a 1.25 or 1.5 ranking on our four-point scale.

able to move from job to job, and Anita stressed the plant's participative policies: "The advantage is probably that I can say whatever I feel like, and they'll listen to me. If I have changes I want to make, I'll go up there and I'll say it, and they'll listen. . . . I like the way they listen to you. They make you part of the plant."

In other words, women may have used individual coping strategies and tactics (setting goals for themselves or complaining to a supervisor about a high quota), but there was little evidence of group-level resistance. Howard's commitment to good pay and benefits and management's successful implementation of job rotation, support of less hierarchical relations between supervisors and workers, and espousal of a high-involvement philosophy had resulted for women workers in positive feelings about their jobs.

Silicon Chip Manufacture and the Team Structure

Two firms had gone even further in altering the labor process, worker-management relations, and work culture than had Computex and Howard Electronics. SystemsPlus, which manufactured silicon chips, and HealthTech, which produced surgical sutures, had dispensed with assembly lines and traditional hierarchies to organize production around "teams." Both espoused a participative management philosophy, and both had instituted unusual shift schedules. SystemsPlus implemented a twelve-hour, three-and-a-half-day shift schedule; HealthTech teams rotated between first and second shift, usually spending two weeks on one before switching to the other. The restructuring of work, along with each firm's participative philosophy, obscured management's control system to an even greater degree than was true at Computex and Howard. The contradictions between management goals for productivity and workers' attempts to control their own work were less apparent. This in turn had implications for women's work practice and strategies for resistance. In contrast, the unusual shift schedules often sharpened the contradictions between women's work and family roles, as women had to rearrange child care and family responsibilities to fit schedules out of sync with the more usual nine-to-five, forty-hour work week. We interviewed only one employee at SystemsPlus, but she gave us important insights into how far innovations were proceeding in high-tech firms in 1982.

SystemsPlus manufactured silicon chips that became parts of integrated circuits, a production process prior to and quite different from that of stuffing boards. The manufacture of wafers and cutting them into chips involved building the wafers from silicon and etching circuitry on them. Each wafer had 300 dies, and each die contained a separate circuit. The plant had several "fabs" (fabrication facilities) composed of "clean rooms" containing the complex machinery necessary to build the wafers. In the fab, workers had to wear special clothing and take special precautions to prevent wafers from becoming contaminated.

There were three departments in the fab that had opened in the Albuquerque plant in 1982: "masking," "diffusion," and "thin film." In the diffusion department, the wafers were constructed by layering oxide and nitrites. In masking, sectors of the wafer were blocked out and others etched with the circuits. In the thin film department, additional layers were built on.

At the time of our interviews the plant had only eighty-five employees, but by 1987 its labor force numbered 599: 43.1 percent women and 56.9 percent men. SystemsPlus was scheduled to run on a twenty-four-hour, seven-day-a-week schedule, but in 1982 only the day shifts were in operation. Shift A started on Sunday at 6:00 A.M. and continued to 6:00 P.M. on Sunday, Monday, and Tuesday and until noon on Wednesday. Shift B started at noon Wednesday, continued to 6:00 P.M., and resumed from 6:00 A.M. to 6:00 P.M. on Thursday, Friday, and Saturday. We interviewed Donna Garcia, a trainer responsible for teaching production jobs to new employees; she worked on shift B.

Within departments, production teams on each shift integrated employees from different supervisory and skill levels: each team had a supervisor, several engineers and technicians, and a number of operators. Since engineers and technicians were usually men and assemblers were women, teams also brought males and females into the same work group. Team organization also emphasized job rotation among the assemblers and control over work scheduling. The plant manager told us that ideally a team would have six to eight assemblers, one for each task to be performed; if possible, each of these workers would be trained for all tasks within the team and would be able to switch off among them.[6] Each team was to have

---

[6] This team structure is commonly used in automobile plants (Harley Shaiken, per-

considerable autonomy and could often decide how to divide up its work.

The importance of job rotation was obvious in Donna's work experience. At the time of our interview she was working in the diffusion department and had learned eleven jobs there. Previously, she had mastered four jobs in masking. Donna described the rationale: "See, everybody is trained to run two different jobs. We run twelve hours a day, and this breaks up their day. Instead of being put on just one piece of equipment, and you're just there the rest of the day, you have a chance to get a little bit of variety."

In addition to job rotation, each team within a department met daily to plan production, a task often directed by an engineer but with the operators' participation.

At 6:00 A.M. I have a meeting in the fab—we have what we call a team meeting. And this is the diffusion team; it's the supervisor of the operators, plus me and the other trainor, [and] the operators, the techs, and the engineers. We all get together, the supervisor lets us know what's in the area, what's priority, and asks the training department what we need for the day, what do you guys want to do? We say, "Well, we want to work on this product over here, so let us have all this product, and your operators can go off and do this other product over here."

The trainers carefully schedule which persons they will work with each day and how they will supervise and monitor their work. Donna and her partner were training two new operators; the other workers in diffusion had completed training.

Donna was a particularly important person in the implementation of management's control system. She had responsibility not only for her trainees' output but also for quality control. Following a checklist of steps for each job, she instructed the workers and then graded them on their quality and quantity: "I have a master timing sheet in which I can get a grade for them; in other words, it's like a percentage. If they get three wrong out of thirty, I can give them a certain percentage. So that's their quality rating for the day." When they had learned the job, she then worked with each trainee to get the job done in a specified amount of time. The trainers used a learning

---

sonal communication), but at SystemsPlus and especially at HealthTech, there was more effort to transform relations between supervisors and workers in order to "de-bureaucratize control."

curve for each operation and also kept a diary of what each person did during the twelve-hour shift. If one trainer monitored three individuals, and each was learning two different jobs, measuring their work and drawing up the charts could be a complex operation.

Once a week the trainers from all the teams had their own team meeting for two hours to discuss the progress of the workers they were supervising. Since we were unable to interview assemblers, we do not know what kinds of strategies and tactics grew up around the learning curves imposed on each job. Workers were being monitored very closely at the beginning of their training; however, the jobs were very complex, and it is possible that if trainers stressed quality rather than quotas, women workers did not feel at odds with a control system.

Donna's interview gives us some sense of how the team structure was used to change relationships between supervisors and workers, between trainers and workers, and between co-workers themselves. In team meetings, trainers could bring up any problems they had and suggest any improvements they wanted to make. An organizational development specialist gave the trainers exercises in role playing and conflict resolution. "Well, like our last team meeting . . . we had a deal on role playing and changing roles, and how communication is involved in that and how some people can only see one side of something, they don't really know all the facts. And why this other person is against them."

Each team, from management on down, also attended a "team concepts" seminar that lasted for three and a half days. "Some people, they don't really like to be involved. And they're the type of people who go to meetings and they don't say a word, you know, they never express themselves, but they are the ones who are having the problems. . . . In the year that I've been there, I can say that yes, it does work. We've matured, our team has matured a lot."

The trainers often solved problems within their group without going to the supervisors. For example, when one trainer was spending too much time away from the fab area, they wanted to encourage her to check more often on her trainees. But instead of criticizing the trainer directly, they suggested, "So and so is in the fab, and they were asking for you." In that way, "we get the person to feel like, 'Well, maybe I should be in the fab more,'" Donna explained. In short, there seemed to be close monitoring of production, but the team structure was being implemented in a manner that produced more cooperative and less hierarchical relationships.

For working mothers, the SystemsPlus shift schedule had the single most important impact on the family. Aware that it might be an issue in recruiting a high-quality labor force, the firm had conducted a survey to find out whether enough people would be willing to work three and a half days on twelve-hour shifts. The results were positive; despite potential problems with family responsibilities, the plant manager thought the schedule would attract a different kind of employee, a younger population, and those who would be interested in a three-and-a-half-day weekend.

For some mothers, the shift schedule sharpened the contradictions between full-time mother and worker. Donna had had to make some adjustments, but she had been able to arrange a place at a day-care center for her three-year-old daughter only on Thursdays and Fridays (Donna's mother kept the child on Wednesday afternoons). Her husband's schedule as a facilitator at HealthTech was flexible enough so that he was able to drop the younger child off and pick her up, and to oversee the eight-year-old during nonschool hours. Thus, Donna had worked through the sharpened contradictions brought about by her unusual schedule.

> I like it. I like it. It's a hard adjustment to get used to when you first start out. And there's some problems involved that you wouldn't have normally in other jobs. One of them is day care, cause you go in at six. We have to be there by twenty to six in the morning, the trainers do; the operators have to be there at six. And the day cares aren't open at that time. And day cares usually close at 6:00 in the evening, and you don't get out of work until six, so that's a problem there. Another problem would be that [on second shift] you don't have a real weekend. That's an adjustment, also.

The job itself had a lot of positive benefits, including the pay. Since Donna worked a forty-two-hour week, she was paid time-and-a-half for the extra two hours. Averaged out, her earnings were about $7.00 an hour, a dollar or two over the wages earned by many other women we interviewed. She felt she was "very lucky" to get her job, rated it highly (a 1 or 2 on all items), and had never thought of quitting this position. "I like the people contact, I like working with people and teaching them. I get a lot of satisfaction out of it when they go through the job and they learn it and they demonstrate. . . . It's like watching your kid graduate from high school or something. You're really proud of them because they know the job, and you know that you taught them right. . . . So it's really satisfying work."

[163]

Donna was an enthusiastic employee who had made adjustments to the unorthodox shift schedule and who was happy with the high pay, benefits, and flexibility of her job. From her perspective, participative management was a success. The story was much more complex at HealthTech.

The Labor Process in Medical Products

Like SystemsPlus, HealthTech had gone beyond piecemeal forms of participation to a complete restructuring of management-worker relations around small groups. The teams at HealthTech were involved not only in training and evaluation (like Donna) but in hiring and firing of fellow workers—prerogatives still reserved for management at SystemsPlus. In the HealthTech philosophy, supervisors were to "facilitate" social relationships within the team, and workers were to help one another with production problems. Employees were coparticipators with management in producing quality medical products. Like Computex and Howard, HealthTech used no time clocks, maintained an open-door policy, and had something like flextime in that workers could come in late and make up the time at the end of the day. Through the team philosophy, management attempted to impart its vision of the company to workers. Thus HealthTech represents the most "radical" of the participative plants we studied and, at the same time, the plant that generated the most conflict over the nature of participative management. During the course of our interviews, the company was the site of a union drive, which met with a great deal of company resistance. In May 1983 the union was defeated by a two-to-one margin in the voting.

Despite the team structure, HealthTech retained some traditional aspects of the labor process and wage system similar to those at Leslie Pants. HealthTech made surgical sutures, using batch processing at individual machines rather than assembly lines. Women in two departments, "channel swaging" and "drill swaging," attached surgical thread to curved steel needles. Swaging (pronounced "swedging") demanded many of the skills important in the garment industry: good hand-eye coordination, manual dexterity, and the ability to work quickly without making mistakes. Employees were trained through the use of "learning curves": each week the trainee was given a production goal of completing so many dozen swaged needles each day; the number increased until the worker reached "100 percent efficiency." Like women at Leslie Pants, HealthTech workers were in effect pushing against a clock and trying to "make their numbers," increasing their daily production, but they were not paid on a piece-rate basis. Rewards and punishments for higher or lower production levels were administered through an hourly wage rate and through the team structure. Thus, the control systems at Leslie Pants and HealthTech stood in marked contrast. Both depended on increasing worker productivity during training and then maintaining it at high levels with high quality control, but they achieved this in opposite ways: one through a more traditional use of the piece rate in combination with supervisory control and public awards, and the other through the "team concept" and peer pressure.

Like SystemsPlus, HealthTech also instituted an unusual shift structure that sharpened the contradictions between family and employment roles. Each department was divided into "production teams" of twelve to fourteen workers; six or seven members of each team worked days from 7:00 A.M. to 3:00 P.M., and the rest worked evenings from 3:00 to 11:00 P.M. The team planned a rotation schedule whereby each individual normally worked two weeks on days followed by two weeks on evenings. For working mothers with small children, this meant that child-care needs also alternated between daytime (when day-care centers and babysitters were available) to afternoon and evening, when husbands or relatives were the most appropriate to fill in for a mother's care. It was difficult for women to find day-care centers that would accept a child on a two-weeks-per-month basis; babysitters were more willing to deal with this arrangement. But some mothers had less than satisfactory arrangements for care during the weeks they were on the evening shift. A few had negotiated with their teammates to work permanently during the day, if there were other members willing to work regularly on the evening shift. Others, however, were unhappy with the lack of fit between their work and mothering responsibilities and with the difficulties they faced in replacing their reproductive labor.

Within the plant other contradictions were sharpened: between management's team structure and high-involvement philosophy on the one hand, and its actual practice on the other. The team concept entailed a massive restructuring of management-worker relations that went much further than at Computex and Howard, where supervisors were more open, sat down with employees at lunch, and arranged potlucks. First, the cultural categories describing worker-management relations were altered. Each team had a "facilitator" rather than a "supervisor," suggesting a shift from imposing policies and watching over workers to "helping out." Second, in terms of actual duties, the facilitator was not a "boss" who meted out rewards and punishments but someone who focused on the interpersonal relationships within a team. In addition, the hiring prerogatives of management were to be shared with the team. Two team members interviewed prospective employees (after they had been interviewed by a personnel administrator and the facilitator), and if their evaluation was negative, the person was usually not hired.

Once a worker was hired, teams were involved in evaluation—and even in firing—after a two-month probationary period and again at the end of each six-month period. Evaluations were based on quality, quantity, attendance, and team support. Each team member filled out a form, checking among other things whether the person in question "works hard to reach production." Nonproduction aspects were also rated, including whether the co-worker "showed a positive attitude towards the job," "took active part in team evaluations," and "understood the team concept/open communication philosophy." That is, team members were asked to evaluate their peers on social behavior and attitudes as well as their ability to cope with the production process. Evaluations were discussed in a team meeting, and a poor evaluation could result in a raise refusal or a termination (especially at the end of the probationary period).

Finally, the company encouraged an informal work culture that utilized the team as its basis, rather than a network or group that could run counter to management structures. Breaks were timed so that teammates went to the snack room together or ate lunch as a unit. Workers from both shifts met weekly with the facilitator at the time of the shift change, and teams were the groups around which potlucks and showers were organized. Building production around small groups rather than large departments meant that management rather than workers created and shaped the form of the "informal work group" long ago discovered by the human relations school of management psychology (Mayo 1933; Roethlisberger, Dickson, and Wright 1939).

Although the structure of the teams, the role of the facilitator, and the involvement of workers seemed to dovetail with a participatory philosophy, there was a clear contradiction between management ideology and practice. For example, a good deal of time was spent at team meetings discussing the production quotas of individual team members and the team as a whole. In a more hierarchical plant, the supervisor or trainer would be responsible for exhorting the worker to do better; at HealthTech, discussion of "numbers" in the team meetings involved the use of public embarrassment and negative comments by co-workers as methods of motivating a worker to perform better.

We argue that behind the public stance of a participatory company lay a hierarchical structure in which management actually retained control of the production process and of hiring and firing. The contradiction between management ideology and practice was undoubtedly present also at Computex and Howard, but at HealthTech it was sharpened: the team structure and management ideology made greater claims for their participatory nature, and the struggle over unionization forced management to take more autocratic action than might have been necessary under ordinary circumstances.

The Labor Process, Wages, and Individual Tactics

Our data on HealthTech derive from interviews with the plant manager and ten working mothers (three Anglos and seven Hispanas, including four single parents). These were supplemented by the interviews with union activists, fieldnotes, and tape-recordings of team sessions collected by Guillermo Grenier, who was conducting a study of participatory management and teams during the union drive (see Grenier 1988).

We particularly focus on the experiences of three women: Lucille Sanchez, an anti-union activist, and Bonnie Anderson and Annette Griego, pro-union activists. Lucille, a Hispana and the mother of three, was a coprovider. Bonnie, an Anglo and also the mother of three, was a mainstay provider. Lucille's husband, as a truck driver for a local beverage company, earned slightly more than her hourly wage. Bonnie's husband was laid off for eight months in 1982 from his job as a cement truck driver because of the recession in the construction industry. Annette, a young widow and single parent, was a sole provider for herself and her son, although she shared household expenses with her sister and boyfriend. Her father was German, but Annette considered herself Spanish, drawing on her mother's heritage and traditions. We use these three cases to show how a woman's place in the production process, her relationship with facilitators, and her family situation influenced her participation. In addition we draw attention to the process of the union drive and the dialectical relationship that evolved as workers responded to management tactics and vice versa.[7]

Since HealthTech was a brand-new facility in 1981, the firm had its pick of workers in an economy where women's jobs usually did not pay as much as HealthTech's $4.50 to $5.00 an hour for an entry-level job. Lucille and Bonnie were among the first 900 who applied, and they were two of the forty who were screened and tested at "selection Saturday," a special one-day session to help identify those who could work with the "team concept." Lucille was assigned to team A in drill swaging in January; Bonnie began to work on team A in channel swaging in March; Annette was hired in September 1981 and joined Team B in channel swaging.

Drill and channel swaging were two different methods of attaching a surgical needle to a gut or silk cord. Since the channel technique involved a step in which the needle was curved, it took eighteen months to master; the drill technique (drill needles had been curved in a previous process) took twelve. Learning curves were used to train women both in swaging and in winding the surgical thread in a figure-eight pattern preparatory to placing the unit in a foil envelope. Unlike Leslie Pants workers, HealthTech women had to "demonstrate"—maintain the 100 percent efficiency level for a period of thirteen weeks at the end of their training period—before receiving a bonus raise. Then they were supposed to enter a year's "payback" period, working at 100 percent efficiency in either drill or channel swaging before they were allowed to learn another job. Only a few workers in drill swaging had completed their demonstration period at the time of our interviews, and virtually no workers had attempted demonstration in channel swaging.

Like sewing, channel swaging takes good hand-eye coordination and an ability to work quickly without making mistakes. Annette described her job:

First this [left] hand is what we are holding the sutures in . . . and you roll them . . . what you do is get one suture and put it out and the

---

[7] See Lamphere and Grenier (1988) for a more detailed explanation of why the union drive failed.

others are still sticking in like this [in my hand], and then with this hand—the right hand—you grab your needle and you put it together on your first groove. . . . You press your pedal . . . and once you get used to it you can do all three steps at once. When you press your pedal with the needle over the suture it closes the needle. And then you bring it to the second groove, and you round it off, and the third groove curves it . . . there's two grooves and one curver. . . . You push the pedal and it will go for the three steps, and then you let up on it and it will stop. And then you get ready for the next one and then you press it again for the three steps.

Bonnie remarked how difficult it was to learn the technique under the pressure of meeting the learning curve:

> I was really scared at first. Because it's very tedious, you know. Right down into the machine. It really took me a month or so to get into it. I really thought I was going to lose it, you know. All that producing. You only had so many days to produce that much. And if you don't make it . . . well, "goodbye." So I was really kind of panicked, but I picked up on it. . . . There was so much to learn that it was really quite scary.

Bonnie soon learned, like Leslie Pants workers, to pace herself. "Every half hour I'd try to do 25 dozen . . . I tried." She also learned what problems to look out for. "Because the needles, they weren't perfect. So you had to hold your needles differently sometimes. And you had to be real careful not to get fins on them . . . [fins are] when it flairs out at the sides. . . . And there are slivers. And if the needle wasn't cut right, then you have to try and work with those needles, and sometimes that slows you down quite a bit."

Annette reported that she had to learn to keep her hands steady. "Because I was taught with the smallest needle there is in channel. And I had problems with keeping my hands steady, because you just like . . . shake trying to aim for those little grooves." Like women at Leslie Pants, workers at HealthTech responded to the learning curve by developing individual tactics for working quickly under pressure.

In swaging as in sewing pants, machine difficulties emerged as a big barrier to keeping up with the learning curve. Women in channel swaging had more difficulty than those in drill. One of the major problems was getting the right dies so that the needle would fit in each groove as it was being shaped and threaded. As Annette explained, "Well, in channel swaging, you get a stubborn product and the dies and the needles don't want to go together and you get defects until you get one that will run with your needle. . . . I've had some batches where I made a lot of needle changes . . . same product . . . just different needles." At the time of our interviews Annette had been having machine problems, and her numbers were low. In addition, "when gut first came in to channel swaging, I was the first one to work with it. I had to learn. The facilitator had me trying different dies to find out which dies the needles worked best with and stuff like that. So my numbers dropped then too."

It was Annette's view that as long as they were working under a learning curve, they should have been paid on a piece rate or bonus system. She also thought the numbers were too high: "You can start and you can work your hardest, and you can do twice as much as the person next to you, and you can be getting the same pay. . . . And they are always comparing us to the other plant. . . . But their swagers have been there an average of fifteen to twenty years, and we've only been swaging a year or a year and a half."

Lucille's difficulties did not come until she needed to maintain 100 percent efficiency during her demonstration period. She had learned both the drill swaging technique and how to wind the sutures quickly and was asked to train new employees in the drill department in March 1981. Her own training continued until December, and then she began her thirteen-week demonstration in winding:

> Well, in the winding department it took several weeks, and I was performing like at 97 or 98 percent. I couldn't get over that 98 or 99 hump. My last week in demonstration is when I went on a daily basis to 117, 124, and that averaged out to make up for the other weeks. . . . So, I took a big step without realizing what position I was putting myself into. And then not only that, I was the first person to demonstrate . . . that made the pressure more severe. You know, there was lots of people behind you and lots of people against you. It was really hard.

Lucille felt that other team members were not supportive and that she was not given credit and praise for finishing her demonstration (and getting a raise). This did not dampen her overall enthusiasm for her job, however, she gave her work top ratings on all aspects from pay to supervisor and job security.

Women responded differently to the labor process and pay system in channel and drill. Many, especially in the more demanding channel department, developed tactics to deal with the pressures of producing but also came to feel that the numbers were too high, that it would be difficult to go through demonstration, and even that a piece-rate system would be fairer. Women in drill, like Lucille, had less difficulty learning the technique, but most felt pressure to work harder to attain 100 percent efficiency.

Approximately 25 percent of the assemblers employed at Health-Tech worked in two other departments: "foil and overwrap" (where the finished needles were packaged) and "devices" (where items made in other plants were packaged). In both departments women worked on a line and were paid by the hour. They did have to achieve production quotas or 100 percent efficiency, but since most of the jobs entailed loading machines or watching the progress of foil wrapping, the quotas did not seem difficult to achieve. And there was job rotation on each line. For example, in the overwrap section, two women worked together: one would feed the machine while the other inspected the wrapped needles and boxed them; then they would switch positions. As Grace Estrada, a single mother (see Chapter 3), described the process: "There's two people on the overwrap machine. . . . one person feeds the foil packages into the machine, and the other person gets them with the serlane on them and boxes them, so you work with a partner all the time. And when you're working with the foil end, you know, feeding it . . . you have to keep moving kind of fast."

Work in devices was similar. Workers rotated between loading a machine and sealing the staples, ligaclips, and cartridges that were being boxed in plastic. Karen Lucas, the only worker we interviewed in that department, had been working at HealthTech only for six months but was hoping to begin her demonstration period soon.

Clearly, those working in the channel and drill departments faced a different kind of work process than those in foil and overwrap and in devices. Not only was there a difference between working on the line versus individual batch processing on a learning curve, but 100 percent efficiency was much more difficult to achieve in the more highly skilled swaging and winding jobs. Management's push to extract more labor from women workers was particularly apparent in channel swaging. And without a piece rate or bonus system to produce consent, it is not surprising that workers on these teams were the first to become interested in unionization. Even so, this collective resistance might not have taken shape if the contradictions between the high-involvement philosophy and management practices within the teams had not become clear.

The Team Structure in Practice

Reactions to the team structure and HealthTech's high-involvement philosophy varied among the workers we interviewed. Experiences with particular facilitators were important in either leading women to feel that worker-management relations were more egalitarian or helping them see through management ideology to the underlying control structure.

Lucille was particularly positive about her team. She enjoyed the team meetings "because you get to communicate real good with the people on your own team, plus with your facilitator, and you get input with everything that goes on. There is really nothing that you can't talk about in your team meeting." Lucille also felt that she had real power in decisions about prospective workers:

> Yes, anybody that we recommend gets hired. We are the final say-so.
> . . . See, we grasp a lot more about that person, because people think
> that the only ones you have to impress are the big people, so they kind
> of let it all hang out when you are interviewing them. They figure that
> all of these are just workers, you know, I don't really have to impress
> them. But they don't realize that we have the final say-so. And there
> have been occasions where the facilitator and the personnel person
> have really liked a person and we haven't, and then they don't hire
> them.

Bonnie, however, reported a very different set of experiences. She had initially acted favorably to team philosophy: "I thought it was kind of nice. It might be kind of fun. It was all new to me: to have somebody . . . if you had a problem in your team you should have somebody to help you out." But Bonnie became disillusioned as the practice of the facilitator for channel teams A and B revealed that he still filled the role of a "supervisor" in pushing workers to produce. Bonnie found it embarrassing to have to justify low production numbers or explain troubles with the machines during a public meeting of team A:

> He was always on us about numbers. It was always his job if our numbers didn't come up, and why did we do so poorly that week. And we'd

[172]

have to go around the table. And I really hated that. If your numbers were 80 percent for the week and the week before, and that week you did only 67 percent, you know, "Why did you do 67 percent? You are supposed to be at 80." At the time, our machines seemed to be breaking down constantly. Down time [would count against us]. . . . But we had to go around [the table]. . . . I hated that. It was so embarrassing. It really was.

Bonnie liked her job on the whole, but she often felt that there were some unfair aspects of the production system, such as having "lost time" due to difficulties with the machine count against her in meeting her production quotas. For her, these problems were only exacerbated by the atmosphere of the team meetings and the pressure to produce.

Participating in a firing, as she did when one male team member was unable to meet his production quotas, was also a difficult process for Bonnie:

Well, it's terrible. That person is sitting right there . . . it was for his numbers. He really was a good worker and a good person . . . to get along with and everything, but his numbers weren't there. He'd had some trouble with his machine, and I guess it had just gotten down to the wire, and they had to fire him. I guess we all agreed that if this was what we are supposed to do, we've got to do it. If you don't make your numbers, you've got to go. . . . It was awful.

For Bonnie, taking over that part of the supervisor's role transformed her own relationship with co-workers into a hierarchical one, a change with which she was very uncomfortable.

Bonnie's ambivalence about the team meetings was echoed by Annette, who was on team B but had the same facilitator:

It would be just like one big "tattle-tale session." That's the way our other facilitator . . . the one before José, he had the meetings being conducted like that. It got to where everybody was fighting with each other and everything. And now José has come in, we've gotten closer, and we look out for each other. Okay, we are supposed to be doing . . . like what they are saying, you know, disciplining each other and stuff like that. But José is getting upset, because he doesn't really know what's going on.

[173]

Annette's complaints, like Bonnie's, were based both on her perception of how difficulties with production were unfairly treated and on her sense that the team concept was not real "participation." Workers on the teams whose production quotas were the most difficult were beginning to see the contradictions between management's ideology and the underlying control system actually in operation.

Group Resistance and Management Response

By late June 1982, six workers from channel teams A and B were willing to form an organizing committee with the goal of unionization. By July 27, a group of fifteen workers had signed a letter to the plant manager stating that they favored a union and asking for a debate to take place on the issue. These workers included Bonnie and three of her female teammates from channel team A, three workers from channel team B, four from devices, one from the "vault" department, and three from the drill department, (including two of Lucille's teammates). Since most were from the earliest group of employees hired and almost half from channel swaging (which had the most difficult jobs with the most demanding production numbers and the most production problems), these workers had begun to develop a critique of how production was administered in the plant. In addition, some had begun to "see through" company ideology and the team structure. Possibly because of the way channel facilitators administered their teams, workers felt that their participation was really only on the surface and under the control of management.

Through the next few months, support for the union grew. A union organizer from the national office began to contact workers emphasizing the higher wages at other unionized company plants, even where there was little difference in the cost of living. The organizing committee began to pass out leaflets, and by October 25 the committee's membership had expanded to include twenty-one workers.

Management's response to union activity in the first months of the campaign (July–December 1982) occurred at several levels. At the level of ideology, management argued that a union would intefere with the effort to get everyone to participate and the company would "lose flexibility" in implementing the high-involvement design. One company document stated: "We give everyone a chance to represent themselves without a 'third party' such as a union." Behind this ideology, however, lay some very important financial considerations. In the decision to come to Albuquerque, the absence of a "strong union environment" had been a factor. Even though other branch plants were unionized, the company would not have located the new plant in an area with a pro-union environment. HealthTech calculated that if it could keep the union out for the first three years, the company would save $5 million in wages, benefits, manpower, and administration. And once it reached its projected employee limit of 500, it would save more than $10 million every three years.

At the level of the team structure and the relationship between facilitators and workers, the company took a "proactive" approach. As the plant psychologist told Guillermo Grenier, "The facilitator sort of orchestrates and initiates the discussion of the union at the QC [team] meetings, and in that way gets across certain ideas about the union to the employees" (Grenier 1988:60). Thus the team meeting became the arena in which the facilitator could mold anti-union opinion, often calling on those who had already taken an anti-union stance to pressure their peers. The use of the team as part of management's anti-union strategy can best be illustrated by what happened in drill teams A, B, and C, where one facilitator, Dennis, used his team meetings to persuade workers to the company point of view.

In team A, Dennis could count on Lucille; she helped organize an anti-union committee which, with the help of the plant manager's and psychologist's secretaries, printed, copied, and distributed anti-union literature. Lucille also worked to "change the minds" of the few union supporters on her team.

In team B, Dennis faced more union sympathizers, including Valerie Mondragon and Delores Maes, two of the Hispanas we interviewed. During one meeting Dennis provoked an anti-union discussion of the Coors strike in Colorado, using comments from a female personnel administrator he had invited to the meeting to voice pro-company sentiments.

In team C, Dennis used the tactic of isolating a union supporter, Rosa, and using peer pressure from other team members against her. It was part of the company's "individual-conflict approach" to isolate pro-union workers at both the team and the individual level (Grenier 1988:60). Rosa was one of two pro-union employees on the Compensation Committee, which dealt with the wage and evaluation system. During a team meeting and later at a mass meeting of the entire drill department, Dennis allowed and even encouraged Rosa's best friend

[175]

Tracy to demand her resignation on the grounds that she was "untrustworthy" and unable to represent her co-workers' opinions. Asked to stand up and be identified, Rosa felt she was "being harassed for my political opinion" and eventually did resign.

Using both the "proactive" and "individual-conflict" approaches, Dennis was able to limit union support in his three teams to two members of team A (Lucille's team), only three or four workers in team B (including Valerie and Delores), and five in team C (including Rosa).

José, the facilitator of channel teams A and B, met with more resistance. Annette described the situation at Team B meetings:

> Well, the thing is he'd ask us our opinion in the team meeting and if we gave it to him, we'd be considered bitchy. If we didn't give it to him . . . we weren't [participating]. So he got really mad one week and he said, "No more team meetings." Because we just weren't getting anything out of them any more. So like every time we did open our mouths to say anything, he'd get . . . he'd just run around in circles with us, and he'd contradict himself. Time after time. And it got to the point where nobody would say anything anymore. But what he wanted was for everyone to rat on each other . . . which we were not.

After José quit holding weekly meetings, Annette said the team had "gotten closer and we look out for each other . . . you know, disciplining each other and stuff like that." Workers on team B were able not only to unite as a team and confront the contradictions they saw between management ideology and practice but also to organize the team internally as a support system on their own terms. Channel teams A and B had been the center of union sentiment from the beginning, and José had come from a union plant, so perhaps he was less committed than others to fighting the union in team meetings.

A measure of the union's support in early December 1982 was the fact that ninety-three workers (both women and men) signed a petition asking the company to investigate a bad smell pervading the plant; workers thought it might be ETO, a dangerous chemical used to sterilize the sutures. Not all the women who eventually voted for the union signed the petition; however, thirty-seven Hispanas and seven Anglo or black women who did sign later did *not* vote for the union. A company statement, read at all team meetings, argued that ETO was not a compound with a smell, and the issue eventually faded into the background. The petition represented a high point of

[176]

pro-union support, however. Only about 50 percent of the employees had signed union cards calling for an election, and in the following months the company began to be more successful in eroding union sentiment.

Most facilitators remained in control of their teams. They continued to use the rhetoric surrounding the high-involvement philosophy in fighting the union and to isolate union supporters as workers with "bad attitudes," who did not believe in the team concept and thus were not trustworthy. Being pro-union was defined by facilitators as being anti-company, and union supporters were labeled "losers." These tactics of labeling and isolation went hand in hand with the company's major illegal strategy: firing pro-union workers.

Firings can have a devastating impact on union campaigns, particularly if a company has already laid the basis for support for its anti-union position in the interpersonal relationships between workers and management. The team system at HealthTech and its use by management to support anti-union workers and isolate the union supporters created the context. The firings also revealed that behind all the rhetoric of participation lay a hierarchical system: management had the right to fire employees without consultation. This revelation supported the suspicions of pro-union activists that Health-Tech management did not really believe in participation. For those who had not yet made up their minds, it demonstrated management power and the vulnerability of individual workers. Siding with those who fit in with the team concept and drew management support must have seemed like the less risky alternative.

Sometime in November the management had met with corporate lawyers who recommended using firing as an anti-union strategy. The first two firings during that month were "trial balloons" to see what the union would do when their supporters were fired allegedly for objective reasons. Although the union filed NLRB charges, the company believed that worker sentiment had not been mobilized and assumed that further firings could be planned. On December 16, Maria telephoned her friend Linda to log her in on the computer (a practice other workers told us was common), saying she would be five minutes late; however, she arrived an hour late, and by the end of the day her facilitator had fired both Maria and Linda for "falsifying company records." Both women were union supporters and members of the organizing committee.

[177]

Worker Resistance

Pro-union women workers and their male peers did not knuckle under to the company's anti-union strategies. Beginning in October, the struggle between pro-union forces and management became more open and confrontational in team meetings and outside the plant. Charges of unfair labor practice were filed with the NLRB on October 27, alleging that workers were being interrogated and threatened with a loss of benefits or jobs if a union was formed. Additional charges were filed after the November 6 and December 16 firings.

The dismissals had created a climate of fear. Supporting the union could mean being threatened with a suspension if one's numbers were down (as in Annette's case), or being fired through the strict application of company policy (more leniently applied to nonunion supporters) as in the case of Maria and Linda. The union was thus faced with the problem of persuading more workers to join, despite the threatening atmosphere and the company's careful screening of new employees to make sure they would be anti-union when they entered the plant.

Then a mechanic who had previously not been associated with the union drive was fired for talking back to his supervisor. His dismissal enlisted a great deal of sympathy from workers, and the union's filing of an unfair labor practice charge on the mechanic's behalf gained his support and that of several other workers in early March. Clearly, the union was continuing to take an aggressive legal stand in trying to protect workers.

The union also planned a trip for five production workers (two anti-union, two undecided, and one afraid of taking a side) to the company's unionized plant in the eastern United States. Although they were not able to see the inside of the plant, they met with a hundred union employees and made a videotape of the meeting, which was later shown to the Albuquerque workers at a union-sponsored meeting. All five workers who made the trip were convinced to take the union's side.

In the meantime, the company continued to isolate union support. The plant psychologist went on breaks with pro-union people, interrupting their conversations and blocking their ability to recruit new members. In this way, he said, he continued to increase the pressure on union activists by "withdrawing status from them using a strong psychological approach." The company was trying to separate the anti-union "winners" from the pro-union "losers."

Women workers reacted in different ways to this strategy of isolating the union supporters. Some resented it and became stronger union supporters. Others took the management rejection more personally. Lorraine, the single parent in devices, felt particularly ostracized once it was known that she had become pro-union: "They ignored me. Before the campaign started, they were always inviting me to go here and there. Then afterwards . . . not even a 'Hi.' . . . They'd come onto the production floor, and they'd stand like two or three and make faces and stand like they were talking about me. And that would bother me. Because they had never done it before."

The union gained some supporters because of the contradictions women faced in integrating their family and work roles around the rotating shift system. The union promised to change the shift policy if it was voted in; this was the strongest incentive for women such as Valerie and Delores on drill team B to remain pro-union, despite the pressures from management. As Valerie said: "When we do have to go nights, it's a real big problem, one of the biggest problems I have there. . . . No babysitter's going to want . . . okay, these two weeks you can take her and then for two hours the next two weeks. I've got to find somebody that can take her at nights. And that's hard on my husband, it's hard on my little girl." Delores was equally adamant that the rotating shift system interfered with her time with her family and kept her away from her five-year-old daughter. The crucial aspect for both in supporting the union was the issue of shift rotation and its impact on them as mothers. The union was able to capitalize on their frustrations and keep their allegiance, despite the climate of fear induced by the firings and other unfair labor practices.

Perhaps typical of the kinds of women workers the union did not win over were Regina Armenta, Grace Estrada, Karen Leyba, and Jenny Phillips, the four of our interviewees—in addition to Lucille— who did not vote for the union. Regina and Grace were single parents; Karen and Jenny were married. Economically, their situations were similar to those of the union supporters we interviewed; for example, Jenny's husband's bouts with unemployment were not dissimilar to those of Bonnie's and Valerie's spouses. But all the non-union women, in contrast to the union supporters, had been at HealthTech a shorter time (with the exception of Lorraine, who had been a union member elsewhere), and all were in departments

[179]

where there was a low level of union support (foil and overwrap, drill team D, and devices). Any complaints these women had about their jobs were outweighed by financial need and job security. These were the kinds of women that the union needed to win over in order to win the election, but it was difficult to do so in the atmosphere created by the company.

As the election approached, HealthTech engaged in a more open public expression of anti-union sentiment. Some of these activities had all the earmarks of the "tough legal campaign" (Freeman and Medhoff 1984). In April the company initiated a Union Strike Contest, asking employees to guess how many strikes the union had engaged in between 1975 and 1983. Memos from the plant manager were frequently circulated to employees, and plantwide meetings were held. At one meeting in May a film on union violence was shown. The motto of the campaign became "Be a Winner! Vote No." Lorraine felt strongly about the way the company handled this part of the campaign and the image of the union it presented:

> I wouldn't have portrayed the image that these people would. This is a free country. Everybody could do what they want. Sure there's rules . . . but they don't have to go around treating us like that. . . . You couldn't say certain things. You couldn't bring in certain papers. I would have let people bring in their papers: you know, equal—both sides. But it wasn't equal. Only one side. And that wasn't right, that wasn't a fair way. Only certain people could walk around and say what they want. . . . You'd get punished if you'd bring in one of these leaflets into the department.

The union's one important strategy during this period was to hold a public meeting on April 12, organized by a group of lawyers and community leaders concerned over the course of the union campaign. At the meeting of this Citizens' Monitoring Committee, Guillermo Grenier, the sociologist conducting his dissertation research on HealthTech teams, read a statement arguing that the teams were being used as part of the company's union-busting strategy. Shortly thereafter, the plant psychologist and the personnel director were dismissed, and Grenier's statement was used by the union in pressing its NLRB charges.

Despite the public exposure of the company's strategies, on May 18, 1982, the union lost the election 71 votes to 141 (with several additional votes contested). An analysis of voting patterns indicates that though men were evenly divided on the union issue (23 against and 22 for), women voted against the union 71.3 percent to 28.7 percent (124 against and 50 for). Moreover, only 23.5 percent of the Mexican-American women and 28.3 percent of the Mexican-American mothers voted for the union, whereas 40 percent of the non-Mexican-American women (22 of fifty-five Anglos, blacks, and Asians) and 65 percent of the non-Mexican-American mothers (13 of 20) voted for the union. There was a much larger proportion of Mexican-American women (68.4 percent, or 114 of 174) in the female labor force at HealthTech, and many of these, though favorable when the ETO petition was signed, dropped from the potentially pro-union ranks during the last five months of the campaign.

Nevertheless, as we have argued elsewhere (Lamphere and Grenier 1988:248–52, 255), the defeat of the union cannot be blamed on the passivity of women workers or traditional Hispano values: that is, on the importance of "difference" in the workplace. The economic vulnerability of Hispanas, particularly mothers, was an important ingredient but must be placed in the context of the campaign as a dialectical process. Both the team structure and management's ideology of participation were important in shaping this process and the initial interaction between facilitators and workers. It was the labor process, the wage system, and management's implementation of them, however, that resulted in both group resistance on the job and the ability of women workers to see through the contradiction between high-involvement ideology and actual practice.

Bonnie, Annette, Valerie, and Delores were located in the teams that were formed early in the plant's history. Bonnie and Annette experienced the contradictions between management ideology and practice; Valerie and Delores were particularly concerned about the contradictions between work and family roles intensified by the rotating shift situation. That Regina, Grace, Karen, and Jenny did not come to share their view of these contradictions was due to a number of factors: the place of different women in the labor process, the careful screening of new employees, the intensity of management's tactics in creating a climate of fear as the campaign progressed, and management's ability to isolate pro-union activists at the individual and team level. For many, this was the best job they had ever had, and it was too important to risk. The union's defeat was a measure of both the company's power and the value women placed on retaining their jobs, even in an atmosphere of considerable conflict and threat.

Women workers in participative plants and hierarchical plants faced very different systems of control. Each of the plants discussed here had taken steps to rearrange some aspects of the labor process, the wage system, management-worker relations, and work culture to make work appear less hierarchical or at least more in concert with a participative ideology. At Howard and Computex, with modified assembly lines, job rotation, and lax quotas, women forged fewer tactics and strategies for coping, since the labor process and wage systems did not push them in that direction, though some resistance did occur at an individual level (when a worker complained to her supervisor about the quota system, for example).

SystemsPlus and HealthTech had gone much further in rearranging the labor process and worker-management relations, using job rotation, teams, and facilitators. At HealthTech where the new structure promised to deliver more and and where a labor process much like the learning curves at Leslie Pants was instituted, women workers came to see the contradictions between management's ideology of participation and the real power relations still in place. Group resistance took the form of a union drive. The union was defeated, but the drive laid bare management's continuing hierarchical nature under the trappings of team structure and participative ideology.

Although many of the women we interviewed at participative plants were more satisfied with their jobs than those at hierarchical plants, the HealthTech drive suggests that we need to be skeptical concerning the claims that participative plants really changed the nature of women's work in sunbelt industries.

[6]

Strategies for the Household Division of Labor

This chapter looks at how working mothers, married and single, divided up household maintenance and perceived their domestic arrangements. We want to document whether married women's participation in the labor force influences husbands to do more work in the household, and whether women are rethinking their notions of who should bear responsibility for the home. We are concerned not with the amount of time spent on household tasks but with the responsibility for tasks. It has been well established that women perform most of the housework and child care (Berk 1985; Hartmann 1981), and that this pattern has held for at least fifty years. Even though the nature of housework and the standards of cleanliness have changed with technological and social changes (Ehrenreich and English 1975; Vanek 1974), the responsibility for household maintenance has remained with women.

For dual-worker households, the contradiction between work and family means replacing women's labor at home, and it sets up a cultural contradiction as well. Within a patriarchal ideology in which men are supposed to be breadwinners, working fathers pose no cultural problem, since to be a father means to provide economic support for the family and, when he is at home, to discipline, play with, and supervise the children (Haas 1982; Hood 1983; LaRossa and LaRossa 1981). Working mothers, on the other hand, embody a cultural problematic because when they take on a provider role they are still expected to bear primary responsibility for nurturing, child care, housework, and organizing the household. Women (and men) may

[183]

contest this ideological framework and organize household work by other means. Therefore it is important to distinguish between taking responsibility for a chore—the thinking, planning, organizing, administering, and supervising—and actually doing the work (Oakley 1974), so that we can see whether women seek "help" from husbands (implying that the "second shift" is really women's responsibility) or whether husbands take full responsibility for household chores themselves. Women's process of negotiation with their partners indicates some attempt to reconcile this cultural contradiction.

Research on the household division of labor has shown that working-class men usually do less household work than those from the middle class (Berk 1985; Berk and Berk 1979; Bott 1957; Coltrane 1990; Pleck 1985). Our own previous research found that in working-class immigrant and Mexican-American families with seasonally working wives, the men did not do much housework (Lamphere 1987; Zavella 1987). Investigators of middle-class dual-career families have found that wives' access to resources—especially salaries or job benefits—increase women's domestic power, and that working wives have more influence in decision-making and the division of household chores than housewives, particularly if they have a strong commitment to remaining in the labor force (Bahr 1974; Rapoport and Rapoport 1971, 1978). Even though working wives get more help, however, "wives typically carry most of the burden even when employed full-time" (Berk and Berk 1979:116). The greater a wife's contribution to family income, the more likely that a husband will do more housework (Huber and Spitze 1981; Model 1982), and husbands tend to do more household work if they are home while their wives are working (Berk and Berk 1979).

In *The Second Shift*, Arlie Hochschild argued that there was a "stalled revolution" between the changes experienced by American women as they combine full-time employment with marriage and motherhood and the absence of change "in much else" (1989:12). For most of the couples she studied, this meant that wives devoted more time to housework than their husbands and proportionately less time to child care, while the husbands "do more of what they'd rather do." The result was tension between husbands and wives and emotionally drained women who coped by performing the "second shift" and abandoning hope that the situation would change. Hochschild found that finances are not the determining factor. Rather, her analysis links individual strategies to gender identity and gender ideology, noting how women and men are socialized to expect different things in marriage, and how women, forming the "peasantry of the labor force," bear the brunt of forging strategies.

Hochschild's analysis is helpful in understanding the national aggregate statistics—which indicate little change in the household division of labor—yet may have limited application for some sectors of the American working class—especially for people of color. Although she did interview some working-class and minority couples, middle-class couples (the sector usually observed in family studies) are the focus of her analysis. The husband in one of her three working-class families was an example of "the new man" who shares the household labor; the other two working-class families had a traditional division of labor. It is unclear how representative these couples are of the working class; further, Hochschild's use of strategies is slightly different from ours. She focuses on gender ideals, including what a woman or man does, thinks, or feels, but gender strategies may sometimes reflect unconscious motivations or emotions that get expressed through behavior.

We define strategies more straightforwardly as those behaviors and practices that people construct in response to circumstances. We include informants' reflections and statements on their strategies but do not attempt to analyze their emotional or psychological meanings. Particularly with respect to gender ideology, we found that informants gave contradictory responses, and it was sometimes impossible to discover how strongly an individual was committed to traditional gender roles. We consider how individuals stategize over cross-cutting constraints and opportunities that may "stall" couples' household arrangements in traditional forms or enable them to share the household chores more equitably. We argue that in working-class couples, the household division of labor differs from the patterns found for the middle class. In contrast to the stereotypes of working-class men and women who mindlessly adhere to patriarchal roles, we found that household maintenance takes place in a context in which gender ideology is mitigated by other important factors: women's economic contribution, day-care arrangements, and the couples' work shifts—all of which can change with little notice. Working-class couples, then, must adapt to exigencies in their lives, sometimes regardless of their values and beliefs about who *should* be taking responsibility for certain chores.

Our data include information on twenty-two housework and six-

[185]

teen child-care chores, and we got a description of a typical work day from each informant.[1] We found that asking both husbands and wives about housework provided important insights. Sometimes spouses would disagree on who usually performed a task: women often over-estimated what their husbands did; men were often more forthright in admitting their lack of participation or more frank in discussing marital conflict over the household division of labor. The data from the typical day were particularly illuminating regarding what taking responsibility for a chore meant in different households.

Our data also confirmed that there is a cultural distinction between "inside" and "outside" work in the American household: women are thought to have responsibility for tasks performed inside the home (with the exception of household repairs), while chores performed outside the home (except hanging laundry and perhaps gardening) are generally regarded as men's work (Yanagisako 1977). Using these symbolic inside-outside distinctions, we found that five of the twenty-two household chores on our interview schedule can be considered "men's chores" (putting out the garbage, taking care of the car, plumbing and electrical repairs, general repairs, and yard work); eleven can be considered "women's chores" (preparing breakfast, lunch, or dinner, setting the table, washing dishes, making beds, vacuuming, washing floors, cleaning the bathroom, washing clothes, and ironing); and six chores can be considered gender-neutral (shopping for groceries, purchasing adult's or children's clothes, taking charge of money, paying monthly bills,[2] and making large purchases).

Parenting chores are also gendered within a traditional ideology, with many of the tasks of parenting—except serious disciplining and supervising homework—considered to be the mother's responsibility (Haas 1982). According to this schema, most items on our list of sixteen child care chores would be "women's chores": awakening the

---

[1] Much of the previous research on the household division of labor used diaries of time spent on chores, or surveys (sometimes relying on wives to report what their husbands did), and focused on the performance of only a few household chores, or did not examine dual-worker families (Berk and Berk 1979; Hartmann 1981). Robinson (1977; Robinson et al. 1988) argues that the actual time spent on household chores has declined since 1965, but people's perceptions that they are strapped for time have increased. To ascertain informants' ideology, we asked them to agree or disagree with a series of statements about gender roles.

[2] Many couples did not have checking accounts, so paying monthly bills involved actually driving to various offices and paying cash.

child, dressing, feeding, diapering, bathing, putting to bed, caring for children's clothing (washing, putting away, mending), giving spending money, taking child to school or activities, supervising chores, daily discipline, taking children to doctor or dentist appointments, and staying home with a sick child.

Our informants often implicitly subscribed to these symbolic systems, yet in their actual practice the distinctions were becoming less rigid, and men were taking on a number of "women's chores." Only about one-third of our informants (fourteen of thirty-seven couples) had explicitly discussed how they would divide up household maintenance; therefore, we argue that their actual practice contained implicit norms. Even those couples who had discussed the division of labor and had preferences regarding who should take responsibility for what work did not always follow those preferences in their practice.

We found a continuum of actual household arrangements, ranging from "traditional" to "semitraditional" to "egalitarian" to "nontraditional." Among couples with traditional arrangements, the distinction between women's and men's domestic responsibility usually held, and wives performed both the women's and the gender-neutral chores; husbands, the men's chores. This meant that wives did most of the housework, and considerably more than their spouses. In semitraditional couples the gendered division of household chores remained and wives did more work than their spouses, but men did some women's chores such as washing dishes or gender-neutral chores such as grocery shopping. In egalitarian couples, men did enough women's chores to make their total household contribution equal to that of their wives. In nontraditional couples, husbands did more housework than their wives.[3]

Using these definitions, we found ten Hispano and two Anglo couples in our sample who had a completely traditional division of housework; five Hispano and six Anglo couples, semitraditional; eight Hispano and four Anglo couples, egalitarian; and one Anglo and one Hispano couple, nontraditional (see Table 18). We found that caring for children often took precedence over housework and was

---

[3] There were a few "women's chores" that men rarely did—cleaning bathrooms was a noticeable one. Virtually all couples decided jointly on large purchases.

[187]

Table 18. The division of housework

Traditional	Semitraditional	Egalitarian	Nontraditional
	Hispano Couples (n = 24)		
42%	21%	33%	4%
Baca	Barela	Benavides	Mondragon
Delgado	Gilbert	Duran	
Garcia	Luna	Griego	
Maes	Tafoya	Olguin	
Peña	Thomas	Rivera	
Perez		Santos	
Ortega		Sena	
Ortiz		Valdez	
Sanchez			
Sandoval			
	Anglo Couples (n = 13)		
15%	46%	31%	8%
Anderson	Bennet	Adams	Pike
Phillips	Chandler	Connelly	
	Hall	Leyba	
	Singleton	Mead	
	Smith		
	Todd		

shared more equitably (see Table 19), confirming the findings of Col-trane (1990), Hochschild (1989), and Staines and Pleck (1983).[4]

Disentangling Household Arrangements

Our analysis began by examining whether the proportion of wom-en's contribution to household income influenced the way chores were divided. Using our categorization of wives as secondary pro-viders, coproviders, mainstay providers, and sole providers, we found that socioeconomic status is correlated with patterns of divid-ing up household chores: in seven Mexican-American couples (out of twenty-four) and one white couple (out of thirteen) the wife was a secondary provider, and these couples had a traditional or semitradi-

---

[4] Only after we had completed the interviews did we realize that our list of house-hold tasks was weighted toward "women's chores." Our definitions of arrangements attempts to compensate for this by noting who took responsibility for a chore.

Table 19. The division of child care compared with housework

Traditional	Semitraditional	Egalitarian	Nontraditional
	Hispano Couples (n = 24)		
21%	38%	33%	8%
Baca TRAD	Barela SEMITRAD	Garcia TRAD	Duran EGAL
Benavides EGAL	Gilbert SEMITRAD	Luna SEMITRAD	Griego EGAL
Delgado TRAD	Olguin EGAL	Mondragon NONTRAD	
Maes TRAD	Ortega TRAD	Ortiz TRAD	
Perez TRAD	Pena TRAD	Sena EGAL	
	Rivera EGAL	Tafoya SEMITRAD	
	Sanchez TRAD	Thomas SEMITRAD	
	Sandoval TRAD	Valdez EGAL	
	Santos EGAL		
	Anglo Couples (n = 13)		
8%	62%	15%	15%
Phillips TRAD	Adams SEMITRAD	Anderson EGAL	Mead EGAL
	Bennett SEMITRAD	Leyba EGAL	Smith SEMITRAD
	Chandler SEMITRAD		
	Connelly EGAL		
	Hall SEMITRAD		
	Pike NONTRAD		
	Singleton SEMITRAD		
	Todd SEMITRAD		

Note: Column heads refer to child care; housework status is indicated with each name.

tional division of housework.[5] In families where the woman was the economic mainstay—seven Hispano and four Anglo—there were a significant number of egalitarian or even nontraditional arrangements, mainly among Hispanos. Coproviding couples in our sample—ten Hispano and eight Anglo—had more varied arrangements, ranging from traditional to egalitarian (see Table 20).

Single mothers in our sample had varied patterns. Those who were in precarious economic circumstances tended to reside with kin (especially female kin) and share household chores with them. The more economically stable, often older single mothers tended to reside alone or with roommates and, to the extent that they did so at all, divided up household chores with their roommates or older chil-

[5] Because Anita Alvarez's interview was incomplete, we do not have information from her about housework, child care, or day care. Thus, only twenty-four married Hispanas are considered in our analysis in Chapter 6, 7, and 8.

Table 20. Wives' provider status and the division of housework

Secondary Provider	Coprovider	Mainstay Provider
	Hispano Couples (n = 24)	
29%	42%	29%
Delgado TRAD	Baca TRAD	Duran EGAL
Garcia TRAD	Barela SEMITRAD	Griego EGAL
Gilbert SEMITRAD	Benavides EGAL	Mondragon NONTRAD
Luna SEMITRAD	Maes TRAD	Ortiz TRAD
Sandoval TRAD	Olguin EGAL	Peña TRAD
Tafoya SEMITRAD	Ortega TRAD	Santos EGAL
Thomas SEMITRAD	Perez TRAD	Valdez EGAL
	Rivera EGAL	
	Sanchez TRAD	
	Sena EGAL	
	Anglo Couples (n = 13)	
8%	61%	31%
Chandler SEMITRAD	Adams EGAL	Anderson TRAD
	Bennet SEMITRAD	Hall SEMITRAD
	Connelly EGAL	Mead EGAL
	Leyba EGAL	Phillips TRAD
	Pike NONTRAD	
	Singleton SEMITRAD	
	Smith SEMITRAD	
	Todd SEMITRAD	

dren. Compared with wives, single mothers performed considerably more of the household chores.

Beyond socioeconomic considerations, three other important factors—the husband's and wife's work shifts, who cared for the children during working hours, and family ideology—affected a couple's arrangements regarding household work. These factors were particularly important in coprovider couples.

Work shifts were important because they were related to child-care arrangements and chores that had to be done at a certain time of day, such as preparing dinner or putting the children to bed (Hood and Golden 1979). But the effects of shifts could go either way. If a couple decided to use a "split-shift" day-care arrangement, in which each parent took care of the children while the other worked, men tended to do more child-care tasks and, in some cases, more housework. Yet if husbands worked evening or night shifts and their wives worked on day shifts, women could end up doing most of the housework when they were home in the evenings. Child-care arrangements were closely related to the shifts a couple worked. Often there was a tradeoff between housework and child care: if a husband took care of his children, the wife would overlook his lack of responsibility for doing housework.

Hood (1983) has shown that couples can negotiate a "marketwork/ housework bargain," a tradeoff between wage work and unpaid household work. This bargain assumes that the male provider role is considered the reciprocal of the housewife/mother role, and if women take on responsibility for providing for the family by engaging in wage work, then the allocation of other household responsibilities should change as well. In our sample, norms about the division of labor could range from traditional views—with the couple committed to the notion that the husband should be the economic provider and the wife should be the housewife/mother—to the egalitarian view that responsibility for providing and household work should be shared equally.

Despite having categorized our informants, we emphasize that household arrangements were quite fluid, changing in response to new work schedules, to a spouse's losing a job or getting hired at a better-paying one (so that the wife's provider role changed), to the need to find another day-care arrangement, or to women's (occasionally men's) pressure on their spouses to take on more tasks. Because there were twice as many couples using semitraditional, egalitarian, or nontraditional arrangements (twenty-five) as couples maintaining a purely traditional arrangement (twelve), we argue that the conditions of women's work in sunbelt factories provided opportunities for a slight but significant shift toward men doing more work in the household.

Finally, we found that strategies for household maintenance were similar for Mexican-Americans and whites, with differences stemming from particular circumstances, such as more Hispanas having access to help from relatives for day care (see Chapter 7), or Mexican-American men being subject to higher unemployment rates, or a couple's ability to arrange a split-shift day-care arrangement. Our research suggests that for working-class couples the household division of labor is more complex than we might assume by interpreting aggregate data.

The following representative case material illustrates how different child-care arrangements, shift schedules, or couple's ideology affected the fluidity of household arrangements.[6]

Wives as Secondary Providers

The Sandovals

Geri Sandoval worked in solder repair on the evening shift at Southwest Electronics; her husband worked days as an engineer specialist at Southwest Telephone (see Chapter 3); and their combined income was over $30,000 a year. The Sandovals combined a split-shift day-care arrangement with a part-time day-care provider. Geri, reared in northern New Mexico, called herself "Spanish," while Ray described himself as "native New Mexican." While Geri had some high school, Ray had completed a few years of college. They were buying a large tract home on the west side.

Geri did virtually all the housework. She believed in the inside-outside distinction, and she had high housekeeping standards; as our conversation shows:

> I usually [make dinner] because he makes a mess out of my kitchen. [*Interviewer*: What about making beds?] I don't like the way he makes the beds. [So you're responsible, huh?] [*Shrugs*] [And vacuuming and washing the floor?] To tell you the truth, I don't like the way he cleans house at all [*laughs*]. [So you feel you're responsible for most of the housework?] Yeah. [And he's more responsible for the yard work and taking care of the house?] Yeah.

Ray, a devoted fan of rock music, spent considerable time watching televised rock concerts or playing music, and he characterized their relationship in the terminology of the performers' world: "Geri's my

[6] Most of the couples we interviewed lived in households made up of husband, wife, and children: that is, nuclear families. Only three had other kin living with them; these relatives helped out with household chores but did not contribute to family income. Thus, in most cases the division of household work was between husband and wife. Very few couples received help from an older child or other kin because their children were too young or kin were not available. Of the single mothers who resided with roommates, none indicated that these were lesbian relationships, but of course this would have been very difficult to admit to an interviewer.

[192]

agent." As befitting a "star," Ray did very little housework—though when asked who usually washed the dishes, he sarcastically replied, "That's my job. [But] sometimes I get really lazy and Geri has to end up doing it. [Did you volunteer for this job?] No, I don't know. It's kind of . . . that's about the only thing I know how to do." Geri's version downplayed the dishwashing question: "I guess whoever feels like doing them [*laughs*], whoever gets tired of looking at them first." Ray did take responsibility for the outside chores: "Definitely me. I'll say to Geri, 'Hey, at least talk to me while I'm working outside.' By the time I turn my back, she's already in the house watching TV." And in taking charge of their money and paying monthly bills, "probably 75 percent of it is Geri. Like I tell you, she's my agent." For large purchases, he said, "we just kind of have a mutual discussion on it." The Sandovals had not discussed the division of labor, Ray indicated: "It's just been like routine. Whenever, we kind of had our arrangements." Geri seemed ambivalent about the household division of labor but was unwilling to discuss her feelings in detail.

The Sandovals started their marriage with the expectation that Ray would be the sole provider. Geri gave the reason she decided to find a job: "I guess I was just getting bored staying at home. I like the fact that, the extra money that I could buy things. Of course, my husband was never stingy with his money, but you know, it's just something that I wanted to do for myself." Ray, however, emphasized his role in the decision: "Well, I guess I kind of pushed her into working. I don't think she wanted to work when we first got married. It was like that concept women can't work. Just the male provider. But I knew I wasn't going to get anywhere just on my paycheck. In fact, I was working overtime, just barely surviving . . . day to day, paycheck to paycheck. . . . I mean, just the reality. I didn't have to convince her that much."

In the seven years from the time that Geri started working, Ray's salary had increased considerably, to $10 an hour. By the time of the interview he was earning almost twice his wife's wages of $5.96 an hour. Yet they agreed that "women need to work to help their families keep up with the high cost of living." Geri reported that she had never considered quitting her job. Neither Ray nor Geri was strongly committed to the notion that husbands should be the only economic providers, and they considered Geri's economic contribution very important. Geri disagreed with the statement "It's much better all

[193]

around if a woman can stay home and take care of her family instead of having to work." Her husband indicated an interest in role reversal and spending his time in leisure activities: "I think it would be better if the guy stayed home to take care of the family. I hate going to work, period. I could see myself at the Friar's Pub at 7:45, y'know, just relaxing, having beers all day long. I could be doing that instead of going to work." Regarding the notion that working is important, Geri said: "It wouldn't be hard for me to give up, but I think then I would be robbing myself of the opportunity to expand and grow. . . . You know they say it's not the amount of time that you spend with your kids, it's the quality of the time." She agreed strongly that even if she didn't need the money, she would continue to work. Thus Geri did not demonstrate a strong commitment to returning home and becoming a full-time housewife-mother, and her husband had no strong preference for that either, although he might have appreciated having that option.

The Sandovals believed in coparenting; Ray stated a strong belief that children should be cared for equally by both parents. Yet this "natural" arrangement, as Ray had characterized it, meant that Ray did a significant number of child-care chores. On a typical work morning, Ray would make the baby a bottle, change his diaper and dress him, then put him into bed with Geri. She would rise about 10:00 A.M., feed the child breakfast, clean house, run errands (including grocery shopping), make dinner, and attend to the child, including giving him a bath and taking him to the day-care provider. After work Ray would pick up his son, feed him dinner, attend to his needs (including diaper changes) and put him to bed. Yet Ray was able to spend evenings with his friends listening to his music collection or watching television: "See I live in the west side of town and I've got this kid and I really don't like to lug him around. So I just stay at home, and people come over here, because I'm an oracle of knowledge, too, with my music. They get entertained very well. They'll come with their six-packs, their herbs, or whatever. We'll have a grand old time. Generally, somebody comes every day." Nevertheless, Ray was taking care of their son while his wife worked. Their overall practice, however, was not fully equitable. When asked who took responsibility for the child when they were both home, Ray said: "I do on weekdays. Weekends I try to slough him off or let Geri put up with his nonsense, since I put up with his nonsense all morning. We kind of trade off." Later he admitted that "the bulk of coping and hassling with this guy is Geri's."

The Sandovals' traditional division of housework and more nearly equitable sharing of child-care chores can be explained by Geri's secondary contribution to family income, their split-shift day-care arrangement, and gender ideology: Geri's belief that housework was her domain and Ray's characterization of his wife as his "agent." Clearly, Ray did significant child-care tasks in the course of babysitting while his wife was at work, but implicit in the way he "sloughed off" his son was a resistance to taking responsibility for housework and child care. Rather he took care of the necessities until his wife was around. She, on the other hand, believed that quality care for her son was important and was provided by their split-shift arrangements. Geri was unwilling to pressure her husband to learn how to do other household chores and was silent about any misgivings she might have had. As long as he did a few outside chores and took care of their son while she worked, Geri was relatively satisfied with this tradeoff. And since he was able to continue partying with his friends while he took care of their child, Ray was satisfied as well. The Sandovals' attempt at reconciling the contradiction of work and family embodied a certain amount of privilege for Ray.

The Garcias

Similar to the other couples in which the wife was a secondary provider, the Garcias had a traditional division of housework but an equitable division of child care. Donna worked at SystemsPlus as a skills trainer; Jimmy worked at HealthTech as a production facilitator. Donna had taken some college nursing courses and was enrolled in business courses at the time of our interviews. Jimmy had completed some college as well, majoring in business. Donna's wages, including overtime, averaged about $7.00 an hour, while Jimmy made an annual salary of about $27,000, for a combined family income of about $40,000. The Garcias were purchasing a home in an upscale west-side neighborhood. Because Donna worked three and a half days and Jimmy's hours were also unconventional, the Garcias' complicated day-care arrangements for their two daughters combined a split shift, a nursery, and Donna's mother (see Chapter 7).

The Garcias had migrated to Albuquerque from central Texas a few years prior, in part to be close to her kin, and Donna considered herself "Chicana or Mexican American."[7]

Donna took responsibility for all cleaning, purchasing food and clothing, and paying bills; she did the household work on her days off. The only household chore the couple shared was preparing dinner: "I'm not one to cook. I'll cook if I have to, but it's not everyday; it's not even every other day. Maybe two days out of the week, and they've never complained. . . . It's a toss-up between me and my husband and going out to eat." Jimmy would occasionally vacuum, and he did all the traditional men's chores. Donna made decisions about large purchases herself, based on a complicated system of financial planning: "The only thing that he's bought was his truck, and that was a surprise. But other than that, I have a budget that I set up, and usually I make a list of everything I want for the next five years, and I prioritize it, and whenever I feel like we can buy it, then we buy it. [So your husband leaves it up to you?] Uh-huh. It's kind of neat; I enjoy it."

Jimmy took more responsibility for child-care chores than for housework. He would get up about 6:30 A.M. (after Donna had already left for work), wake the girls, give them breakfast, and drive them to school or day care. In the evenings, Donna supervised baths and putting the girls to bed, then prepared their bag lunches and laid out their clothes for the next day. "And if he has to pay the nursery or whatever, I leave a check." The Garcias shared helping their daughters with homework, staying home when they were sick, and diapering them when they were babies. Donna usually gave the girls their spending money, supervised chores, and took them to doctor or dentist appointments on her days off.

Although Donna was generally satisfied with their domestic arrangements, she had tried to get Jimmy to do more housework:

> I would say that [the chores] are pretty fairly divided. There's sometimes when I get mad at him, because he likes to play golf and stuff like that. Sometimes I feel like he gets a little bit more pleasure than I do, and I'll bitch about it. And then he'll come and help me. But there's not any real problem there at all. He's real helpful, he really is. [Q: So you have talked about doing things differently, then?] Yeah. Usually its

---

[7] Jimmy's interview was incomplete and did not include the questions about either household division of labor or ethnic identity.

telling him the same thing over and over again, you know [*mimics own voice*]: "From now on . . . I said the same thing last . . ." But it's no big deal. It's not any big problem or anything.

Donna had strong egalitarian views regarding gender roles. She disputed the truisms that men should be the primary providers, that it's better if husbands earn more than wives, and that it's better all around if a woman can stay home instead of going out to work. Regarding the notion that working mothers miss the best years of their children's lives, Donna responded: "I disagree strongly. I think if a person is cut out to work, they're going to be happier working, and they're going to be able to spend time with their family. But if a person is staying at home and they're unhappy, that's going to cause problems too. I know I am a person who's cut out for work. I've always felt responsible for myself, and along with that comes a job." Donna had been unemployed for five months after moving to Albuquerque, before she got her job at SystemsPlus, and was strongly committed to remaining in the labor force.

The Garcias' fairly traditional division of housework but more equitable division of child care can be explained by Donna's status as a secondary provider, the couples' need for a split-shift arrangement because of the impossibility of using a day-care center and the unavailability of kin who could provide full-time day care, and Jimmy's resistance to taking on more housework. Donna was very satisfied with her job, and her unusual work schedule allowed her significant time at home to take care of the housework that Jimmy did not do. Though Donna would have liked more help from her husband, she believed that housework was her responsibility and that Jimmy's help with the children offset his lack of responsibility for cleaning up and managing the house. Like the Sandovals', the Garcias' attempt at reconciling the contradiction of work and family meant that the wife essentially took on a second shift of housework in exchange for child care. Unlike Geri Sandoval, however, Donna was not silent about her occasional unhappiness but contested Jimmy's privilege.

In these two couples with wives as secondary providers, the division of labor—though not explicitly arranged and a source of ambivalence for both women—took fairly traditional forms: though both men did more child-care chores while taking care of their children, they did not necessarily do more housework. Ray Sandoval had contradictory yet ultimately traditional norms regarding the division of labor; Jimmy Garcia indicated to his wife that he had flexible views about family roles, yet his practice, like that of Ray Sandoval, was passive resistance. We conclude that because these husbands regarded their wives' income as important but secondary, their practice reflected a belief that responsibility for the housework rested primarily with their wives.

Wives as Mainstay Providers

The mainstay couples contrasted sharply with those couples in which the wife was a secondary provider. Mainstay couples also often used split-shift day-care arrangements, but the division of labor was more equitable, and in some cases men were taking major responsibility for women's chores and the care of their children. Women's economic contribution was the crucial factor that pushed these couples toward more equitable practice.

The Mondragons

Edward Mondragon took on responsibility for more housework than his wife, and they had an equitable division of child care. Valerie was a mainstay provider who worked as a swager and winder at HealthTech and earned a higher income than her husband. Edward worked in construction, framing houses (though he was unemployed at the time of the interview). The Mondragons (introduced in Chapter 3) had a split-shift day-care arrangement, trading off the care of their twenty-one-month-old daughter around Valerie's rotating shift at HealthTech. They lived with his parents in a small house in Old Town, and described themselves as "Spanish." Valerie was satisfied with this arrangement: "I like it. It's a lot less pressure on me because he really takes the trouble, because it's his kid, and he helps me with my housework and all that, so that's good" (see also Chapter 7).

The "help" that Edward provided with housework was substantial. He did all the men's chores and took sole responsibility for setting the table, vacuuming, and ironing: "He usually does mine because he says I don't know how to iron too good [*laughs*]." They shared a number of chores, including cooking, cleaning up, purchasing food and clothing, and paying monthly bills (Edward did even more while he was unemployed).

[198]

The Mondragons had not discussed the division of labor, but again, Valerie was satisfied with their arrangements: "It looks like he does more stuff, but, you know, I do a lot of it general. I don't let him, I don't, uh, handle him as a slave, you know, 'you do this,' or 'you do that.' . . . He just helps me. When he wants to. [Q: But has he kind of decided to do that on his own?] Mmm-hmm. I don't tell him."

The Mondragons did not articulate an egalitarian ideology about housework; rather, each noted that Edward helped Valerie, implying that it was her responsibility. In describing a typical Saturday, Edward said, "I usually help my wife clean up the house" while Valerie said: "After I eat, I have to do the dishes. Get the clothes off the dryer and then start dusting or whatever. He helps me most of the time. . . . Like if we're having potatoes and stuff, he'll peel the potatoes. And he helps me with dusting and vacuuming and stuff." When asked how he felt about the way chores were divided, Edward said: "It's all right with me. It doesn't bother me. [Q: You haven't considered doing it a different way?] No."

Although Edward actually did more housework than she, Valerie strongly agreed with the statements "I have sometimes felt it was unfair that I have to work and also spend so much time taking care of my home and children," and "I sometimes think I cannot do enough for my family when I work." Implicit in her comments was the assumption that the housework was generally her responsibility, with which he helped, even if it was considerable help.

Edward and Valerie strongly agreed that taking care of children should be shared equally, and their practice was consistent with this view. But while Edward was not working, he also took his daughter to appointments and cared for her whenever she got sick.

Valerie had been working at an apparel factory when she was pregnant and worked until her daughter's birth, then stayed out of the labor force for three months before getting another job. She had discussed the decision to return to work with her husband, and she recalled his feelings: "He said that I had to work: 'If we want to make it and buy a house, you have to work.' [So he was really for your working, the whole time?] Yes, and so am I. . . . I have to be out doing something. Although I like spending time with [my daughter]. I wish I could go to school, though." Edward described his feelings about his wife's going back to work: "We needed the help. It's hard to get by nowadays with just one [income]." Although Valerie was not strongly committed to the notion of becoming a full-time homemaker, she was intrigued with the idea of leaving the labor force, and her husband believed that it would be better if she could. Their precarious economic situation, however, would not allow them to explore that possibility.

Because of HealthTech's rotating work schedule, the Mondragons had to rearrange their domestic living arrangements periodically. Valerie said: "When they first gave me the job, they said, 'Well, you know you're going to have to go nights.' And I was all, you know, 'I need a job, I'd better do it.' But then I guess I got so spoiled on days. And my whole life changes when I go on nights. It's like a whole different . . . I don't know what I'm going to do. I'll probably stay there and take it, [but] I don't like it."

In sum, the Mondragons had to adapt their household arrangements to Valerie's shift changes and to Edward's bouts of unemployment. Their practice was such that Edward actually did more housework than his wife, apparently without any prompting on her part, and they both felt good about this. Although his wife would normally do more child care, Edward took on more of those chores as well when he was not working. This couple's division of labor can be explained by her status as mainstay provider, his periodic unemployment, and Valerie's rotating work schedule, which created a situation in which Edward was available to perform more work in the household. Edward did not seem to resent doing more housework than his wife, and she seemed satisfied with their arrangement. To the Mondragons, reconciling the contradiction between work and family meant sharing strategies to adapt to their precarious places in the labor market.

The Meads

Like Valerie Mondragon, Connie Mead was the mainstay provider in her family. Connie worked as an assembler on second shift at Howard Electronics and made $5.55 an hour. Jack was a radio announcer who normally worked from 6:00 A.M. to 1:00 P.M., but he was unemployed at the time of the interview. The previous year, because he had been unemployed and she had taken maternity leave, their income was about $15,000. The Meads had a son who was ten months old. They had an equitable division of housework and a nontraditional division of child-care chores.

Connie usually vacuumed, cleaned the bathroom, and took charge of their money. Jack would normally take responsibility for car maintenance and some household repairs, although Connie indicated that she did minor repairs as well. They shared the rest of the chores. The Meads agreed that taking care of children should be shared equally between husband and wife, but their arrangement was nontraditional in that he actually did slightly more child care.

Connie had a strong commitment to the labor force. Before moving to Albuquerque, she had held a number of different jobs; then she worked hard to get hired at Howard. Yet when her maternity leave was up, she was ambivalent about returning to work. She would have preferred to stay on leave for at least six months, but "I felt like that steady flow of income needed to be coming in." Her husband had more conservative views and had sometimes expressed his wish that she didn't have to work at all, but on the whole, she said, it was "fine with him, more or less." In response to the statement "Men should get most of the higher-paying jobs because they have families to support," Jack at first was equivocal, saying that he could "see both sides of the coin. I'm enough of a chauvinist to think that, you know. When I was growing up, my mother was always in the home, see—of course she had to be, with eleven kids. But a lot of kids that I knew who had both parents working, even back in the '60s there, they had to have both wages coming into the house, which is a sad deal, not very good." Connie said: "I think that varies a lot because the situation is a lot different now. I think women are holding more jobs than men, and I think they are having easier access to jobs than men are."

Connie agreed that it was "better for a marriage if a husband earns more money than his wife." Jack disagreed: "I'd be real happy if Connie walked in tomorrow and said 'Hey I just got a raise, I'm making $25,000 a year.' I'd take her out to dinner [*laughs*]." Connie was interested in the possibility of becoming a full-time housewife. She agreed that it would be much better if she could stay home and take care of her family instead of having to work, but noted that "it doesn't work out that way." If she didn't need the money she would work only part time.

The Meads were unusual in having explicitly discussed the division of labor and considered changing their arrangement. When asked how he felt about the division of chores, Jack said:

> Sometimes it can get kind of nerve-racking. If I have to do yard work, car work, screwing around with these appliances and shit, you know, since the other things are fifty-fifty. . . . But for the sake of peace and

[201]

tranquillity it's best to keep your mouth shut. [*Q*: So have you ever talked about doing things differently?] Yeah. [*Q*: Did you come to any conclusions?] No, the more things change, the more they stay the same [*laughs*]. Ah, it's all right, you know. She's working and putting in hours and bringing home money and so, you know, I'd probably have more to say about it if I was the only one working. There was a time when I *was* the only one working, and I did have more to say about it. But now, since we're both working (although I'm not working now), since both of us are more or less throwing equal pay into the pot, so to speak, we both have a say.

The Meads' equitable division of labor can be explained by their explicit wage work–housework bargain, which involved a tradeoff between Connie's economic contribution and Jack's help with the housework. With equal responsibility between husband and wife for supporting the family and Connie the primary provider, Jack believed that he should do more housework. The couple's decision to use a split-shift day-care arrangement, fueled by their unstable economic situation, meant that Jack did more child-care tasks. Yet in contrast to the Mondragons, neither one was entirely happy with this situation.

Wives as Coproviders

Among the couples with coproviding wives, there was more variation in household arrangements than among the secondary or mainstay couples. Not just women's economic contribution but other factors—such as work shifts or a spouse's ideology—pushed couples into traditional or equitable arrangements. We contrast four families: the Riveras and the Smiths with relatively high incomes, and the Bacas and the Pikes with low incomes.

The Riveras

Deborah and Sabine Rivera both worked the day shift (7:20 A.M. to 3:50 P.M.) as modular testers (GR-8) at Southwest Electronics and were earning similar hourly wages. He earned $7.74 an hour, but because of the layoff, Deborah had less job tenure and earned $6.25. They were on the high end of the economic scale, with a combined income of almost $27,000 a year. Deborah, reared in a northern New

Mexican village, called herself "Spanish," while Sabine, born in Mexico, described his ethnic identity as "Mexican." The Riveras took their two-year-old son to a day-care center and were satisfied with the quality of care (see Chapter 7). They had explicitly discussed the division of labor and were in the process of negotiating a more egalitarian division of housework. Yet they were similar to other couples in their semitraditional arrangement for caring for their son.

Deborah clearly expressed her views on the distinction between women's and men's work. She believed that she was responsible for chores inside the house, while "things around the house that need to be done, or outside, or repairs, I just tell him to do it. I'm not going to go outside. . . . So everything in here, really [is my responsibility]." Yet the Riveras' behavior was not entirely consistent with these views. Deborah usually took responsibility for seven of the women's chores on our list, and she also took charge of their money and paid monthly bills, although they both decided on major purchases. They shared in preparing breakfast, lunch, and dinner and in setting the table, shopping for groceries and clothing, and washing clothes. Sabine took responsibility for the men's chores—including such major maintenance as installing a security system on his truck, as well as care of the yard and garden surrounding their large west-side home.

Deborah had initiated a new division of labor, asking for more help with housework, especially dishwashing: "I've told him, 'I can't be doing here and outside; you've got to help me with some stuff.' Especially when we both work, its hard." She was satisfied with the change that occurred.

The Riveras had egalitarian views on coparenting, with Deborah strongly believing that child care should be shared equally. Yet in the actual care of their fifteen-month-old son, Deborah took on more responsibility. Sabine said: "We share some things pretty well, evenly. A lot of the times she does most of it, and some of the other times I do most of it. But I think she ends up doing more than I do." In part, this result could be attributed to Deborah's "shorter patience." In disciplining the child, Sabine pointed out, his wife had a lower tolerance level, and she'd "probably blow up before I would." Deborah acknowledged, "It's usually me, because I get more frustrated." Implicit in her greater intolerance was the traditional notion that women should care for children.

The Riveras had egalitarian views about family support: neither partner expressed strong commitment to the notion that men should be the breadwinners, "especially now that, you know, everything is so high," Deborah said. "We bought our house and everything, our payments are real high, our truck payment. So we both have to work and he doesn't mind it at all." About his wife's working, Sabine said: "I like it. It helps quite a bit. Her income is not the same as mine— I've been there longer so I get more than she does, but at the same time her income is quite a bit. . . . And without her it would be really tight for me to make the bills. . . . I think it would be too much pressure. And since she actually likes to work, it's been really good, easy for me to be in this situation. Actually making it easy for me. At the same time she's doing what she wants to do."

Deborah did not like the idea of quitting her job and becoming a homemaker: "I don't think so, because right now I do have a little baby, and I have to work in order to keep up with our bills too. It's not the thing that I don't like to be home; it's just that we have to pay our bills. And with his check, you know, we wouldn't have money enough to spend otherwise."

Sabine was more ambivalent:

> I believe for her to be working if that's what she wants. Also, we spend as much time as we can with my little boy, like we want to, but yet it would be better if one of us wasn't working. But then in another sense, he also spends a lot of time in a nursery with a lot of other kids. I think he learns a lot more there in relation to sharing and playing with other kids. I think a lot of times if the parents don't know how to approach some things, the kid can actually get bored being at home.

Deborah too became more ambivalent as she reflected further:

> It's kind of hard. I do like to work, but I think my family is more important. If I had the money—but I don't, so . . . [So if you didn't need the money would you continue to work?] I don't think so, no. Like I said, I like to work now, maybe because I do need the money [*laughs*]. And I'd probably spend more time with my family then [if I didn't need the money].

Several factors contribute to the Riveras' equitable division of housework. Deborah's wages were almost equal to her husband's, and she was making an important contribution to their standard of living. Because they both worked the same shift in the same plant,

[204]

they did some chores together—such as taking their son to the doctor after work, or shopping for groceries—and could trade off housework and child care in the evenings, in contrast to couples who had a split-shift arrangement.

This was another family in which there was a tradeoff between wage work and housework. Deborah believed that as she took on responsibility for the provider role, Sabine should take on more responsibility for housework, and he seemed to be complying. Their relatively equal wages and same work shift made them appear to be equal partners and enabled them to carry out their egalitarian views, so that after some discussion they had divided up the household chores more equitably.

The Smiths

Though the Smiths were high-income coproviders like the Riveras, Karen Smith took responsibility for more housework, or seeing to it that the older children performed their chores, while Rex took more responsibility for child care. Like the Sandovals and other couples, the Smiths' arrangement stemmed in large part from their decision to use a split-shift day-care arrangement. Karen and Rex both worked at Aerospace, Inc.: he as a machinist on first shift, she as an inspector on second shift both making about $10 an hour (see Chapter 3). In addition, Karen was a paid union officer, working two Saturdays a month and some afternoons for a monthly income of $450. The Smiths, on the high end of the income scale, had a combined annual income of about $45,000. They had four children, ages twenty-one, eighteen, twelve, and six. Karen took care of the youngest son during the days, and Rex took responsibility for the children while his wife worked.

In the actual division of chores, Karen did five of the women's chores; Rex purchased all the groceries; Rex and the oldest son would usually cook dinner, although occasionally Karen would leave dinner for them to heat up in the microwave oven. Rex (or the oldest son) would take care of car maintenance. Rex did not do many men's chores himself, leaving electrical and plumbing repairs to professionals and the yard work and garbage detail to his older children. The children had plenty of other chores, as well, including being responsible for packing their own school lunches and making their beds, occasionally vacuuming, and taking turns washing dishes, setting the table, and cleaning bathrooms. The Smiths shared in buying their children's clothing and their own, taking charge of the money, and deciding on large purchases. They had two checking accounts and a system of dividing up household expenditures, further evidence of their status as coproviders: normal monthly bills were paid out of Karen's account; food and recreation expenses out of Rex's. Karen was not entirely happy about the division of housework, but Rex seemed satisfied, noting "I think the kids have had a pretty decent life" because of the split-shift arrangement. He did not like their limited time together, however: "We wave goodbye and hello to each other [during the week] and make love, where we can, on the weekends."

The division of child-care tasks had changed since the children were younger. Then Karen normally had done all of the work, although Rex would usually see to it that they went to bed. Now that they were older and she worked evenings, Rex had taken on more child-care tasks than his wife. The couple noted, however, that if the children neglected their chores, Karen would sometimes do them: for example, washing dishes after her work shift had ended. The Smiths now strongly believed in sharing child care equally.

On a typical work day during the school year, Rex would get up about 6:00 A.M., get ready for work, and awaken his oldest son, Randy, before he left. Randy would wake up the other children, who prepared their own breakfasts. Karen got up in time to supervise the children's departure, then she would clean house, get the youngest son ready for kindergarten, then go to the union hall for a couple of hours of work. The twelve-year-old daughter would pick up the six-year-old from school and take care of him for the half-hour or so before Rex came home. After his shift, Rex would either cook dinner with Randy or heat up the dinner Karen had prepared. Then the children would do homework or watch television, and be in bed by 9:00 P.M. Karen would come home and either do some housecleaning or catch up on union work before going to sleep around 2:00 A.M..

The Smiths had relatively egalitarian views about gender roles. They both agreed that economic support should be shared by husband and wife, and Karen was strongly committed to remaining in the labor force. Their division of labor can be explained, first, by Karen's significant economic contribution and, second, by the couple's decision to divide up child care. Karen had started at Aerospace before her husband did. She went to work after the birth of her fourth child because she wanted to and "for the extra income." For a time Rex was unemployed, so Karen was a mainstay provider until she was able to get him a job at Aerospace as a janitor. He later moved up to his machinist's job. Because of her greater seniority, Karen made slightly higher wages than Rex. Then, when their work schedules made a split-shift arrangement best for taking care of their four children and Rex was home alone in the evening, he became responsible for more child-care chores than previously. Finally, neither spouse was strongly wedded to traditional notions that the man should be the provider and the woman solely responsible for household chores. Though their division of housework leaned toward the traditional—especially considering that she generally took responsibility for seeing that the children's chores got done—clearly, Rex was doing some housework and a significant amount of child care.

The Bacas

Like Karen Mead, Delores Baca was a coprovider but earned only about two-thirds of the weekly income of her husband Albert, who worked as a grocery stocker (see Chapter 3). The Bacas had a traditional division of housework and child care. They were economically stable, but their combined income of about $18,000 put them at the low end of the scale. Delores worked as a sewing operator on the first shift at Leslie Pants but, because of the recession, was working short weeks during 1982, which sometimes meant that she came home around noon. Albert worked the graveyard shift (11:00 P.M. to 7:00 A.M.). Delores's mother, who lived across the street in a small adobe house similar to the Bacas', took care of their six-month-old daughter while Delores worked and her husband slept during the day. Well integrated into a large Bernalillo-based kin network (see Chapter 8), Delores described herself as "Spanish-Mexican," while Albert called himself "Spanish-Chicano."

Delores performed most of the housework, with the exception of making beds—"I do [that]—no, my husband helps me once in a while, so it's like both, I guess"—and ironing, which they both did. He noted that his wife didn't like the way he vacuumed, so she usually did that chore. Albert did all of the men's chores, although he got help with yard work from his wife and a brother-in-law who slept at their home. As to who took charge of their finances, Delores said they both did; Albert said, "I give her all the money; she gets all the money." But they agreed that they both paid monthly bills.

On a typical work day, Delores got up at 5:00 A.M., prepared the diaper bag, and took the baby to her mother's house. After work, she would pick up the baby, come home and cook dinner, and take care of her daughter while trying to do housework: "So I'm running back and forth with her, you know, and then trying to straighten up the house, because my husband really doesn't do anything like that. Once in a while, like the days he's off . . . he'll help me." Once the baby was asleep, Delores would iron her clothes for work and sometimes her brother's clothes, then would go to bed. Her husband usually got up for dinner but took another nap before starting his work shift. Delores would wake up at 11:00 P.M. to make sure he got off to work on time, before she retired for the night: "I don't do anything [like prepare lunch] for him before he goes to work. . . . [But] I can't sleep really comfortable until I see that he is up."

The Bacas had fairly traditional notions about who should be responsible for housework. Delores said: "All the house chores, I'm responsible for [*laughs*]. [*Interviewer*: And the outside things, he's responsible?] I think so, yeah. [Did you guys talk about that, or you just do it like that?] We just do it; we never really talked about it." Yet despite her view that housework was her responsibility, Delores agreed with the statement: "I have sometimes felt it was unfair that I have to work and also spend so much time taking care of my home and my children." Of course, Albert's work on the graveyard shift meant that he slept during the day and evenings, and this limited the amount of housework he was able to do.

The Bacas had had conflict over housework, although Albert was more willing than Delores to discuss it:

Sometimes we get into it about washing the dishes. . . . She'll say "Come and help me," you know, and I'll have something to do and she'll say "Wait till later." I'll tell *her* to wait till later, you know, it's just a runaround. And like dinner, too, because sometimes she comes home really tired, you know, and she tells me she don't want to make it. I tell her, "Well, don't make it," you know? [So then do you make it?] Yeah, well I do, I just go in there and scrounge up something to eat. [You feel you ever get in serious discussions about work?] No, we haven't had [a serious fight] yet. We came close to it, but I broke down and went and helped, washing the dishes. I remember that night we had company over, there was a lot of dishes and she was tired, and she

[208]

said she wanted help, so I had to help her. [You almost didn't?] I wasn't [going to], because I remember that night I had to go in early [to work].

The conflict was over whether Albert would take on responsibility for some of his wife's inside chores. When he needed to sleep or relax before his night shift, Albert balked at helping with the housework, even though he seemed to agree that his wife was right in requesting more help from him. He did not like working nights and was hoping to find a better-paying day job.

Albert and Delores strongly agreed that caring for children should be shared equally between fathers and mothers. Yet Delores took major responsibility for the baby, and Albert would help out occasionally. He noted the difference between ideals and practice: "I say it should [be shared equally], but in my position and our hours it's impossible for us."

The Bacas had a fairly traditional ideology regarding family roles. Both agreed that men should be breadwinners, but they could not afford that option. Delores was already working at Leslie Pants when she and Albert married. When she was pregnant with their first child, she had considered quitting her job, but "we really couldn't afford it," so she returned to work when her daughter was two months old. Delores had somewhat more traditional views regarding gender roles, believing that men should earn higher wages than their wives. Albert disagreed:

That's not true because . . . sometimes, you know, the families, they do depend on the father's earnings, but the mothers, they make good money, too. I know a couple of families where the wives make more than the husbands, you know. He really feels kind of bad about it . . . she's making all the money, you know, and he's barely. . . . [Do you think he should feel that way?] No. As long as they're happy. [Why does he feel that way?] I guess he's a macho type. . . . But as long as they're happy, the way I see it, it doesn't really matter.

Delores had a strong desire to leave the labor market: "Because being with your kids all day long, you know what they're learning and what they're not learning." Asked whether she would continue to work if she didn't need the money, Delores said, "No, I think I'd rather stay home and take care of my family."

The Bacas' child-care arrangement affected their household divi-

[209]

sion of labor. Besides the convenience and low cost of having Delores's mother take care of the baby (the grandmother refused payment, but they occasionally paid one of her bills), there was another
advantage: "Well, I get to rest during the day," Albert said. He expressed some ambivalence about this arrangement for his daughter
but noted, "There ain't no way that I could take her anywhere else,
you know, without starting a big fight." Asked about the possibility of
other day care if his mother-in-law were not available, Albert said:
"I'd just have to take care of her when I got home from work if I still
worked graveyard. I'd just, you know, have to take care of her. See,
my mother-in-law's doing this for me, you know, to help me out too.
So I can rest during the day. So I won't have a breakdown [*laughs*],
twenty-five years old." It is doubtful that Albert would be able to
handle working the graveyard shift and taking care of an infant during the day for very long. Having his mother-in-law care for the baby
enabled Albert to continue working nights and sleeping during the
days. Further, as a result of his work schedule, he could legitimately
claim that he was too tired to do much housework.

The Bacas' traditional division of labor can be explained by their
shift schedules and day-care arrangement, as well as their fairly traditional views about gender roles. Albert's night shift and the grandmother's babysitting created barriers to Delores's ability to get her
husband to perform more housework. The Bacas were consistent in
their ideology and their actual practice of doing housework and caring for their child, but there were indications that Delores would like
a more equitable division of labor and that Albert was willing to help
more. If he could get a job on the day shift, this couple might move
toward a more equitable division of housework.

The Pikes

Like Delores Baca, Mary Pike worked days as a sewing operator at
Leslie Pants, earning an average of $5.12 an hour (see Chapter 3).
Her husband was one of those who had "skidded" down the occupational scale: Don had been working as a roughneck on an oil rig,
making $11.95 an hour, until he was fired for missing a day of work.
After being unemployed, he got a job in receiving at Leslie Pants,
making $4.80 an hour. Like the Bacas, too, the Pikes were coprovid-
ers, and their annual income of about $18,000 put them on the low
end of the income scale. The Pikes both worked on the day shift,

from 7:00 A.M. to 3:30 P.M.; a neighbor took care of their four-month-old daughter while they worked.

Yet unlike the Bacas, the Pikes divided up chores in a nontraditional way. In addition to doing most of the men's chores, Don took responsibility for several women's chores: he usually set the table, vacuumed, and washed the floor. He paid the monthly bills and said he took charge of their money (though Mary said they shared that task). Don also shared a considerable number of chores with his wife, including preparing meals, washing dishes (although they agreed that he could do them more often), doing laundry, cleaning the bathroom, buying food, purchasing adult clothing, doing yard work, and deciding on large purchases. Mary did two chores on her own: making their bed and buying the baby's clothing (although baby gifts had made the purchase of babywear unecessary at the time of the interview).

Mary Pike did not believe that parenting should be shared equally; her husband did, but Mary in fact took more responsibility for the care of their daughter. In particular, Don admitted that about "75 percent" of the time Mary would change diapers, and Mary noted that "I do most of the getting-ready-for-the-babysitter work." Mary was satisfied with their household arrangement:

> I think I do more of the child care than he does. I take care of her when we're both here. And he takes care of her if I need to go somewhere. . . . Oh sometimes I would like him to help me with her more. But I know that sometimes he does more housework than I do. He's neater than I am. He will start cleaning before I will. So he usually winds up starting the housework, and he does more of it usually than I do. Of course I'm so busy with her that I don't have any time anymore. [Q: Are you happy about that? *Nods affirmatively*].

When asked how he felt about the division of chores, Don indicated that the couple had gone through some struggle, that he had wanted more help with housework:

> They're about right [now]. For a while I was doing everything, but now she's got to where she's interested in doing a lot more. . . . I was cleaning the house, and doing the yard work, and everything. [How did that happen?] I don't know. I just like to have everything neat. And she doesn't care, she just sits, she doesn't care. And so I end up always being the one to clean it up. It got worse and worse until I started

[211]

blowing up the last couple of weeks, and now it's about fifty-fifty. . . .
Now she does most of the cooking, but I'm still the one who sets the
table; I do most of the housework, but she takes care of the baby most
of the time.

The Pikes had relatively nontraditional views about gender roles.
They agreed that they needed Mary's wages, though Mary was ambivalent about being in the labor force permanently:

> I thought about how nice it would be to be able to stay home and raise
> the baby, but I don't get as frustrated working as he does. I get bored
> at home. I like to be out and talk to people. For him, it would be
> better if he was the "househusband," and if it came down to that, it
> might work out that way, where he would get off and I would work.
> And he's real good with the baby. He cooks, he just does stuff like that.
> . . . For some reason people think the husband's lazy if he doesn't
> work; if a wife doesn't work, that's okay. Well, everything else about
> sex roles is changing; I don't see what's so different about [a husband
> not working].

The overriding consideration for the Pikes' division of labor was
that Mary was a coprovider, making slightly higher wages than her
husband, who had been displaced from his role as primary breadwinner. Another factor was the Pikes' ideology. Both believed that it was
proper that Mary should work, and that housework and child care
should be shared. The Pikes were flexible regarding gender roles in
the family, and their wage work–housework bargain meant that the
way they divided up chores was nonconventional, with Don taking
more responsibility for the housework and Mary taking most of the
child-care chores. Reinforcing factors were Don's meticulousness and
his discomfort with caring for a very young infant. Don did not like
his job, and both he and Mary were considering the possibility of
changing roles, giving him major responsibility for the household and
making Mary the main provider. Given that there were few opportunities in the Albuquerque labor market for Don to return to the
wages he had once earned as an oil-rig roughneck, being a househus-
band seemed attractive.

In sum, women who were coproviders made arrangements with
their spouses based on their particular circumstances. When their
economic contribution did not push men into doing more housework, they strategized around work shifts and day-care arrangements; ideology was not necessarily the determinant.

Women as Sole Providers

Only four of the fifteen single parents had partners who contributed any income toward the support of their children, much less performed household duties. Single parents had two major patterns in the way they organized family life—younger women often lived with relatives or friends; older women usually resided only with their children (see Chapter 3)—and three major patterns in managing household chores. Susan Anaya represents those women who lived alone with children too young to help out; Grace Estrada lived with her parents and divided housework and child care with her mother and other kin; Christina Espinosa's children had become teenagers and shared her household chores.

Susan Anaya

At the time of our interview, Susan had been living alone with her son in a small "efficiency apartment" in the North Valley for several months. Before that she had had a long list of moves and had lived with her sister and mother for a period of time. Susan (who was introduced in Chapter 3, and described herself as "Spanish") worked at Southwest Electronics, making $5.46 an hour. She was on the low end of the income scale of single parents, with an annual income of $10,000. The mother of a friend from work took care of her eight-month-old son, Jason, charging her only $20 a week (see Chapter 7). Susan got considerable help from her day-care provider—who would wash the baby's diapers and occasionally his clothes if they got soiled during the day—and her sister, who drove the baby to the provider's house and picked him up after work.

Other than that, Susan did all the household and child-care chores herself. She cleaned house in the evenings or on weekends and did whatever men's chores her landlord did not handle, though her brother did help with car maintenance. She made all decisions about finances by herself.

Susan had an egalitarian ideology, which partially explained why she was a single parent to begin with. She had decided not to marry the father of the child because he was too independent and not sufficiently responsible: "He just liked his freedom a lot, you know. And then I thought now that I was having a baby, we just couldn't stay like that." Further, Susan believed in shared parenting and a wage work-housework bargain. If she were married, she said, "we'd go half, depending on who worked when, you know, if he worked nights or days. [*Interviewer*: So you would expect him to help out quite a bit?] Oh yes. I mean if I stayed home all day and I didn't work, then no, but being that I was working and he was working, I think we'd divide it. There is a lot of men that don't think that way, but mine would have to, definitely [*laughs*]." Although she felt ambivalent about working while her son was so young—"You do miss a lot"— she had a strong commitment to her job, and expected to remain in the labor force even if she married.

When asked what had changed since she had her son and went back to work, Susan said:

> I've settled down a lot. And I enjoy him so much. The double work that I have, it's great. It's nice to have somebody to come home to and say, "Wow, this is my son," you know, I just love it. It was so much easier before because I just had to think of myself and that's no problem, like the responsibilities were nothing. Now it's a whole different world because I have this little one that I have to think of. It's a lot more work, like I say, more laundry, more everything, but it's worth it.

Susan Anaya had little recourse once she made the decision to rear her child alone. She considered herself very fortunate to have an extraordinary day-care provider and a sister who helped out as well. Even though, beyond their help, she managed the child care and housework by herself, she was satisfied with her situation.

Grace Estrada

Grace Estrada's life contrasted sharply with that of Susan Anaya (Grace too was introduced in Chapter 3 and described herself as "Spanish"). After becoming pregnant, she had been pressured into marriage but left her batterer husband five months later and, at twenty-one, went on welfare. Eventually, she and her year-old daughter, Yvette, moved into her parents' home in Los Lunas, where the household included Grace's mother and father, her older brother with his wife and daughter, and two younger siblings.

Grace's father worked days in construction; while her mother worked an evening shift and took care of Yvette during the days while Grace worked at HealthTech. Grace's annual income was $10,000. She did not pay regular fees to her mother for babysitting; instead, "I give her what I can" every week. Grace occasionally gave her father small sums of money or bought a few groceries, but she paid no rent for the use of the room that she shared with her daughter and was not asked to share utility costs or other household expenses.

Grace had to arrive at work by 6:50 A.M., so most child-care chores were done by her mother until evening, when Grace bathed Yvette, fed her dinner, and put her to bed. The division of household chores was varied and complex. Her mother purchased food and prepared dinners. Grace, her mother, sister-in-law, and sister divided up other chores: setting the table, washing dishes, making beds, vacuuming, and mopping floors. The chores that Grace took care of herself included cleaning the bathroom, doing her own laundry, purchasing her clothing and Yvette's, and having her car maintained. Her father and brother did all the men's chores, except for yard work, which was shared by everyone except the two small children. Her parents, her brother and his wife, and Grace had separate budgets. She refused to accept child support from Yvette's father.

Grace had contradictory views about gender roles. She believed that a man should be the breadwinner and that a woman should stay home and take care of her family, because "I feel that's her job." Yet she said she would continue to work even if she didn't have to and strongly believed that work was an important part of her life. Grace was socially isolated, noting that "I usually stick to myself" and that she talked openly only with her sister-in-law. Though living with her parents was an improvement over her marriage or living alone on welfare, Grace still felt pressured: the hardest part of being a working mother was "making sure the meal's on the table and everything's done—housework. I got to bring money in and [do] everything." Grace hoped for a raise so she could afford to put her daughter in a day-care center and give her mother, who was deprived of adequate sleep, some rest (see Chapter 7). She seemed depressed and admitted that she sometimes broke into tears over her situation. But Grace's job at HealthTech stood between her and abject poverty, and she was committed to keeping her job.

Christina Espinosa

Christina Espinosa (see Chapter 3), who earned $9.75 an hour at Aerospace, was the sole support of her two sons, Todd and Michael, who were fifteen and thirteen years old. Christina had been married for five years but left her husband because of domestic violence. Her mother had been a single parent as well, and when the mother died she left her house in the Northeast Heights to Christina. Christina was half Anglo and half Hispana and identified herself as "Albuquerquian." She had one of the highest annual incomes of all the single mothers, having made between $16,000 and $18,000 the previous year.

Christina did not enter the labor force full time until after she and her husband had separated (nine years before our interview); except for brief periods of part-time work as a housekeeper, she had been a full-time housewife. Once she left her husband, she lived with her mother and started working (first at Southwest Electronics, then Aerospace), so she divided up housework with her mother, who also provided day care for the boys.

Christina got considerable help from her sons as well. The boys were responsible for preparing their own breakfasts and lunches, making their own beds, vacuuming, washing floors, putting out the garbage, cleaning the car, and doing yard work. Christina hired a professional to take care of all car maintenance and major plumbing or electrical problems. Christina and Todd, the older son, would figure out the monthly bills together, and the whole family would decide on major purchases. Christina did the rest of the chores herself.

When the boys were younger, Christina had taken major responsibility for child care. Now that the boys were older and their maternal grandmother was dead, they mainly took care of themselves. Christina supervised their homework and chores, and she disciplined them and gave them spending money. She was fairly satisfied with the division of labor: "They seem to do it all right. I mean they complain now and then to me, but I guess that's the way it's going to be all the time. . . . they still do what they want when I'm not here."

Christina had strong traditional views about gender expectations: she believed that men should support families, and women should remain homemakers: "That's what I'd rather do, but I can't." She found it very difficult to work and take care of her family, and would have liked to spend more time with her boys.

[216]

After leaving her husband, Christina had been able to divide housework and child-care chores with her mother for several years. With her mother gone, she had the option of pulling a second shift or getting her sons to help out. Christina made it a point to include them in figuring out how to spend her money and deciding on major purchases, indications that she wanted them even more involved in running the household. Although she made high hourly wages, it was hard to support two teenage boys on her income. Still, though she would have liked the option of leaving the labor market, Christina was relatively satisfied with her situation.

In contrast to working middle-class women who can purchase services to replace their domestic labor, these working-class women constructed arrangements with spouses or, in the case of single parents, with kin, day-care providers, roommates, or children. We are not arguing that women's work itself leads to more egalitarian family structures (Ybarra 1981; Zinn 1980); rather we argue that specific conditions of women's work are what turn the tide. Our informants shared some features with the predominantly middle-class couples that Hochschild (1989) studied: for the most part, neither group had explicitly discussed the household division of labor; arrangements were implicit or "just happened." Nor did couples often live out their gender ideologies: their practice revolved around the availability of day care. With a few exceptions, parents in both studies agreed that parenting should be shared equally, and men generally did more child care than housework, confirming the findings of other studies.

Yet we found some important contrasts with Hochschild's study. Most of our informants started their marriages as full-time workers who planned to remain in the labor force indefinitely. Our data confirm that working wives' contribution to family income is an important factor in the division of labor: women who earn significantly less than their husbands tend to perform more housework and child care. There were indications that a wife's shift to mainstay provider—especially among Hispanos—leads to a more equitable division of housework, with a few men performing even more household and child-care chores than their wives. The importance of Mexican-American wives' income on the household division of labor confirms the findings of Beatriz Pesquera (1985). In her comparative analysis of Chicana professional, clerical, and blue-collar workers, Pesquera found that women with higher income and employment status—particularly professional and blue-collar wives—had an advantage in the struggle over the household division of labor.

This shift toward a nontraditional division of labor certainly is unexpected for working-class men. It contrasts sharply with the predominantly traditional or semitraditional arrangements of working-class informants in our previous studies, and with the findings of Beneria and Roldan (1987:165) on working women in Mexico City: "We did not find that women's control over their incomes empowered them significantly in the bargaining of gender relations within the home." This leads us to pose a question for further research: under what cultural and economic conditions do wives' wages push spouses toward more involvement in household labor?[8] Our findings and those of Pesquera suggest that wives' wages can be an important bargaining chip for working-class women.

Though the majority of our informants had traditional or semitraditional divisions of housework, we have highlighted the egalitarian and nontraditional couples among our cases in order to illustrate the variation and the processes through which couples move toward more equitable sharing. We believe that the shift of wives to becoming mainstay providers and the accompanying egalitarian or nontraditional division of household chores is significant. As more wives enter the labor force, the proportion of the family income they contribute may well influence how much husbands contribute to domestic chores. Though women generally earn much lower wages than men, some families—especially in those households where men have been displaced in the labor market—are relying increasingly on women's wages for economic support. The overall standard of living of mainstay families will generally be lower than if the woman rather than the man is the primary provider, but ironically, women in these families may be able to get a more equal division of household chores. Wives who are secondary providers, unless they can arrange a split-shift day-care arrangement with their spouses or instill more egalitarian views about household responsibility, usually have greater difficulty in breaking away from a traditional division of labor in the home.

A second major point is that beyond socioeconomic considerations,

---

[8] Arlie Hochschild looked for this relationship between wives' income and gender relations in her data and did not find it (personal communication). Thanks to her for suggesting this question.

how a couple arranges for the daily performance of necessary chores is often complex (the result of a combination of factors) and frequently shifts as conditions of work get rearranged. In some families in our sample, wives' secondary income, the use of a split-shift day-care arrangement, and adherence to traditional ideology on the part of either spouse (as in the case of the Sandovals) resulted in wives' doing most of the housework but husbands' doing a significant amount of child-care chores. In these families there was a tradeoff between housework and child care, with women unwilling or unable to push for more help with housework so long as their husbands took care of the children. When wives were mainstay providers, couples often had more equitable arrangements than their traditional ideology would have led us to expect; here the tradeoff seemed to be between wage work and domestic chores, but it was often implicit and rarely openly discussed. The woman's greater economic contribution offset whatever traditional views either spouse might have about gender roles in the family. Combined with using a split-shift arrangement for the care of their children, mainstay couples' division of household labor became more equitable.

It is interesting that virtually every informant agreed that parenting should be shared equally, and that child care was usually shared to a greater degree than was housework, confirming the findings in the literature. In parenting, there was a closer congruence between egalitarian views and a couple's actual behavior.

Married couples' actual practice took precedence over their ideology. Since the majority of our married informants had not discussed the division of household labor, we had to make sense of the implicit understandings where arrangements "just happened" or "came natural." Often the implicit meanings were quite traditional; only when marital conflict emerged did couples explicitly negotiate a change— often at the wife's insistence. Most often, a couple's primary concern was with the care of the children, so that the bargain (again, often implicit) was wagework for child care; whatever housework wives could extract from their husbands was seen as a bonus. For each couple, the strategies were constructed differently and open to change when their work circumstances altered.

For single mothers, domestic arrangements necessarily took on different forms. When women lived alone with their young children, they performed most of the household chores themselves, relegating some men's chores to relatives, landlords, professionals, or friends if possible. Only if single mothers lived with kin, roommates, or older children were they able to divide the chores—and even then, single mothers did considerably more housework than their married counterparts.

Our data also confirm that wives' availability is crucial in how household chores get divided up. When managers experiment with shift schedules—setting up three-and-a-half-day work weeks like SystemsPlus, or rotating shifts like HealthTech—working mothers and members of their households have to make significant accommodations in how they arrange for child care and household maintenance. There are indications that unusual work schedules place married women at a disadvantage regarding the division of household chores. Of the seven couples with unusual shifts, five (the Andersons, Garcias, Maeses, Phillipses, and Sanchezes) had a traditional division of housework. The two exceptions were the Mondragons, where the husband was unemployed, and the Leybas, who had an explicitly egalitarian commitment to dividing up housework. Interestingly enough, Bret Anderson had also shared the housework when he was unemployed during 1982, but the Andersons had assumed a traditional division of labor at the time of our interview, when he was working and she was on maternity leave.

Finally, we found more convergences than differences between Anglos and Hispanos in their domestic arrangements; the proportion of traditional and semitraditional arrangements was the same. All our informants worked within the constraints imposed by their jobs and, for married women, their husbands' jobs. An unusual shift schedule, long-term male unemployment, and the difficulty of finding day care could be problematic for all women workers and their families, and their accommodations to these situations varied.

[7]

Strategies for Day Care
while Mothers Work

Probably the most difficult decision facing working mothers (who usually make the day-care arrangements) is who will care for their children while they are away from the home. Replacing the care of children that is usually done by women goes to the heart of the contradiction between women's paid and unpaid labor (Lamb 1986; Uttal 1990).

On the one hand, day care is an important economic consideration, particularly when women's wages are devalued in the labor market and available day care is expensive. According to Dornbusch and Strober, "Child care is the fourth largest expense for working families, after food, housing, and taxes. Families with one preschool child typically spend 10% of their income on child care, while those with two preschoolers often spend as much as 30%" (1988:123). One study found that the first concern of parents seeking day care was affordability (Skold, Siegel, and Lawrence 1983, cited in Dornbusch and Strober 1988:123).

On the other hand, when day care is seen as replacing mothering, there are specific culturally defined notions regarding what constitutes quality care. Finding quality day care mediates the contradiction between women's paid and domestic labor by filling in the need for women's labor, and by providing women with a sense that their obligations to their children are being fulfilled in a satisfactory way. In a society in which there is debate whether women's employment will have detrimental effects on children's well-being (Kahn and Kamerman 1987), there is a startling absence of debate about conflicts between fathering and employment. "As long as work continues to be organized without regard for the time demands of parenting it may seem that a mother's decision to work outside the home conflicts with her child's need for a close bond with at least one parent" (Dornbusch and Strober 1988:116). Particularly when children are infants or toddlers, parents want them closely and lovingly supervised, and few day-care centers meets these standards.

The search for satisfactory day care, then, often involved the first series of strategies the women we interviewed engaged in, once they decided to return to work after the birth of a child. Finding an acceptable balance between the conflicting needs of quality and affordability often seemed like a juggling act. This chapter considers the kinds of child-care provision that these women made. We argue that cost was neither the sole nor the primary criterion for our informants; rather, parents equally weighed the "three Cs": caring attention, convenience, and cost. In achieving these qualities, couples were constrained by the ages of their children, the availability of either parent or another relative, and the shifts they themselves worked.

We found that the major differences between Hispano and Anglo families in making day-care arrangements was that Hispanos had a greater preference for kin to care for their children, that Hispanos had more kin available to provide day care, and that day-care centers were located predominantly in Anglo areas of Albuquerque, making them accessible to fewer Hispanos.

Our discussion is cast first against census statistics, which provide a national profile of child-care practices by wives in blue-collar and professional occupations and by single mothers. Then we look at actual strategies for day care and how they related to women's (and, their spouses') values, differences according to the age of children, and difficulties the women experienced.

Sunbelt Women and the National Day-Care Picture

According to national census data published in 1982, married mothers who had blue-collar jobs and whose youngest child was under age five were most likely to have their children cared for by relatives. Over one third of blue-collar wives had their children cared for by kin (14 percent in their own home and 21 percent in another home). Care by fathers was another important form, used by 19 percent of blue-collar working women (see Table 21). Professional (and managerial) women were far less likely to have their children cared for by relatives (a total of 17 percent in their own and other homes), and significantly fewer used care provided by the child's father—only 9 percent. Blue-collar wives were less likely to use day-care centers than professional women: 7 percent, compared with 17 percent (U.S. Bureau of the Census 1982b:20-22).[1]

Of the thirty-seven married women in our sample, sixteen (43 percent) had their youngest child cared for at home primarily by the child's father (see Table 21) in a split-shift arrangement made possible by the parents' different work shifts. This was more than twice the national figures. Nineteen percent of these sunbelt wives had their children cared for in another home by relatives, and 24 percent in another home by nonrelatives (usually unlicensed day-care providers). In contrast to the 20 percent of married blue-collar mothers

Table 21. Day-care arrangements of married women with youngest child under age five

Arrangement	Professional[a]	Blue-Collar[a]	Albuquerque Sample
In child's home	23%	38%	43%
by father (split shift)	9%	19%	43%
by relative	4%	14%	0
by nonrelative	10%	6%	0
In other home	53%	42%	43%
by relatives	13%	21%	19%
by nonrelatives	40%	21%	24%
Group care center	17%	7%	14%

[a]U.S. Bureau of the Census 1982b:20–22 (figures rounded; do not include categories "mother caring for child while working" or "child taking care of self").

[1] Although published in 1982, the data reported in Table 21 are from 1977—the closest we could find to correspond to our 1982–83 data. Since then, the national picture on day care has changed somewhat: in 1988, for all employed mothers, 16 percent of children were cared for by their fathers, 8 percent by relatives, and 8 percent by nonrelatives in their own homes; care in another home was provided by relatives in 13 percent of the cases, by nonrelatives in 24 percent; 24 percent of children were cared for in a nursery, preschool, or day-care center (Dawson 1990:5; this report did not provide categories of care by mother's occupational status).

in the national statistics, none of the married women we interviewed had either relatives or nonrelatives come into *their* homes for primary day care. Finally, 14 percent of our married informants utilized day-care centers for the primary care of their children, twice as many as reported by the census for blue-collar wives. In short, there were clear differences between the arrangements made by the wives in our sample and those of other working-class wives.

Single parents faced additional problems in arranging for day care. As the census reported: "The problems that unmarried women encounter in securing daytime care for their young children may be accentuated by the loss of support from the child's father both financially and as a caretaker. Since more unmarried than married women are forced to seek full-time employment, flexibility in working hours is reduced and periods of child care are of greater duration" (U.S. Bureau of the Census 1982b:15–16). In other ways too, child-care options could be more restricted for single mothers. For example, the mother's estrangement from the child's father would likely preclude the use of in-laws as potential care providers. Even so, census data show that "31 percent of unmarried women still managed to arrange in-home care for the child, about the same percentage as that provided by currently married women (33 percent)," suggesting that

> the use of relatives by women in these two marital status groups is actually a function of different social and economic characteristics of the women rather than marital status per se. Unmarried women are more likely to have economic and social characteristics which are associated with a high incidence of the use of relatives for child care; a disproportionate number of unmarried women are in low-income categories, with blue-collar/service worker jobs, and living in households where other adult females are present. . . . Where there may be an extended family situation, the time of female relatives [is] used as substitute for parental or nonrelative child care. (U.S. Bureau of the Census, 1982b:16–17)

Moreover, relatives who did not reside with single mothers were an important source of day care for single parents nationally. Employed single mothers used day care in another home 45 percent of the time, with 21 percent using relatives and 24 percent using nonrelatives (see Table 22). On the use of day-care centers, the census noted: "Ironically, it is the unmarried woman who can probably least

Table 22. Day-care arrangements of unmarried women nationally and in Albuquerque sample

Arrangement	Unmarried Mothers (national)[a]	Single Parents (ABQ sample)
In child's home	31%	6% (1)
by father (split shift)	1%	0
by relative	24%	6% (1)
by nonrelative	6%	0
In other home	45%	80% (12)
by relatives	21%	40% (6)
by nonrelatives	24%	40% (6)
Group care center	19%	13% (2)

[a]U.S. Bureau of the Census 1982b:16 (figures rounded; do not include categories "mother caring for child while working" and "child taking care of self").

afford the cost of group care, yet she uses it the most. In 1977, 19 percent of unmarried women used group care services for their youngest child under 5 years old, compared with 12 percent for [all] currently married women" (U.S. Bureau of the Census 1982b:17).

The single mothers we interviewed did not conform to the national pattern. About half (all Hispanas) of the fifteen single mothers had their children cared for by a close relative (see Table 22). One had day care provided by a relative in her own home, and the rest took their children to another person's home. Forty percent (six) of our single mothers used nonrelated day-care providers; only two utilized established day-care centers for the primary care of their children. Compared with married informants, single parents relied heavily on kin for day care (see Table 23).

Despite differences between blue-collar working women nationally and within our sample, the figures emphasize the importance of kin in the choices of child care. The research on Mexican-American use of social networks also leads us to expect that working-class families would turn first to the possibility of keeping the care of small children within the home and under the care of a parent or other kin (Keefe and Padilla 1987; Wagner and Schaefer 1980). As the following discussion shows, the child-care arrangements described by our interviewees generally conformed, though with variation, to census figures and to patterns found in the literature.

Table 23. Day-care arrangements of Anglo and Hispano informants

	Split Shift	Relative	Provider	Center
Married Hispanas (*n* = 24)	12 (50%)	5 (21%)	4 (16%)	3 (13%)
Married Anglos (*n* = 13)	4 (31%)	2 (15%)	5 (38%)	2 (15%)
Single parents (*n* = 15)	n/a	7 (47%)	6 (40%)	2 (13%)
TOTAL (*n* = 52)	16 (31%)	14 (27%)	15 (29%)	7 (13%)

Our interviews recorded detailed care histories for each child, permitting a more complete analysis than can be provided by aggregate data. For example, among the sixteen married women who had a split-shift arrangement with their husbands, in which each parent took care of the children while the other worked, over two-thirds (eleven) did not have perfectly compatible work schedules with their husbands and so were dependent on others to cover the of overlaps in the parents' work time. The situation was complicated in families with children whose different ages created the need for more than one form of child care. Aid in supplementing the split-shift arrangements in these cases was provided by the husband's or wife's kin, neighbors, hired providers (licensed and unlicensed), a nursery, or combinations of these. The actual arrangements were complex, and some women had had to make changes several times.

The following descriptions include the use of split shifts, close relatives, care providers who worked in their own homes, and day-care centers. For each type of child care, we compare the Mexican-American and white working wives and single parents to examine variation within each group. Like Auerbach (1975), we are concerned with the parents' perceptions of strategies, values, difficulties, and change in their overall child-care experiences.

Split-Shift Arrangements

Using a split shift, where each parent takes care of the children while the other works, best expresses the concerns of working mothers and their spouses for quality care, convenience, and reasonable cost. Besides maintaining family ties and easing financial burdens, other advantages of the split-shift arrangement mentioned by wives included not having to take children out in the morning, children's safety, and a general reduction of worry.

The decision to arrange a split shift was made easy if a couple's work schedules were already different before a child was born, as in the Mondragons' experience. The Mondragons had a nontraditional division of labor (see Chapter 6) because Edward was periodically unemployed, and their twenty-one-month-old daughter was too young for most day-care centers. Valerie worked on rotating shifts at HealthTech: two weeks on days, then two weeks on evenings. She described their initial adjustment when she started working at HealthTech:

> That was a mess. Because they told me I was going to be working nights, every two weeks, I would rotate.[2] So I couldn't really get a nursery, because nurseries, you have to pay for a whole month whether you come or not. It was a hassle because I'd have to pay for a month, and half that month I'd be working nights, and it's not very common to have a day-care center open nights. [So] we used a babysitter. When I finally went on nights and my husband was working days, then we didn't have to pay for a babysitter. And he would take her to his grandmother's house. Then he'd pick her up after work.

When her spouse was laid off, he began taking care of their daughter full time, and Valerie was satisfied with this arrangement: "I like it. It's a lot less pressure on me because he really takes the trouble, because it's his kid." Valerie would have been willing to place her child in a day-care center if it met her standards of licensing, location, diet, and supervision, but she realized that centers were not an option:

> My whole life changes when I go on nights. . . . I don't like it. I probably won't enjoy my job that much. . . . I'm not a night person. I have to be to bed by a certain time. And my little girl wakes up at 6:00 [A.M.], and if you come home at 12:30 [A.M.] and don't fall asleep till

---

[2] Technically speaking, the night (or third) shift is from 11:00 P.M. to 7:00 A.M. Valerie was working the evening (second) shift but preferred to call it the night shift.

1:30, that's not good for your health either. . . . I'd rather have a normal schedule, like a normal person.

It was Valerie's concerns about working the unusual shifts that led to her strong union support (see Chapter 5).

This couple preferred using a split shift, but once Edward began working again, they would have to call on kin or find a day-care provider when Valerie worked days. When Valerie went back on evenings, they could return to the split-shift arrangement, which met their concern with quality, was the most convenient option, and had the side benefit of low cost.

Of course wives experienced some disadvantages on the split-shift system. Elena Ortega, for example, said that her spouse let her two-year-old son "do whatever he wants. When I come home, this place is upside down, [*laughs*] and he doesn't tell him anything or, you know, help me pick up or anything; he just lets it go."

Establishing a split-shift arrangement became a greater strategic objective for those couples whose work schedules were not already synchronized; they often had to go through a series of other child care arrangements first. Of the twelve Hispano couples using split-shift day care, seven couples depended on relatives rather than care providers when they were both working. Most of the women who needed help with a split-shift arrangement got it from a mother, sister, or mother-in-law. Mexican-Americans had more female kin available to provide day care: about two-thirds of Hispano wives but only one-third of Anglo wives had mothers who were not in the labor force. In at least three cases, a Hispana's mother resolved the day-care problem after the birth of a child by volunteering to care for the newborn. Five of the thirteen white wives used a split-shift arrangement, and three combined a split-shift with part-time help from someone else. Only one Anglo couple used kin to supplement a split-shift arrangement.

Reliance on Close Kin

Those Hispano wives who used relatives for their child-care needs often felt strongly that their mothers or other female relatives provided the best care because they could be trusted and had had experience raising their own children. For example, the Thomases (a

Mexican-American woman married to an Anglo man), left their four-year-old daughter and 16-month-old son with Leona's mother (who lived next door). They considered their situation ideal. The mother initially refused any payment for day care but then agreed to accept $40 a week, which she used to buy diapers and other things for the children. Carl would drop off the children on his way to work, and Leona would pick them up in the afternoon. "The advantages are if the children are sick, I don't have to worry about it, I don't have to stay home from work. And if it snows, she just walks over here. . . . My mother will read to them, she plays games with them, she takes them to the movies, swimming. There's really no disadvantage." Leona said she would quit working if her mother were unavailable. But the combination of having her mother available for low-cost, quality day care, a spouse who shared transporting the children, and a work schedule which—thanks to Computex's flextime—allowed her to come in any time between 6:00 and 8:30 A.M. made Leona very satisfied with her day-care arrangements: "You can't have it better than that."

There were some difficulties in having a grandmother care for a small child. Lucia Benavides expressed a common complaint, that her children were "spoiled rotten." Another problem was conflict between women and their mothers-in-law over the children. For example, Josephine Perez, a migrant from a small New Mexico town, had no female kin of her own nearby but did have her mother-in-law, "someone who would be, you know, more loving. . . . She would buy [my daughter] clothes and toys, and I know she took care of her like she was her own child." Her mother-in-law, however, had become too possessive: "After a while she tried to take over completely. She would try and tell me how to take care of her, interfering with the way I was trying to raise her. So I didn't like that at all. But I've never told her anything." Manuel said, "The only disadvantage was [our daughter] seemed to be really confused as to who her mother really was. . . . We both felt it was a problem."

Nevertheless, the value of family was often expressed in terms of a contrast with and distinct mistrust of day-care centers and nurseries. Most of the women using kin made this judgment even though they had little direct experience with day-care centers. Prelinda Duran, for example, said that no one in her family had tried day-care centers, she was apprehensive about them: "You read so much; that's why it worries you. Like what happened up there . . . where the kids

[229]

were being abused? Well, you know." Nina Griego too had strong reservations: "I don't like to leave my kids with somebody I don't know. And if I can't take care of them or somebody that I know, I'd just quit."

It is somewhat surprising, in view of the importance of sisters to Hispano wives' social networks (see Chapter 8), that sisters did not play a larger role in the care of children. Often, however, that was because the burden was considered too much. Lucy Valdez had left children with her sister for a brief time but recalled that "it was kind of hard on her because she had three kids of her own, and then my three. That's when I couldn't even afford a babysitter." In addition, many of the sisters of Hispanas were also working and were therefore not available.

The one Mexican-American woman who did rely on her sisters was a single mother in an unusual situation. Maria Apodaca was a forty-one-year-old immigrant from Mexico, an abandoned wife with three children aged six, eight, and ten. At the time of our interview, Maria's seventeen-year-old sister from Mexico was living with her and provided after-school and, in summer, full-time child care (in addition to being a familiar person to her kids, Maria thought it important to give her sister this kind of responsibility). Maria had kept the care of her children either at home or within family. In the two years since her husband left her, she had taken in two other women from Mexico who took care of the children as partial rent payment. Maria's steadiest, most dependable child-care resources, however, were two other sisters—one of whom was a housewife—who also came from Mexico: "If I can't take them to one sister then I take them to another. . . . That's how I've done it up to now." The extensive use of sisters in Maria's case reflected an aspect of immigrant social organization: Maria provided a way for her sisters to migrate to the United States and to fulfill a need for her as well.

Six other Hispana single mothers also depended on close kin for day care. Four women had live-in arrangements with their mothers, two of whom were themselves divorced. The provision of child care in these cases was part of a family bonding that served the emotional interests of the caretaking grandmother as well as the practical interests of the young mother.

Annette Griego, who became pregnant at sixteen, began living with her divorced mother after her own marital separation and then her husband's suicide. Annette returned to work soon after the birth of her son in 1978; she described her day-care arrangements as having "always been in my family." Her younger brother and two sisters were in school, "so my mom did the watching." At first, with Annette working the day and her mother the graveyard shift, they worked out the same sort of split-shift arrangement as had many husbands and wives. Annette described one problem: "The baby at the time was sleeping a lot. He would wake up every three or four hours, so she would sleep with him, and then when he'd get up, she'd stick a bottle in his mouth . . . she'd get as much [sleep] in as she could. If she didn't get enough, she'd go to sleep before she'd leave for work, when I was home."

At the time of our interview, however, Annette's mother had moved to Los Lunas, twenty miles away, while Annette's sister— who herself alternated three shifts as manager of a fast food place— remained with her in the Albuquerque house. Annette was working the second shift at HealthTech, and her mother had changed to working days. Annette's complex child-care system involved her live-in sister and her mother in Los Lunas: "I take Eddie [to my mom's] at three [P.M.] . . . even when my sister works days . . . because when she works days, she gets off at five. So any day that she works during the week that I work nights, then I take him at three and drop him off, and my mom, on the way to work, drops him back off over here . . . in the early morning." When Annette worked days, her mother "picked him up, and for a while there, he'd have to stay a couple of days [at the Los Lunas house with other kin] and then come [back]. But now that she's on days [and I'm on nights], it's working to where she can just take him at night and then bring him back in the morning. So I see him every day." Annette explained that to alleviate the difficulty of this situation, she planned to move next door to her mother. Her son would come home after school and take care of himself until his grandmother got home: "That's what I'm planning on doing, is get a trailer next to my mom's. And my mom would be able to keep an eye on him and he'd be able to do for himself—if I ever ran into the problem, if nobody could take him . . . I could probably basically depend on my mom."

Carmen Archuleta's case illustrates that having her mother to provide child care can serve as a safety net for a young inexperienced mother yet can also cause pressure on the young woman and become an imposition on her caretaking mother. Carmen started working at Leslie Pants when her baby was three months old. Initially, her

[231]

mother, who had for some years cared for the children of Carmen's older sisters, chose not to assume responsibility for this baby: "She gets real tired." But then a series of crises occurred. Carmen had problems making the rate on a new job (see Chapter 4) and experienced a drop in pay; she changed her residence several times and finally moved in with her parents. Further, she discovered the inadequacy of the young woman taking care of Steve when the provider's seven-year-old daughter informed her that Steve was "a crybaby; my mom spanks him all the time." Carmen said, "I thought she was a good mother. Maybe she is to her own kids. Some people, you know, when it's not their kids, they just don't care that much. . . . A three-month-old baby should not be spanked." After this, Carmen's mother agreed to take care of Steve for $40 for forty hours per week. With babysitters, Carmen said she worried: "I could never sit down at ease; I was always wondering. But with my mom, you know, I go to work—nothing. I don't even call her during the day to see how he is because I know he's fine."

Still, Carmen felt constrained by living with her parents: "You always want your own domain; like now, you know, it's real hard." Carmen said her mother did not even like her in the kitchen and that she yearned for her own privacy: "That's what I miss the most; and, you know, it's hard with Stevie, [now two and a half] because he can't do anything he wants, you know; there's always limits. There would be limits anyway, but *your* limits." Besides the differences in parenting styles, Carmen was concerned for her son's peer socialization, and she decided to move out and enroll him in a nursery two days a week "as soon as things get better. . . . I feel better when I'm on my own." Given the pressure she felt living in her parents' house, Carmen's view of day-care centers was positive, even though her family had had no experience with them.

Unlike the majority of Mexican-American mothers, the greater portion of white mothers were migrants to the area from other states, so they had fewer neighboring relatives. None used sisters as full-time day care providers, and only one used her mother and another her mother-in-law. Maggie and Johnny Todd worked second (evening) shift at Southwest Electronics. Maggie's mother had been taking care of their one-year-old son since he was three months old: "She's only about three blocks away, you know; we have to pick him up so late at night that, you know, we don't have to lug him clear across town, which is nice . . . I like him at my mom's, yeah. There's always a lot of people in and out of the house, and he does real good with people." Maggie added, "And she had seven kids of her own— she knows what she's doing." She paid her mother $20 a week and provided diapers, food, and other baby needs. Maggie Todd's arrangement, like those of the Hispanas who preferred the use of close kin, combined loving care, convenience, and low cost.

There may be some evidence of ethnic difference in values regarding the use of kin as day-care providers. Not all Anglo women felt that their relatives were the most appropriate caretakers. For example, Sherrie Smith had exchanged child care with sisters and in-laws off and on, but even with relatives close by, she resorted mostly to day-care providers or a split shift and avoided using her mother: "My mother . . . said she had hers; I could take care of mine. . . . I have a funny family: a lot of them wouldn't be too useful." If any Hispanas felt such sentiments, none volunteered them in the interviews. Moreover, even white women who relied on relatives for day care did not exhibit the kind of bias against day-care centers that most of the Mexican Americans had. Connie Mead, for example, had had no experience with such centers; she said that she simply preferred someone personal for her baby but quickly added that nurseries would be fine once her daughter was older, "because of the socialization with kids, you know, being able to be around others."

Thus, Hispanas not only placed greater value on kin as child-care providers; they also had more kin available. In contrast, whatever their feelings about leaving children with relatives, most Anglo women were forced to depend on outside providers and day-care centers.

Nonrelated Day-Care Providers

For those women who were not able to arrange a split-shift form of child care and who did not have close kin available, the need to look for nonrelatives involved definite strategic choices. In all cases, they wanted a loving and caring individual who would take the children's and the parents' interests to heart.

Mothers found satisfactory day-care providers principally through someone else personally known to them. Lucy Valdez used her neighbor: "I was able to see her work with other kids and I really enjoyed the way she was babysitting other kids so that's how I got her." When her children were older, Lucy placed them in a city low-income preschool program, but, "I didn't like it, because the kids weren't happy. There were a lot of kids there." Though the preschool offered some advantages (such as potty training), she nevertheless changed to a person to whom she was referred by her church and who lived close by. Asked if she would use a day-care program, Lucy said, "If I didn't have to, I'd rather not. . . . I think they get more attention from a [provider]. I think kids need attention, I mean, you know, being the parents aren't there."

Among Anglo wives, more than a third (five of thirteen), relied on day-care providers, compared with only four of twenty-four Mexican-American wives. Yet like Hispana mothers, white mothers found day care primarily through personal references. The testimony of Ann Singleton suggests that in a neighbor, a friend, a friend's relative, or a hired provider, she looked for a replication of the home environment, a personal loving commitment to the child, and reasonable cost. Ann was an Albuquerque native whose mother worked full time and whose other relatives and in-laws lived out of state. She tried several options for their two-year-old daughter, including a home day-care provider and a day-care center. Then

> we turned her over to my mother's neighbor. I've known her for a while. She's about the same age as I am, and she took excellent care of Jessica. We'll never find anybody who takes as good care of her as she did. . . . She had [a] boy, a year younger . . . well, she took care of Jessica just like one of her own. She did things with both of them. . . . It was like they were both her children. That's the way she took care of them both. She was immaculate. She'd take them places and do things with them and play with them and stuff like that.

Ann was forced to find another provider because this one entered the labor market: "I haven't found another babysitter who was that loving."

While sometimes there were benefits with children being kept in the care of a loving provider, women found problems as well. Mary and Don Pike, who both worked at Leslie Pants on the day shift, used their neighbor, a former co-worker, to care for their four-month-old daughter. They paid her $30 a week and provided diapers and food. Mary said: "Once in a while I get a little jealous because the baby will cry when I hold her, and I'll have to hand her to [the

[234]

neighbor], and she'll just talk to her, and she'll start smiling at her. Once in a while I feel like, you know." Yet Mary realized that despite missing her daughter, "it's nice being able to get away from her and coming home. I think I've gotten closer to her since I go and leave her. When I come home, I love her to pieces. I think she gets more attention from me coming home from work than she did when I was there with her all day." Don was generally satisfied with this arrangement as well: "I like that she's right there, she's someone we've known for a while. We can trust her and she has her own kids. Even when she's not there, her mother lives there, so there's always someone to watch [the children]." Mary preferred to leave her child with this care provider rather than with her own mother, because her mother "raised me real well, but I just want to raise [my daughter] in my own way." If the day-care provider were no longer available, Mary and Don would look for another babysitter who lived in the neighborhood. They had no aversion to day-care centers but preferred to wait until their child was older before taking her to a center, because "I don't think they would get the personal attention that a little baby needs."

Proportionately more single parents relied on kin for day care than married women did, especially the younger single mothers, but older single parents tended to use day-care providers. All six of the single mothers who did so lived independently, and their average age was thirty-two. Three of them were Hispanas and native to the Albuquerque area, and three were Anglo migrants.

Like the testimony of married mothers, that of single parents makes clear that when it is necessary to work, the hope is to find a substitute home environment with quality care, and the belief is that these qualities are most likely to be found through a connection to someone known personally. Twenty-eight-year-old Susan Anaya's son Jason was born nine months before our interview with her; she had chosen not to marry the father and had returned to Southwest Electronics when her son was seven months old (see Chapter 6). The only day-care arrangement she had had was with the mother of a close work-related friend, who had offered to care for the baby. As Susan explained: "I was very fortunate because . . . I have Tracy's mom, and she's a real sweet lady. She just couldn't wait for Jason to come . . . because she wanted a baby around the house. And she has helped me a lot. If I can't pay her that week, she'll say, 'Well, wait to pay me next week or wait till Monday.' And instead of me using

Pampers all the time . . . when Jason's over there, she uses diapers, cloth diapers. She's got a washer, and she washes them. . . . She buys all the food that he eats over there. . . . They're really good people. I thank God; I was lucky." Susan paid Tracy's mother $20 a week for forty hours of care. Susan also needed the help of her sister, because the babysitter lived somewhat out of the way: "See, what happens is my sister goes out [that way to work], so she picks Jason up for me. I'm lucky in a lot of ways. So when she's going by there anyway, she drops him off at Tracy's mom's and then Tracy picks me up." Susan was applying for a low-income loan for a house that would place her closer to her babysitter.

Two of the single parents who used day-care providers were not enthusiastic about day-care centers. Patricia Torres, for example, had experienced problems with babysitters and had had only a brief experience with a nursery, yet she said of nurseries, "I don't like them, no. They charge too much and, I don't know, I like a little more attention . . . [they have] children all together."

All three of the Anglo single parents used day-care providers. In their mid- or late thirties, these women were considerably older than the average in our sample and had relied on day-care providers as their primary child-care strategy throughout their relatively long work histories.

Betty Thompson, thirty-seven, had older teenage children, and her youngest was two. Betty had a hearsay bias against day-care centers, fearing illnesses, "bad habits," and the large child-caretaker ratio. While married and living in Minnesota, Betty had employed teenage girls for day care, and at one point a friend who lived with her had kept the children while Betty worked. Her youngest child was born after she divorced her spouse. Returning to work two months later, she took up her previous strategy of employing neighboring teenage girls. Betty was able to use her two older daughters for child care during periods between babysitters until they, like their two older brothers, went to live with their father. Betty said, "Then I found a babysitter where I could take the baby to her . . . she lived on the way to work. I could drop the baby off and pick her up afterwards." This arrangement cost Betty $40 a week. Of the various types of child care she'd used, Betty said she preferred a live-in: "The little ones stay in their familiar surroundings. They don't feel so insecure."

[236]

Even though Betty had used teenagers, her ideal provider would have conformed to a stereotype:

> I would love to find an old lady from Mexico, and she's almost starving to death down there, and bring her in here to live. She could be like a nanny. And from what I hear, they do a lot of work. They're cheap; they're clean. I wouldn't want no young one because then they'd . . . want to go out. From what I hear, these older ladies are terrific. But you can't do that because that's against the law.

Such a strategy might have been possible in a U.S.-Mexico border community like El Paso (Ruiz 1983), only four hours' drive to the south, but with Albuquerque's relatively small immigrant community, it was not an option.

Day-Care Centers

On the basis of interviews conducted in San Francisco, Auerbach (1975:139–40) reported that working mothers wanted from child care centers "the assurance that the centers care about them and their children as human beings; and so strong is this need, that it almost doesn't matter what the program contains. . . . They want a safe, bright, cheerful place with a loving, knowledgeable staff willing and able to give their children individual attention. . . . They need day care operators who show compassion and genuine interest in their children." These expectations were echoed by the few interviewees in our study who used day-care centers in Albuquerque. Only three of twenty-four Hispano wives in our sample and very few Anglo wives relied on day-care centers for the primary care of children while they and their husbands worked.

Besides their qualms about a probable high child-caretaker ratio and its negative effect on individual attention to the children, a principal reason why most of these women did not choose day-care centers was their unavailability in the areas where our Hispano interviewees lived. In an attempt to help its women workers find day care, Computex had provided a comprehensive list, which shows that thirty-three of sixty-four day-care centers and seventeen of thirty-eight licensed home-care providers were located in the northeast quadrant of the city—the Heights, which is predominantly Anglo and middle class. Only two of our twenty-four Hispano wives and

[237]

nine of thirteen Anglo wives lived there. Twelve Hispano wives and twelve of the fifteen single parents lived in Albuquerque's southwest quadrant (the South Valley), which had only six (9 percent) of the day-care centers on the list and five (13 percent) of the home-care providers. A fourth of our Hispano wives (six) lived in the northwest quadrant (the North Valley), which had only 16 percent of Albuquerque's day-care centers. Undoubtedly, the bias expressed by so many of our Hispano interviewees was related to the scarcity of such facilities in the sections of the city where they could most likely find affordable housing.

Another reason was the lack of evening care. Of sixty-three centers for which data are available only five offered service during evening hours, and only seven of thirty-six home providers did so. Finally, the cost of center care was relatively high: in 1982–83, for children under two, the average weekly fee among forty-nine centers was $44.61; for thirty home-care providers it was $31.77.

Given these disadvantages, it appears that wives will turn to day-care centers and nurseries under two conditions: first, when other alternatives have been closed off (by the impossibility of arranging a split-shift schedule with the husband, the unavailability of close kin, or perhaps bad experiences with private babysitters); second, when parents come to value peer socialization and education for their pre-school children.

The average age of youngest child among the three Hispanas who did use day-care centers or nurseries was almost three. Two of these women were native to Albuquerque, with mothers and close kin nearby; the third had migrated from a small northern New Mexico town. All three were relatively satisfied with their day-care arrangements.

Socorro Peña had in fact previously used her mother for the care of both her children. They were seven and three years old when we interviewed her, but the baby had been only eight months when Socorro got her Computex job. At that time she was living with her mother, having just returned from California while her husband served in the Marine Corps. Socorro said that originally her mother was "talking of wanting to get a job herself" but that instead, she told Socorro, "No, I'll go ahead and take care of the kids. . . . You go ahead and go work." For this reason, Socorro felt that she did not want to accept her mother's sacrifice for too long, and she moved out of her mother's house shortly before Computex distributed its informational packet on child-care centers in Albuquerque. When it came out, "I went to this book and I started calling people, and I went and talked to them and everything, and then I found one. . . . It's their personal home in the back; towards the side, they have a nursery. And she's licensed and everything."

Socorro praised Computex for providing the informational service and found the fee she was paying reasonable: $25 a week for full-time care for the younger child and one hour after school each day for the older. Her children liked the nursery, especially her son: "He thinks he's going to a school you know, cause she teaches them . . . shows them how to draw shapes . . . puts like Mr. Rogers on, educational-type things for them to watch, which is really good."

Each of two Anglo mothers using day-care centers had only one child, two and a half years old. Both had moved with their husbands to Albuquerque from out of state in the 1970s. Both would have preferred not to use day care centers because of past experiences with contagious diseases. For example, Lynn Connelly, returning to work a year after the birth of her daughter, had needed two hours of care a day and so decided on a children's center. She quit the center after only two weeks, however, because "they refused to let [my daughter] use the toilet since she wasn't two years old. And I got furious. And she kept getting sick because . . . their young children's room wasn't exactly as clean as it should have been, and the kids were coming in sick, and mouthing all over the toys, and then the other kids would put them in their mouths, you know. . . . [They picked up] eye infections and ear infections and everything else under the sun because they had so many children and not enough teachers." Lynn also complained about the lack of adequate discipline: "Deeana developed a terrible attitude, very sarcastic. She didn't have to do anything. She refused to talk. She'd grunt and point. Deeana had a very good vocabulary, she always has. It made me pretty angry that they didn't discipline her at all and they didn't make her talk. She could just . . . cry, kick, anything she wanted." Lynn then got a friend to watch her daughter: "I didn't particularly want her to do it, but she was better than the nursery." Lynn paid her friend $30 a week for two months but said she did not "particularly care for the way she raises her [own] youngster." Lynn said she quit work at this point because her daughter developed a serious eye infection which, she was convinced, was the result of conditions at the day nursery.

[239]

When she went to work at Leslie Pants in 1981, Lynn placed Deeana in a large day-care center. She said this place was better than the other: "They have a lot of supervision. . . . She does real good there, and the lady who runs her class is real good with her. . . . But Deeana is a little bit too advanced for the stuff that they go into, and they won't allow her to be moved up a grade to the three-year-old class . . . and it's not doing anything for her intellectual stimulation. . . . Deeana regresses quite a bit every time I put her into day care." Reflecting, Lynn thought that her sister-in-law would provide the right combination of care, discipline, and learning environment that she wanted, "but her youngest baby isn't quite out of diapers yet, and I don't want to burden her with another child. . . . [Deeana] loves her aunt, and . . . her kids—well Allie her oldest—is about on the same mentality level as Dee. She's about 7 months older than she is. . . . She enjoys having them and teaching them at the same time, with a good amount of discipline, but not overly disciplined. I would just prefer Lisa to do it, but it's just impossible right now. . . . She lives on the base and we live way over here, and it's just too much . . . on an everyday basis."

Other Anglo women, though not using day-care centers at the time of our interviews, spoke favorably about them. Ann Singleton, whose only child was two, had had difficulties with several babysitters and recalled "all kinds of advantages" to a center she had used in the past: "She got to play with children her own age; got a lot of fresh air during that time, you know, she'd get outside all the time. She had good care. The ladies were good."

The two single mothers who were using day-care centers had been reluctant initially but were eventually satisfied because of the quality of the care. Betty Saiz, who worked at Southwest Electronics, was at a transitional point in her child-care arrangement when we interviewed her. Her six-year-old daughter had just completed kindergarten and had been going to a group care center in the mornings. Her five-year-old son had been cared for by a Mormon family but was preparing for kindergarten and so would also soon be enrolled in his sister's center. At first, Betty had been hesitant:

> I was so afraid to take my kids to a nursery; I just didn't want to do it. . . . I worked in a nursery for about two weeks and . . . I was told not to tell the parents whether the kids were happy; whether they had eaten; you know, "Their life there was perfect." And I didn't agree with

that, because the kids weren't always happy; they didn't always get their food. They sat them down, if they ate, fine; if they didn't, they didn't care to make sure that they ate well. . . . They were told to sleep: "Go to sleep!" It's not the way you raise children.

However when it became inconvenient to continue taking the children to the Mormon family that had been caring for both of them, Betty turned to the center that several of her co-workers were using. Asked for the difference between this center and the one where she had worked, Betty said that "a lot of the people that I work with have their kids there, and it's like a family. . . . I think the people that are taking care of them do become attached to the kids . . . and they're kind to my kids. That's all that matters, if they love them, and are kind to them. . . . Oh, I'd rather have a family, the reason being that [my kids] don't have a mother and father, you know, at the same place."

The contrast to nurseries in Betty's mind were the two Mormon families she had found through friends. As an example of the quality of their care, Betty mentioned that Monday night was "family night," and "they spend a lot of time with their kids; that was really good." Betty's strategy when she first became a new single parent in need of child care stemmed from the fact that she had been estranged from her own family. Having found a job at Southwest Electronics when her son was five months old, she placed a newspaper advertisement, "Loving family wanted to care for two children," which was answered by a woman Betty still considered a close friend. Betty gave her advice on advertising for a sitter: "It depends on the wording. You find 'Babysitter: cheapest rate available . . .' That won't bring anything, but if you specify what you want and talk to the person and see how they are coping, then it's okay."

Sometimes a day-care center was only part of the complicated arrangements that women with unusual work schedules had to construct. Donna Garcia (see Chapter 6) worked at SystemsPlus six hours on Wednesday afternoons and twelve hours on Thursdays, Fridays, and Saturdays. Her husband also worked unusual hours: on Mondays, Tuesdays, and Wednesdays from 1:00 to 10:00 P.M.; on Thursdays and Fridays from 8:00 A.M. to 5:00 P.M. As a result, the Garcias used a combination of the split-shift, a nursery on a part-time basis, and Donna's mother for half a day a week. On Wednesday afternoons Donna's mother would take care of the girls until Jimmy could pick them up after work; on Thursdays and Fridays the girls attended a nursery for a few hours until Jimmy picked them up; on Saturdays Jimmy was home to take care of them; on Sundays both parents were off; then on Mondays, Tuesdays, and half of Wednesdays Donna would take care of them. Even so, there were difficulties. "Sometimes," Donna said, "my husband has to work late—he has a meeting that runs over—and . . . I don't get out of work until six, so I have to call my mom and ask her to pick up the kids, which she doesn't really mind. But it's just a disadvantage, you know." While Donna Garcia preferred the three-and-a-half-day week because it enabled her to get her domestic duties done (she had a traditional division of labor but was pushing for more help from her spouse) such an unusual work shift was possible only with the help of her spouse, kin, and a day-care center.

Early in the chapter we suggested that especially for younger children, loving attention and convenience are just as important to parents as the cost of day care. This point was illustrated by the complex strategies developed by women. Their testimonies support Auerbach's (1975) point concerning the importance of the quality of the care working mothers seek for their children. Split-shift arrangements, representing the optimal combination of care, convenience, and cost effectiveness, embody an important change; mothers and fathers sharing responsibility for the care of their children. In our study, more Hispano than Anglo couples were in circumstances that allowed them to provide for the care of their children between themselves.

Yet it is rare that parents' schedules permit the split shift as the exclusive form of day care, and so strategies must be devised to fill the gaps of time. We found that women's mothers or mothers-in-law took on a significantly greater amount of child care than sisters or other close kin, but that this relationship—especially for single mothers—was not without its pressures and its limits. More Hispanas than the predominantly migrant Anglos had kin available to call on for child care. In the absence of available relatives, making contact with a care provider or a center was often achieved through a mother's personal connections, allowing her to feel some trust in the stranger who cared for her children.

As we have seen, finding adequate care for young children enables women to fulfill their obligations as full-time workers and thus helps mediate the contradiction they face as workers and mothers. The women we interviewed had definite values and clear notions about what constitutes quality care, and preferences for the type of day care, depending on the age of the child. Our informants had limited options for replacing their labor within Albuquerque: the number and quality of day-care centers was limited; they were geographically concentrated in areas away from those where most of our Mexican-American informants resided; and there were few that remained open in the evenings, which greatly restricted their utility for women who worked evening or rotating shifts. Further, some women had had problems or had heard of problems with day-care centers. Given these constraints, many women (and their husbands) found that replacing their own labor with that of kin was preferable. Those working mothers who could not rely on relatives chose day-care providers on the basis of referrals from kin or friends, often taking chances that everything would work out, occasionally having to change their arrangements to accommodate changes in their work schedules or their children's needs. Clearly, finding quality day care was an ongoing "juggling act" for these women.

[8]

Kin, Friends, and Husbands:
Support Networks for Working Mothers

In the last two chapters we have analyzed the ways that women faced the contradictory nature of being full-time workers and mothers: reworking the division of labor around child-care tasks and household chores outside of working hours, and replacing their reproductive labor by finding ways to have young children taken care of during working hours. This chapter deals with another important range of tasks and support. These are not the everyday pressing arrangements that replace a mother's reproductive labor; they are the more occasional needs, both instrumental and emotional, that involve calling on kin and friends as well as a husband or partner. We think of this bundle of tasks and requests for advice and communication as a working mother's support system.

In our second interview with working wives, husbands, and single mothers, we asked about relationships with parents and siblings, godparents, friends, and neighbors; their residential location and our interviewees' frequency of contact (phone calls, letters, visits) with them; and who from this list participated in the exchange of goods and services. We found four kinds of support that working families often need and exchange: (1) financial support (borrowing and lending money); (2) household support (borrowing a car, borrowing clothes or furniture, help with car or household repairs, yard work, or pet care); (3) child-care support (babysitting or caring for sick children); and (4) emergency support (temporary residence or care during an illness). We saw these exchanges between working families and their relatives, friends, and neighbors as instrumental support.

We also asked working mothers and husbands who they would ask for advice concerning personal issues, work, finances, their marriage, or child rearing. We view this as emotional support for working mothers and their partners.

These are important issues for all working mothers, but we argue that working-class women have fewer financial resources for dealing with household, child care, and financial needs that come up on an irregular basis. Middle-class and professional working mothers often have more discretionary income and can purchase such services as live-in day care, cleaning, and yard work; they can pay for counseling to deal with job stress and marital problems. This is made quite clear in Arlie Hochschild's study *The Second Shift*: many of her informants had day-care providers who came to their homes (more expensive than using relatives, day-care centers, or care providers who work in their own homes); others hired full-time maids (1989:99, 116, 159). Middle-class women can pick up prepared food from the deli and send out the laundry, whereas working-class women do more of the work themselves or share it with their husbands and, for occasional tasks, kin and friends. They engage in exchanges in situations where middle-class women make purchases. In other words, working-class women forge exchange networks among kin, friends, co-workers, and neighbors. The practice of everyday life and mediating the contradictions between family and work means both calling for and giving support within the network.

The pioneering work of Elizabeth Bott (1957) and Michael Young and Peter Willmott (1957) demonstrated the ways in which social networks, composed primarily of extended family members, were important for British working-class families. Mothers and daughters emerged as particularly strong dyads. Carol Stack's (1974) study of urban black families in the United States documented the importance of social networks for poor families. Women emerged as crucial in swapping goods and services and in child care. Mothers were often the central focus of social networks composed of daughters, sisters, and male kin in a number of dispersed households.

While these studies have highlighted the economic and social functions of kin networks, Sylvia Yanagisako has emphasized the cultural and symbolic processes that lie behind women-centered networks. Among second-generation Japanese-American families the ideal of nuclear family independence became important, assigning men to "outside" and women to "inside" roles. But women's roles

[245]

included the creation of links between households: "As symbolic representatives of the affective and domestic domains, women could establish close solidary ties without threatening the economic and jural independence of nuclear families" (1977:219). In a similar vein, di Leonardo (1987) has argued that women facilitate communication and family organization by doing "kinship work": sending Christmas cards, organizing holiday rituals, and keeping relatives in touch with one another.

All these studies have shown that kin networks are often female centered, based on close relationships between a woman, her sisters, and her mother; that they have both instrumental and cultural functions; and that they are particularly important for working-class women and women from diverse ethnic and racial backgrounds. These researchers have not focused on the support systems of working mothers, however, nor do they integrate data on friends and kin into the same study. While the literature on kin networks emphasizes their women-centered nature, much of the literature on friendship focuses on gender contrasts—the differences between women's friendships and men's. Women emphasize trust, self-revelation, nurturance, and intimacy in their friendships and talk about family and personal matters. Men tend to be less expressive in their friendships, to talk about impersonal things such as sports, politics, and business, and to share activities rather than intimate conversation (Aries and Johnson 1983; Davidson and Duberman 1982; Fox, Gibbs, and Auerback 1985; Pogrebin 1987, Rubin 1985; Wright 1982).

But again these studies on friendship do not deal with the role of friends in working-women's lives, and many studies lump middle-class and working-class responses together, so that it is not clear how male-female differences in friendship may be constructed among working-class or ethnic women and men. Our study of two contrasting working-class populations, which does combine data on friendship and kinship, also helps to counter the middle-class bias of the literature.

Patricia Zavella's research on Chicano seasonal women workers paved the way for our interest in female friendships among working-class women. In summarizing her data on the importance of both friends and kin (1987:160), she says:

> Friendships established at work were clearly important to my informants. Women's work friends were in similar situations, and therefore

they could understand each other's problems. My data do not contradict the familistic behavior previously reported for Chicanos. Rather, women enlarged support networks to include friends from work. Those Chicanas who had nearby relatives relied on kin and friends; those who did not relied on friends. I suggest that friendship networks are more important than previously noted and that we examine the conditions under which Chicanos expand kinship networks to include friends, work mates, and neighbors.

Using Zavella's conclusions as a base, we were able to differentiate the roles friends and kin play in providing instrumental exchange and emotional support.

Other literature has led us to suspect that the networks women construct are sensitive to a local political economy and patterns of migration. For example, in Central Falls, Rhode Island, in 1977, recent Colombian immigrant families were in the process of reassembling their kin networks by bringing parents and siblings to the United States, while Portuguese couples were experiencing the dispersal of their kin networks. On arrival, Colombian immigrant women had been relatively isolated and relied on employers, ethnic acquaintances, and impersonal sources to obtain housing, jobs, and other support. Portuguese immigrants, by contrast, had come to Rhode Island through relatives already located there and were initially able to use kin connections to find jobs and housing. The local economy, however, with a number of plant closings and layoffs during the recession years of the mid-1970s, had forced siblings to move to new towns in order to find jobs. Kin were being pushed apart and thus were often unavailable for support (Lamphere 1987).

These findings are similar to those of Keefe and Padilla's study (1987:166) of Mexican, Mexican-American, and Anglo networks in the Santa Barbara, California, area. First-generation Mexican immigrants had relatively few kin and friends, compared with second- and third-generation Mexican Americans, who could rely on a large pool of relatives, friends, and neighbors. Native-born Mexicans who had come to the United States as children had a local kin network and relations with friends and neighbors approximating that of second- and third-generation Mexican-Americans. Yet even the recent Mexican immigrants had a larger pool of relatives than did Anglos in the same neighborhoods. These Anglos (who had higher incomes and were probably more middle class) were much more isolated from kin;

[247]

friends, co-workers, and neighbors made up a larger proportion of their potential contacts.

There may be subtle cultural differences in the value accorded the proximity of kin. Keefe (1984:68) argues that both Anglos and Mexican Americans value extended family ties, but "Mexican Americans value the physical presence of family members while Anglo-Americans are satisfied with intermittent meetings with kin supplemented by telephone calls and letters." She stresses that Mexican Americans were likely to settle in one geographic place and remain there for several generations, whereas most of Keefe and Padilla's white respondents had not been born in California, and almost half had lived in town less than ten years. Clearly, in their study, international migration had disrupted kin networks and forced recent Mexican immigrants to rely on a small number of kin, friends, co-workers, and neighbors. Migration for Anglos (primarily middle class) had created a similar pattern but with even lower numbers of locally available kin and greater reliance on friends. Residential stability for second- and third-generation Mexican Americans in this case created larger kin networks, but friends and co-workers added important supplementary support.[1]

On the basis of these studies and our own findings, we argue that working mothers constructed their support networks from their available kin, acquaintances, and friends in Albuquerque. The persons available depended upon (1) a woman's migration history (whether she was native to Albuqerque, arrived as a child and went to school in the city, or came to the city as an adult); (2) the demography of her family of orientation (the number of her brothers and sisters, the pattern of divorce and death for her parents and siblings, and so on); and (3) her job experience and length of time at her 1982 workplace, which created the possibility of making friends at work. (Husbands' networks, although we will give less attention to them in this chapter, were shaped by the same three factors.)

We view a woman's network as having three major components: the wife's primary kin (her mother, father, sisters, and brothers), her in-laws (the husband's primary kin) and her friends. We identified

---

[1] These data are based on potential contacts. Keefe and Padilla do not include tables on actual exchanges; they do say that these are chiefly with spouse's primary kin, not with the more distant aunts, uncles, and cousins who make up a large part of the "secondary kin" category.

four different kinds of networks. In "plural networks" a woman and her husband had forged a network in which exchanges, advice, and support were relatively evenly distributed among the three categories: primary kin, in-laws and friends. All three corners of the triangle were important. In a second kind, "wife's kin-focused networks," the working mother relied particularly on her primary kin, with the husband's relatives playing a very minor role; nevertheless friends remained important for her. In some cases, migration to Albuquerque had given particular prominence to the wife's relatives. Most of the plural and wife's kin-focused networks were large, since either or both husband and wife had many siblings in Albuquerque. In contrast, the other two types, "in-law-centered" and "friend-centered" networks, were smaller and less interconnected. Again, migration to Albuquerque, particularly by the wife, had affected both their size and shape.

In general, we found that the support networks of all working mothers were woman-centered but that Mexican-American women relied on mothers, sisters, and work friends, white women on mothers and friends. Furthermore, there was a functional specialization among members of the network. Mothers provided support for child-rearing problems, friends for work issues, and both husbands and friends for general emotional support. Friends, many of them met at the workplace, turned out to be much more important than the literature on working-class women suggests, confirming Patricia Zavella's earlier findings. Within these general parameters there was a great deal of variability in the way both Hispano and Anglo women constructed and utilized their support networks. These variations have implications for the ways we theorize difference as it emerges in the lives of working mothers.

The Plural Networks of Hispana Working Mothers

The Bacas had a plural support network that was female-centered and combined her extended family, his primary relatives, and a number of friends—especially two of Delores's friends from her workplace, and others from Albert's connections. They offered the best example of a plural network constructed from a large number of kin, many living in the same neighborhood, whose support functions were supplemented by work friendships.

[249]

Delores came from a large family of nine children. She and her husband and their baby daughter lived next door to her parents in Bernalillo, the small town north of Albuquerque where she had grown up. This residential decision meant that her primary and secondary relatives lived nearby or were part of the immediate neighborhood. Two older brothers (one married) lived in mobile homes on land they had bought in a trailer park about a mile away. A third brother lived with his wife and daughter elsewhere in Bernalillo. Four other sisters and a brother were still members of her parents' household. Two of her father's sisters lived next door; a paternal uncle and a maternal aunt had houses about a block away. Both sets of grandparents had lived close by (though her father's parents were deceased by 1982), and several great-aunts were part of the neighborhood.

Delores had an intense and often conflicting relationship with her twenty-four-year-old sister, Connie, primarily over the sister's treatment of her son, Jason, whom Connie had left in the care of her parents during her early years as a single parent. Delores was very close to her next younger sister, Maria, who was twenty years old in 1982. Maria also worked for Leslie Pants, a job she got when Delores took her application to the personnel manager, and the two of them drove to work together each day.

Like many other Mexican-American women, Delores's female-centered network was functionally differentiated. She utilized kin primarily for exchanges and asked friends (who were her co-workers at Leslie Pants) for advice and emotional support. Despite the conflict with Connie, all of Delores's sisters and most of her brothers were mentioned in answers to questions about exchanges. She had borrowed money from nineteen-year-old Lucia, lent money to Connie, and exchanged clothes often with Maria. Her sisters often babysat, and she went on errands with Maria and Rose. Her brother Pat installed a stereo for her, and her youngest brother Art helped Albert repair and clean the car.

Although she had not been close to her mother during her stormy teenage years, she said, "We get along a lot better now that I've gotten married." Her father had been a strict disciplinarian, but her more distant relationship with him, too, had mellowed since her marriage. She saw her parents daily and occasionally ate dinner at their house. Her mother took care of Delores's six-month-old baby while she was at work, as well as two other grandchildren. Her mother had given the couple a lot of furniture, and the Bacas had given Delores's mother $50 to help out with a particularly high electric bill. Relatives played important roles as godparents. Delores's father's sister who lived in back of her parents' house was her godmother for her baptism. Her brother John and sister-in-law Diane were wedding godparents (*padrinos*). Delores was the *madrina* of Connie's son Jason. Friends were also important in these roles: her husband's friend Ruben and his wife (who was also one of Delores's best friends) were the *padrinos* for the Bacas' daughter's baptism. And Delores was the *madrina* for her friend Margaret's son Joe.

Delores's three best friends included two other women who worked at Leslie Pants. Demetria was part of her lunch group of seven women, six of whom were Spanish from New Mexico; the seventh was from Mexico. This group of women also celebrated one another's birthdays. "We get along real good. . . . Somebody brings the cake, and we just have cake and buy a Coke or whatever, but we give each other a gift." Delores sat next to Demetria, and they both worked on belt loops. They also went to home decorating parties together and often visited outside work. "She's a real good person," Delores commented.

Her second work friend, Margaret, had been a high school friend; they became reacquainted when both started to work at Leslie Pants. Margaret sometimes dropped by Delores's home for a visit. "We have fun together. Before we got married I used to go everywhere with Margaret. I used to babysit for her, her and her husband John; they used to go out, and do things, and I used to babysit. I've gotten to be real close to her."

Rebecca, her wedding godmother, was married to Ruben, Albert's close friend, whom he had met at work. Delores recounted how she had met her future husband through Ruben: "My brother Pat used to work with Ruben . . . so I got introduced to Ruben with Pat. . . . And then from Ruben he introduced me to Albert." Later Albert introduced Delores to Rebecca, who would sometimes babysit for the Bacas, and the two couples usually visited once a week and planned to go camping.

As was typical of the Hispanas we interviewed, Delores relied on her friends for advice. For personal or marital problems, she said she would seek out Rebecca or Margaret. She would not usually confide in her mother. "Once in a while I'll tell my Mom something, but I don't like to get her too much involved in that because I don't like

[251]

for her to turn against Albert or something. But once I'll tell her something, and she'll tell me, 'Ah, all men are alike.'" For problems at work, Delores would turn to Demetria. "Demetria and I really communicate. All of us ladies together. We're always bitching about this and that." When she was feeling down and needed to talk, Delores usually sought out Demetria. "When I get, like in the morning sometimes I get up, and if something's happened between me and Albert and it's bothering me, I talk to Demetria at work. . . . She's a real good friend to me." For other kinds of advice and support, however, her parents were important. Delores said she would consult her parents about financial problems and her mother about child rearing. This preference for using parents or a mother-in-law for a sounding board concerning financial and child-rearing issues was also a common way in which emotional support was functionally differentiated for our Hispana interviewees.

Albert was well integrated into Delores's network. He saw her parents every day and felt close to his mother-in-law, "She's always given me a lot of support." He was more ambivalent about Delores's father. "With him, too, [I am close, except] he ain't nobody to work with. He's really . . . you got to do it his way or no way, you know." When asked how he liked living next door to his in-laws, Albert replied, "There ain't no problem. They don't hassle us. If me and Delores have an argument, you know, it's our argument. They don't come over here and get in it. I like it. It's pretty comfortable." Of all the members of Delores's family, he got along and could communicate best with Connie, but was also close to Art, who lived at their house: "In case anything happens, you know, he can just run across the street."

Albert had important contacts with his own primary kin, and Delores herself was frequently in touch with Albert's mother, who was divorced. Albert saw his mother about three times a week: "I talk to her every day on the phone, you know. . . . When I go to my mom's, I mainly go so she can see my daughter . . . so she can spend some time with her . . . and spoil her her way." Delores said she got along well with her mother-in-law: "Albert's mom's been kind of sick, so we call her almost every day." Delores mentioned that they had lent money to Albert's mother, that her mother-in-law often babysat, and that she would certainly call her for advice if the baby were sick.

Albert did not know all of Delores' relatives and acquaintances in the neighborhood where she had grown up and where they lived in

1982, but, he was involved in more exchanges with his in-laws than with his own family (though he did lend money to his mother and brother). He was helping remodel his mother-in-law's kitchen with her brothers; he often repaired Connie's and Maria's cars and sometimes borrowed Connie's. He borrowed tools from Delores's brothers, as well as from his friend Ruben.

Albert Baca was one of only two Mexican-American husbands who relied on his male friends rather than his wife for emotional support, though she, her mother, and her brothers were important for several kinds of advice. His three closest friends were all men he had met through various jobs and whom he often saw outside the workplace—"every weekend whenever we can get away from the old ladies." Since his best friend, Ruben was married to Rebecca, who has become a good friend of Delores, the two couples often socialized together. In seeking advice, Albert turned to his friends and one of his younger brothers but also relied on Delores's brother Pat for financial advice and his mother-in-law (as well as his own mother) for child-rearing advice. He would talk with Delores herself about marital or child-rearing problems. From Albert's point of view, his three friends were a kind of "countervailing weight" to his wife's family, and he would rely on them when he was feeling down.

Delores Baca had forged a support network revolving around her mother, sisters, and work friends. If Albert's ties are considered as well, the couple's network was wife-dominated, since the Bacas lived next door to Delores's parents, and Albert was well integrated into her family. Albert still had important contacts and exchanges with his own mother and siblings, however, and spent a good deal of time with male friends. We have called this a "plural network" because, from the wife's point of view, it included three segments: her kin, her in-laws, and her work friends. Since Delores had been a lifelong resident of Bernalillo, kin ties were coterminous with neighborhood ties. Finally, both kin and close friends had been given important roles as godparents.

Valerie Mondragon's support system was another example of a plural network, but one in which the husband's relatives emerged as important because, in 1982, the couple lived in the same house as his mother and father. In contrast to the Bacas, Valerie was more integrated into Edward's network than vice versa, but she was still in close contact with her mother, sister, and brother. Since she had only two siblings and Edward was an only child, the Mondragons'

[253]

network was smaller than the Bacas', and they relied more on each other and their parents for advice and support.

As in Delores's network, Valerie's work-related friends were an important third component; Edward, however (unlike Albert Baca), rarely called on his friends but relied instead on his wife, especially for emotional support. Valerie's closest friend was Anita, who had lived four houses away when they were in high school together. "She's the baby-sitter for my little girl, and she takes real good care of her. And she's a good friend. I've known her a long time now." Other friends were Debbie, whom she had met on a previous job, and Lucille, who also worked at HealthTech. Valerie's team members at work were very important to her. They ate together every day and were all invited to her brother's wedding. Valerie would consult one team member, Diane, about personal problems but go to her team facilitator if work problems came up. Valerie relied on her husband to discuss marital or financial problems, consulted her mother about child rearing, and relied on her sister for emotional support when she was feeling down.

Like most Hispano husbands, Edward had a much more constricted network. His best friends were Manuel, whom he had known for twelve years, and Manuel's wife. His third friend was Anita's husband, Andres. His friends were not part of his exchange network, however, nor were they important to him for advice and emotional support. He would ask his parents' advice on personal problems, work problems, and child rearing, but, like twelve other Mexican-American husbands, he would turn to his wife when he was feeling down: "That is what she is there for."

Four other Hispana working wives had constructed plural networks with the same three components: wife's kin, in-laws, and female friends. Toni Sena's network was much like that of Delores Baca except that *both* her primary kin and her husband's were located in the same neighborhood. Soccoro Peña's network was much smaller, more like that of Valerie Mondragon, and work friends were important sources of advice and support. Thelma Barela's and Inez Luna's networks were somewhere in between in their size and composition.

Though the plural network was not the most prevalent of the four patterns among Hispano couples, Hispanas who were born and raised in Albuquerque and came from large families were most easily able to forge one. It was much more difficult for women whose in-laws, siblings, or parents did not live in New Mexico.

Hispana Wives' Networks Focused on Primary Kin

One-third (eight) of the Mexican-American wives in our sample constructed support networks focused on their own kin. The role of friends ranged from a relatively minor to a coequal place with female relatives. In the former case, the woman's network depended primarily on one corner of the component triangle, her own mothers and sisters; in the latter, two corners of the triangle were important. Unlike the plural networks described above, these networks did not include the husband's relatives. To understand the reasons, we need to examine the role of social and demographic factors—migration patterns, the size of the husband's sibling set, and the divorce or death of his parents, the extent of his friendships—in shaping the pool of potential relatives on which a working wife and her husband could call.

The Riveras provide an excellent example of a situation in which migration was the primary factor. Deborah Rivera came from Mora, one of the larger Hispano villages in northern New Mexico. She described herself as "Hispanic or Spanish," while Sabine described himself as "Mexican." Deborah's mother had died just a few weeks before our interview, and her father had died six years earlier, while she was in the armed services. Of her ten brothers and sisters, the five youngest were still living at home with her mother in Rainsville, New Mexico. A sister and two older brothers and their families still lived in Mora, while one other brother was a miner in Grants.

Deborah and Sabine established themselves in Albuquerque after they returned from the service and were married. This meant that except for two of her married sisters, who had moved to Albuquerque and with whom she was in close contact, Deborah saw her siblings and mother much less. Returning to Mora for the funeral service, she realized, "I got married and I came here and I hardly ever see them now. . . . Even students that I graduated with. Everybody just seemed to go everywhere." Nevertheless, a sister and a brother (with their spouses) served as wedding *padrinos*, and one of her Albuquerque sisters is godmother to her young son.

Sabine Rivera was born in Mexico but grew up in a small town in

[255]

the state of Washington. He had met Deborah in the army. Sabine was an only child but had five step-siblings, whom he saw only on his rare visits to Washington.

With such a small kin network in Albuquerque, Deborah and Sabine turned to work-related friendships in constructing a support system. Sabine's friends were Roger and Andrew, who were employed at Southwest Electronics, and Freddie, an electronics engineer who was a friend of Roger. Roger and his wife, Betty, who also worked at Southwest, lived down the street from the Riveras; Deborah counted Betty as her closest friend, and listed Roger as a second friend, and a woman from work as a third. Roger and Freddie and their wives often went on picnics or out to dinner with the Riveras; all three couples had small children.

Still, Deborah relied primarily on her two Albuquerque sisters for borrowing money, a car, or a temporary residence. Both sisters babysat for the Riveras, and they, in turn, sometimes took care of a sister's little girl. Deborah also turned to her sisters for advice on personal problems, marital problems, or child rearing. Sabine was pulled into his wife's network as well; he would lend tools to his brothers-in-law, for example. Friends played an equally important role, however. Sabine often borrowed from or lent money to his friend Roger, and Roger might borrow a circular saw or give Sabine a ride to pick up his car after repairs. And Sabine sometimes consulted his friend Andrew about child rearing.

As a couple with a small network, Deborah and Sabine often turned to each other for advice and support. For example, Sabine did the household repairs and yard work, and they cared for their own children when they were ill. Deborah consulted her husband about work and financial problems, and like most Hispano husbands he relied on his wife when he was feeling down. "I usually talk to my wife. If I am actually really down—sometimes work, stress, or something—she relates to it."

In other cases, it was the small size of the husband's network, rather than his migration to Albuquerque, that led to the predominance of the wife's kin in a couple's network. Women built their support system around their mothers and sisters, and husbands who had few kin of their own relied on those ties. For example, Leona Thomas lived next door to her mother (who also took care of Leona's two children) and father. She had no sisters, and only two brothers, one of whom lived in California. Her husband, Carl, an

Anglo, was also from the South Valley of Albuquerque; his father was deceased, but his handicapped brother lived at home with his mother. He saw them two or three times a week but got together with his sister and her family only once a month. It was the couple's proximity to her parents and his small kin network, rather than an absence of kin brought about by migration, that pulled Carl into daily interaction with his in-laws.

Leona relied on friends from both school and work as an important supplement to the focal relationship with her parents. She listed Adela and Dora, from junior high and high school, as her two best friends. Adela and her husband had lent the Thomases money; Adela and Leona exchanged clothes; and Adela babysat with the Thomas baby when the couple went out. A third friend was Jean, a fifty-year-old co-worker at Computex. Like several working wives who turned to older women as surrogate mothers, Leona found Jean an important source of advice, a role model: "She's sort of my motherly figure at work . . . my mother away from home." Jean was the confidant to whom she could talk about personal relationships, work problems, marital difficulties, and even child-rearing: "She was a nurse and she knows a lot of things about kids and sicknesses." Jean, rather than her mother, was the person Leona would turn to when she was feeling down.

In-Law and Friend-Centered Networks of Hispana Wives

Three of the networks formed by married Hispanas were what we have called "in-law centered," two were "friend centered." Three other couples were relatively isolated and relied chiefly on each other and perhaps one or two siblings or one set of parents.[2]

These networks are much smaller than the others we have discussed, and in each case the wife had migrated to Albuquerque, either from rural New Mexico or from outside the state. In some cases, the husband was a migrant as well, from rural New Mexico or from Mexico. In other words, migration had an important impact on the shape of these networks, just as it did on the construction of networks focused on a wife's primary kin.

[2] For the remaining three of the twenty-four Mexican-American wives, we did not have enough data for analysis.

Josephine Perez is a good example of a working mother who constructed a support system primarily around her husband's relatives rather than her own. Migration and the divorce of Josephine's parents were the major factors in shaping her choices. Josephine and Manuel were both from Española, a small city seventy miles north of Albuquerque. They had met and married there but moved to Albuquerque in 1979. Manuel's parents and one sister had also moved to Albuquerque; his other five siblings had remained in Española, as had Josephine's divorced mother and a younger brother. Her father had remarried and lived in Las Vegas, Nevada, with her two youngest siblings and two half-brothers. An older brother was in the Marine Corps. Although Josephine was closer to her father, she saw her mother several times a month, usually on visits home, and her youngest sister, age eleven, was living with her for the summer. Manuel's youngest brother and his wife often visited in Albuquerque, and Josephine and Manuel stayed at their house when they were in Española. Manuel also frequently went fishing with his two brothers in the northern part of the state.

The Perezes were godparents to a nephew, the son of Manuel's oldest sister, and Manuel's parents were important to the Perezes in many ways. His mother babysat for their two young children (one aged two and the other three months in 1982), and Josephine was well integrated into her husband's kin network. They borrowed money from his parents, and sometimes lent them money as well. Manuel's mother brought in meals when Josephine was sick and took care of their pets when they were on trips to Española. His sisters and sisters-in-law were important too. Josephine lent clothes to the wives of his two younger brothers. Manuel's sister Cecilia babysat for the Perez children, and Josephine often talked to her about personal problems. Manuel's parents were a source of financial advice, and Josephine talked to her mother-in-law about child rearing and personal issues. But both were "loners" when it came to confiding in others. Josephine said, "I just stick it out, or I cry and get it over with, and then I'll feel better." Manuel said that he would probably go to his parents about financial problems and listen to his brothers and sisters about child-rearing matters, but did not ask anyone for advice on personal, work, or marital problems. When he was feeling down, Manuel said, "well, I used to, when I do feel that way, just go outside and then split wood or something."

In addition to her mother-in-law and sister-in-law, Josephine had a number of work-related friends from Computex, where both she and Manuel worked. Josephine exercised with Bernadette, a black co-worker, and would confide in Laurie, a Mexican American, about marital problems. Josephine and Bernadette worked on the same line, often went shopping together, and had played on the same softball team. Of Elizabeth, a third friend and an Anglo, Josephine said, "We've gone swimming, we've gone shopping, we've gone to the spa. We go to her house, she's come to our house . . . she's just cute. You know, she's young, and she acts real young, and she makes me laugh." Margaret, another Hispana, was an older confidant (like Leona's friend Jean). Margaret was one of the women Josephine went out with after work, stopping for a drink. "She's very wise. She can really help me a lot in a lot of problems. She's got all this experience with men."

Manuel mentioned a couple he had met through a previous job and a woman friend from Española. He saw these friends about once a month, but they were not important in terms of exchanges or advice. Manuel took breaks with two men who worked in his department but ate his lunch by himself. He did not have as well-developed a set of friends on the job at Computex as Josephine did.

Migration to Albuquerque had shaped Josephine's female network in the direction of her mother-in-law and sister-in-law, but like Delores Baca or Deborah Rivera, who had constructed plural networks, she gave work friends an important place in her life.

Anglo Wives: Substituting Friends for Siblings

There were important differences in the networks constructed by Mexican-American and Anglo working wives. The Anglo women in our study had fewer sisters and relied more on their mothers, compared with Hispano working wives, although those who did have sisters in Albuquerque depended on them for the exchange of goods and services. Friends substituted where siblings were absent, but Anglo wives did not have many work-based friends; most friends were met elsewhere and were important for some kinds of advice and for emotional support. But husbands filled an even more vital role in this regard. When we examine the individual shape of the support systems constructed by Anglo wives, we see that these generalizations mask two very different patterns.

[259]

Four white working mothers constructed networks that focused on their own kin and their husband's primary kin, two corners of the triangle. In four other cases the husband's kin were not important, either because they lived out of state or because there had been a divorce and a history of family conflict. The second four women forged ties among their primary kin, creating networks similar to those of Mexican-American women such as Deborah Rivera or Leona Thomas. All eight of these networks were smaller than most Hispano plural or wife's kin-focused networks, since the families of Anglo women were smaller, and many siblings had moved away from Albuquerque. Also, for most of these eight Anglo women, work friends did not complement the role of siblings and parents. Instead, women relied on their husbands or their relatively small networks for advice and support.

Five other Anglo wives, in contrast, had friend-centered support networks, substituting friends where both the wife's and husband's primary kin were lacking. These women had only one corner of the triangle on which to rely, in contrast to many of their Hispana counterparts. Of the eight women in the first group (who had small networks of primary kin), those born outside New Mexico had migrated to Albuquerque as children and graduated from high school there. The five women in the second group who constructed friend-centered networks, had come to Albuquerque as adults. The larger proportion of friend-centered networks in the Anglo sample points to the important role of migration, as well as family size, in shaping social support.

The support network forged by Linda Bennett and her husband, Macky Garduno, shared some similarities with the plural network of Delores Baca, since both sets of primary kin were important. Linda had grown up with her grandparents in the North Valley and had three brothers and sisters. Her parents had divorced and remarried several times, and she had only recently reestablished a close relationship with her mother. Two of her brothers lived in Missouri, the third in Carlsbad with his wife and two children. Linda and Macky lived in a trailer in Bernalillo (about half a mile from Delores Baca's house) and next door to her oldest sister, Rhonda, who was married and had two children of her own. Macky Garduno had grown up in Placitas, a small community east of Bernalillo, in a family descended from the original land-grant holders. Macky had three brothers and two sisters. His older siblings lived in Placitas near his mother, but he interacted primarily with his younger brother and wife who lived in Alameda, about seven miles south of Bernalillo on the north edge of Albuquerque. He also saw his brother Charlie, who had recently moved to northern New Mexico. A younger sister lived with his mother but was ostracized somewhat by the family.

Linda and her neighboring sister participated in an intense set of interactions and exchanges that involved the husbands as well. In the months prior to our interviews, Linda had done babysitting for Rhonda's children; Rhonda had taken care of Linda's daughter, Christy, and helped when Christy was sick. Linda and Macky used Rhonda's lawn mower and had borrowed furniture and children's clothes from her. Macky commented that Rhonda had also helped out after his accident at work: "She's brought me over a bowl of soup. It was nice and warm. I was working . . . on the roof, and it caved in and I went down with it. And I was hurting there pretty bad for about a week. And just everybody came to see me, really." Linda's mother was part of her support system as well. The couple had borrowed money from her, and Macky had fixed his mother-in-law's sink and dug her septic tank. Macky's brothers were also part of his exchange network, despite some tension among his siblings over rights to the family land in Placitas. Macky helped with the plumbing at his oldest brother's house in Placitas, and Macky's brother Barney and his wife were Christy's godparents.

Linda's best friend was Carolyn, whom she met in school and saw once or twice a week (sometimes with another friend and former neighbor). A second friend worked with her at Leslie Pants; they often took breaks or lunch together and also saw each other outside of work. Macky could think of only two friends, one a childhood buddy whom he saw every two weeks, and another from grade school, whom he had not seen in three years. Friends played no role in exchanges or advice for either Linda or Macky.

For advice and emotional support, Linda felt ambivalent about confiding in her sister: "That's tough, because I've been trying to find somebody, because I don't tell my sister, because she goes to my mom, and if I want my mom to know, I'll tell her. But usually, it used to be Lilly [her husband's older sister] or his mom, but now . . . I tell Rhonda. I hope she doesn't tell everybody." For financial, work, child-rearing, and marital problems, she generally confided in her husband but said, "We go to my mom too, and his." When she's feeling down, Linda felt she could talk to most of the women in her network. "I'd go to Rhonda or call my [other] sister . . . or my mom, or just a friend . . . like if I can get hold of Carolyn or Debbie or Jeanette or anybody . . . just a friend." Macky's best friend could be counted on to discuss personal problems, but he would also talk about marital problems with his neighboring brother-in-law and consult him if he was feeling down: "If Gus is around I usually go over there. If Gus isn't around, I usually take a walk. That don't happen very often. It has a couple of times. We go camping a lot together. We work on each other's vehicles. We discuss each other's wives, they're sisters."

Connie Mead is a good example of the four Anglo women whose small networks were focused on the wife's kin, with very little support from or exchange with the husband's kin. These women had utilized only one side of our metaphorical triangle that includes wife's kin, husband's kin, and friends. When we interviewed Connie in 1982, she had had ten years of electronics experience and was so intent on keeping her new Howard Electronics job that she returned to work six weeks after her son was born. Like Linda Bennett, she had grown up in Albuquerque; her Finnish-American parents had moved there from Minnesota when she was a child. She had married a man who was not from Albuquerque, however, whose kin were nonresident and since her siblings had dispersed, their network focused primarily on her parents. A few friends, played a minimal role, as they did in Linda's network. The birth of their baby a few months before the interview seemed to have pulled Connie and Jack into themselves as a couple and left them little time for other relationships.

Connie met her husband when he was a college student in Iowa, and they spent a number of years in the Midwest, where he worked as a radio announcer, before moving to New Mexico. Her four brothers and sisters lived in as distant places as Minnesota, California, and Maryland; Jack's older siblings were spread from Minnesota to Kansas and North Dakota, and two younger children lived with his parents in Iowa.

Connie had one close friend at work whom she saw every day. She and Donna had met at a previous job, and Donna had helped Connie get the position at Howard Electronics, but they had not seen each other since the Meads' baby was born. Connie had met two other friends when she was employed at other electronics firms, and a fourth friend was from childhood. She kept in touch mostly by phone, since motherhood had cut down on her nonfamily socializing.

Connie felt that only close family would be important for ex-changes, and the only concrete examples she mentioned were her father's help with car repairs and her mother's offer to babysit. "We haven't had to do it yet. I don't know if I would call her. I think I would maybe ask the lady across the street. She said that, you know, if we ever needed someone to take care of Kyle that she'd do it, but we never have." Connie's husband, Jack, was even clearer that they did most things on their own. For example, they had never bor-rowed or lent money; he would probably rent rather than buy or borrow an expensive tool; and he did household repairs on his own. He could not remember going on an errand with anyone or having borrowed a car. He had, however, helped his neighbor install an evaporative cooler and helped others with car repairs.

Jack mentioned turning to his parents or his father-in-law concern-ing personal problems or financial matters, but he would discuss work problems or even marital problems with Connie. Connie said she would either try to sort something out on her own or turn to her husband. For emotional support, Jack would rely on Connie; Connie mentioned her younger sister (who lived in Maryland) or her mother. Compared with Mexican-American women, whose support systems were skewed toward a large number of the wife's primary kin, Connie relied only on her parents; siblings were not crucial, and friends did not fill the important advice-giving role that they did for Leona Thomas. Instead, Connie and Jack leaned on each other for support and advice.

Migration from out of state was a particularly important force in shaping the support networks of five married Anglo women who had moved to Albuquerque as adults. Although almost the same propor-tion of the Hispano sample were migrants to Albuquerque (38 per-cent), many Hispano migrants came from elsewhere in the state and were still able to visit relatives and encourage others to move to the city as well. Only three Hispano working wives (12 percent) had mi-grated from out of state as adults.

Two of these Anglo couples, the Connellys and the Halls, had fol-lowed the husband's parents to Albuquerque, so these parents (and one husband's siblings) were important parts of the working mothers' support networks. However, for these women and three other cou-ples who had virtually no kin in Albuquerque, friends emerged as the chief sources of material and emotional support.

Sally Hall is an example of an Anglo working mother who con-

[263]

structed a friend-centered network in which some kin were important. Sally was born in California. Both of her parents were deceased, and she moved to Albuquerque when her husband, Guy,
was able to get a job at Leslie Pants through his father, who had
worked for the company most of his life. Sally had an older brother
and two older sisters but had little contact with them, because she
was considered the "black sheep of the family."

Sally had a grudging relationship with her mother-in-law. "You
know, his mother tolerates me. She's reached the point to where I'm
here to stay . . . she knows it. It's 'Get along with her. She ain't
going nowhere.' I guess she realized I'm not as big a screw-up as she
thought I was." She was on better terms and had a joking relationship with Guy's father. They saw his parents once a week, and Guy
often helped his parents: for example, he had his father had laid sod
in a friend's back yard.

Sally mentioned one friend at work, Lynn Connelly (another Anglo
interviewee); her other friends, Lee and Marty, were neighbors.
Sally exchanged goods and services and asked advice of both of these
Anglo women, who formed the core of her support system. Sally
acknowledged the importance of reciprocity in these relationships:
"It's like a two-way street. You know, like Lee'll feed me dinner.
She'll send spaghetti one night, and I went to the store and bought
tomatoes, and I gave her some tomatoes. . . . [and] like her son came
over and his friend and helped me move the furniture around. . . .
So I went over to see her that night and I did her dishes and I took
out her trash, and I kind of dusted and everything." And Marty, she
recalled, "loaned me some medicine for Kara when she had chicken
pox. And I send scraps over for their pig." Guy and Sally also had
friendly relations with a Mexican-American family in the neighborhood. The husband, Benny, had changed light bulbs for Sally, and
his friend Tony helped Guy repair his car.

Guy had three friends among his fellow mechanics at Leslie Pants.
They often got together outside work and would "sit around, drink
beer, and play with the Atari." Guy was quite unaware of his wife's
network of neighbors. He mentioned that he had helped his father
with yard work and his father, in turn, helped repair the car. A
friend who lived in Texas at the time of the interview had asked to
borrow the car and stayed temporarily with Guy and Sally. Otherwise, his parents and his friend Mario provided advice and support.
Sally was more clearly dependent on her friends. She said she would

turn to Marty or Lee for all kinds of advice, and either one would listen if she needed emotional support: "Who's at home and has the time for me, you know. Talk to me, I'm depressed, you know."

Mary Pike too had forged a friend-centered support system because neither her own nor her husband's primary kin were available. But even these friendships were very weak, since Mary and Don had been in Albuquerque only six months at the time of the interview. Mary did visit her mother in eastern New Mexico once or twice a month, but her father was hospitalized with a severe alcohol problem. She saw her older brother rarely and her younger brother only on visits to her mother's home. Don was completely estranged from his parents, who were also divorced. He had not seen his mother in eight years. He had grown up with stepbrothers and -sisters, since he lived with his father and a second wife.

Mary's closest friends were from her school years, and she had little contact with them by 1982. "I don't really have any close friends here. And all my other friends, other best friends I have, I knew back when I was in fourth grade. But I really haven't heard from her for years." Mary had, however, become friendly with Marilyn, a supervisor at the Hobbs plant of Leslie Pants, where she had worked previously. She also had an important relationship with Alice, who lived across the street and had formerly worked for Leslie Pants. When Alice was laid off, Mary asked her to care for the Pikes' newborn child while Mary went back to work.

Mary was not sure she knew these friends well enough to borrow a car or stay with them in an emergency, but "Alice and Sam are always giving us stuff or loaning us things. If we need something and they have it, they'll loan it to us." Alice would also water the lawn when the Pikes were gone or take care of the dog, and Sam was willing to help with repairs. Basically, Mary tried to rely on her relationship with her husband for advice and support. She did not feel she would turn to anyone else with a marital problem: "I don't know that I would go to anybody. . . . You know it would take a first momentous step to even agree that there's a problem, first of all. But I would do that and then try to talk to him what we could do to change it before it would . . . ruin the marriage." She would, she said, consult her mother about personal problems and perhaps go to Alice if she needed to talk.

Don was even more isolated, as was typical of Anglo males in our sample. He mentioned three friends from work. One, Mark, was

[265]

someone Don would confide in. "He's just more my type of person. He likes a lot of sports and working out, stuff like that. He likes rock music." Don often went bowling or out for a drink with Jeff or David who worked with him in the packing section of Leslie Pants. His mother-in-law would supply advice for personal, financial, or marital problems, and Don said he would talk to either Mark or his wife, Mary.

For Anglo working wives, then, we see two patterns. Those women who had been adolescents in Albuquerque often relied on parents or one or two siblings, in addition to depending on their husbands, both for particular tasks and for emotional support. Eight Anglo women forged a support system that included both husband's and wife's kin, but their networks were not as large as the plural networks of Hispano wives. Other white women created networks that were focused on their own primary kin, but none of these relied on friends to complement their kin relationships to the extent that Mexican-American wives did. Migration to Albuquerque as adults, on the other hand, placed many Anglo wives in the position of substituting friends for kin. These women did not have very extensive networks, and again, couples relied on each other. In fact, Anglo men and women both relied heavily on their spouses for advice and support. Some Anglo women would turn to a mother or friend, but for others the husband was the most important sounding board.

Sisters and Friends: Support Networks of Single Mothers

The support systems of single mothers contrasted sharply with those of Hispano and Anglo wives. Unlike married women, they did not have the resources of the husband's primary kin on which to draw, either directly (through a relationship with a mother-in-law) or indirectly (as when a husband utilized parents or siblings in exchanges that supported the household as a whole). Just as single mothers could not rely on a husband's income to support their families, those we interviewed had no links to a husband's kin. For them, one corner of the triangle that made up the plural networks forged by many Mexican-American women (own kin, in-laws, and friends) was entirely missing. Nor did single mothers have the kind of material support, advice, and emotional support that husbands provided especially for many of the Anglo wives in our study. Instead, single mothers built their support systems primarily on ties with sisters and friends.

All three of the Anglo women we interviewed were divorced and had moved to Albuquerque as adult women with children. They were all living independently, two in houses they were purchasing, one in her own apartment. Of the twelve Mexican-American single mothers, ten were from the Albuquerque area and had at least one parent (usually the mother) living in the city or in Los Lunas or Bernalillo—towns within short distances to the south and north of Albuquerque. Six of the twelve women were sharing a household with parents, sister, cousin, or roommate; five were living independently; one was housesitting for her sister and hoped soon to get an apartment on her own. One woman's parents lived in a small town in New Mexico, and another's mother was in Mexico. As was generally true of the married sample, then, the Anglo single parents were migrants and the Hispanas local.

Migration to the Albuquerque economy had a powerful effect on the shape of kin networks, as indicated by the number of siblings available to single mothers. Anglo women had either two sisters or no sisters or brothers in Albuquerque, while the Hispanas had an average of five or six siblings in the area—three more than the average for married Mexican-American women in our sample.

Two Hispana single mothers lived with their parents, and one shared with her sister a house that was owned by their mother. Nonetheless, parents were less important in material exchanges for single parents than they were for married Mexican-American and white women. (Mexican-American wives had an average of five exchanges with their parents, while both white and Hispana single parents averaged three exchanges with parents.) Nor were mothers as important in giving advice to single parents, or an important source of support when they were feeling down. In fact, many single mothers were somewhat distant or even estranged from their own parents, especially if they had been teenage mothers.

Single parents tended to rely instead on their sisters. Sisters emerged as more important for Mexican-American single mothers in the construction of support networks than they did even for Mexican-American wives. Hispana single parents often had two or three sisters within a large range of kin; two of the white single mothers each had two sisters in Albuquerque and a central relationship with one of them (the third Anglo had six sisters, but they were all living in

[267]

Minnesota and Florida). For both Anglos and Hispanas, friends—often from the workplace—were an important complement to siblings in the three areas of exchange, advice, and emotional support.

We can examine the balance between sisters and friends in the lives of single mothers by looking at the networks of two Hispana single mothers, Susan Anaya and Grace Estrada, and one Anglo single mother, Linda Henry.

Susan Anaya was the middle child in a large family of seven sons and eight daughters. Her father had died in 1971, but in 1982 her mother still lived in the South Valley with two of the younger children and one granddaughter. All the older siblings except one brother also lived in Albuquerque: "We all go to visit my mom on weekends, so we all see each other." Susan, who was twenty-eight when we interviewed her, was especially close to the three sisters closest to her in age: Josephine, an assembler at an Albuquerque electronics firm; Diane, who also worked at Southwest Electronics; and Elena, an assembler at a third electronics plant. Her older sister Ramona, thirty-three, was an important confidant: "I don't get to see her as often as I like to, but we talk on the phone every now and then, or either I go have lunch with her."

Susan had lived with Elena after her baby's birth, and during this period she had done babysitting for Elena's daughter and Josephine's children. In 1982 she had her own apartment, but "we usually drop by each other's cause we live so close, you know, or if one wants to borrow something. . . . Like Josephine yesterday, she was short of money, so she came by and asked for $5.00, so I gave it to her. And . . . she came by this morning to pick up [the baby] to take him to Elena's, cause Elena was kind of running late and I didn't want to be late, so it worked out all right."

Susan's closest friend was Tracy, who also worked on the progressive line at Southwest Electronics. They not only saw each other at work but often got together on weekends to "go night clubbing, to the show . . . I mean just spend a lot of time together . . . visit." Susan thought her friend's most important quality was "honesty, she's dependable. She's just, you know, a good friend." When Susan was three months pregnant, Tracy's mother had offered to care for the new baby when Susan went back to work after her maternity leave. Susan was pleased with the relationship she had established with Tracy and her mother. "Tracy, she's my best friend, and yet her mother takes care of Jason and all like that. I lucked out having a babysitter—a good one, you know, that I can depend on."

Another friend was her co-worker Sandra, whom Susan had known for two years when we interviewed her. Sandra was a stock keeper at Southwest Electronics at a grade higher than Susan, but previously they had worked on the progessive line together: "She's always been there to help, you know. She's a good friend." An example of her support was that she had helped Susan move into her new apartment.

Susan's three closest sisters, her friend Tracy, and Tracy's mother gave Susan material support and advice. Susan had borrowed money from Tracy, lent small sums to Elena and Josephine, and lent her car to Elena. "Me and Elena are more about the same size, so I usually exchange [clothes] with her, like if she's got a top I want to wear or I got a top she wants to wear . . . but that's not very often. It used to be when we used to live together." Josephine's husband and Susan's younger brother had repaired Susan's car, and all four sisters had been involved in babysitting exchanges. Susan said she would confide in her older sister Ramona concerning personal problems and go to her mother for advice about child rearing; she would talk to Tracy about work problems and rely on her or Elena if she needed emotional support.

Susan's support network bears some resemblance to that of Delores Baca in that sisters and work-based friends were important components, but Susan relied less on her mother (who was older and did not live nearby), and there was no supportive mother-in-law in the picture. Nor was there a husband to provide support or couples with whom to socialize. Susan's distance from her mother was typical of many Hispana single parents, in contrast to their married counterparts (of Hispana married women, 44 percent felt "very close" to their mothers and 32 percent felt "close," while only 33 percent of the single mothers felt "very close" and 25 percent said they had a "close" relationship). Some Mexican-American wives (20 percent) but more Mexican-American single mothers (41 percent) said they were not close to their fathers. As Susan said of her own father, "I was close to him, but not as close. It was hard to talk to my dad."

A small number of Mexican-American single mothers were more estranged from their families than Susan Anaya. For example, Betty Saiz, another Southwest Electronics worker, told us that conflictual relationships in her family went back to her childhood. She said she did not see her widowed father often: "I love my dad very much, but it's that I was brought up so strict that I'm afraid that if he comes over and sees something he doesn't like, or if I do something or say something [he'll not like it]. . . . I try to stay out of his way, and I know it shouldn't be that way, but I guess that's my defense." Betty was not close to her three sisters and three brothers either. She appeared extremely independent except for the relationship with her boyfriend, who also worked at Southwest Electronics. He and a couple from work and the mother of her children's friends formed Betty's network of closest relationships.

Grace Estrada was one of the six single mothers who lived with kin. Like Delores Baca, she had lived in the Albuquerque area all her life. Grace had been briefly married to the father of her child, who had a drinking problem and physically abused her; she left him and went on welfare for a period, and then returned to her parents' house in Los Lunas, fifteen miles south of Albuquerque and a thirty-minute drive to her job at HealthTech. Besides the siblings who resided with her in her parents' household, her older sister—a divorced mother of two children—lived in Los Lunas with a divorced younger brother; two married brothers and their families had made their homes in Los Lunas as well, and her father's brothers and their families were neighbors. Nevertheless, Grace explained, "I like to stick mostly to myself. I'm kind of close to my mom. I hardly ever see Dad. We hardly ever talk." Asked if she and her father did not get along, she continued, "No, we get along. We all get along. It's just that we never talk; we don't know what to say to each other."

Grace's closest friend was her sister-in-law, Florence, who was married to her twenty-six-year-old brother, Claude. Her second best friend was her current boyfriend. On weekends they would watch television, take an automobile ride, go out for a soft drink. Grace found him very understanding and sympathetic, and he no longer pressured her to marry. A third friend was her partner in the foil and overwrap section at HealthTech. They saw each other only at work, but because both had been raised by strict parents, they could share their problems and experiences.

In general, single mothers were "thrown more on their own" in forging a support network. Though many Hispana single mothers had a large number of siblings and were fortunate to have close relations with sisters, some did not have close or consistently supportive relations with parents, particularly fathers. Without a husband or a husband's kin and friends, their networks were not plural, like those of Delores Baca and Valerie Mondragon. Even the married Hispanas whose networks focused on their own primary kin and friends tended to gain more support from their parents than did single mothers and, of course, could rely on their husbands. And even the Hispana single parents who were able to utilize their mothers or a babysitter for child care seemed much more limited than Hispana married women in their options for constructing support relationships. Those who came from large local families, however, had a larger kin network on which to rely than their white counterparts.

A number of white women had as many siblings as some of the Mexican-American women, yet the Anglo single parents we interviewed had less extensive support networks and tended to rely on a very few siblings and work-based friends. Migration to Albuquerque was even more important in shaping the social support system of these working mothers. They found their work-based friends to be particularly important, though two were lucky enough to have sisters living in Albuquerque as well.

Linda Henry was thirty-seven, divorced, and the mother of two children when we interviewed her. She came from a large family of nine brothers and sisters in Wisconsin. Her mother was eighty years old, and Linda was able to visit her only on yearly vacations. Two sisters lived in Alburquerque, however: Martha, a widow with two grown children; and Brenda, her husband, and two married daughters. These sisters had moved to Albuquerque years earlier, and Linda had spent summers with them as a teenager—a major factor in attracting her to the city after her divorce. Brenda's daughter Susie was also an important relative: "We're more like sisters; we share babysitting." Linda was the godmother of one of Susie's children.

Linda's three best friends were other divorced women. She had met Kristen and Roxanne at "Parents without Partners," and Gloria was a friend from work: "We worked at Southwest together. We were laid off, and then she picked up the applications [for jobs at Howard Electronics]. I got the job first, and then I got her a job there, so now she works there." Linda commented on how much they had in common: "We both come from a big family. We both come from a divorced family, and we have . . . well, we can discuss anything and we talk about everything."

Although she had forged some congenial relationships with neighbors—she could borrow a grill from one, and another could borrow a hoe from her—Linda's most important exchanges were with her sisters and her friend Kristen. As divorced parents, she and Kristen often exchanged babysitting, and Linda felt that Kristen would put her up if she needed a temporary residence. Linda had also kept Susie's children while she and her husband took a trip, and Susie returned the favor when Linda had to stay at work for mandatory inventory. Brenda's husband had fixed her car, but she would rely on a professional for household repairs.

For advice, Linda would consult Susie about personal problems, and Gloria about work problems. She would confide in Kristen about financial problems, and her sister Brenda about problems with men. This constellation of friends, sister, and niece provided her with emotional support as well.

Undoubtedly, if Linda had still been living in Wisconsin, she would have had a kin network that looked more like Susan Anaya's, since her large family was a very close one. Her post-divorce migration to Albuquerque, however, had restricted the number of relatives she could depend on and made a small number of divorced mothers—including a close friend at work—equally important.

Laura Davidson, an Anglo divorcee from a family of six children, also had two sisters in the city; these and her friends from work provided her major support. Betty Thompson, the third Anglo single mother, was one of twelve children, but none of her sisters lived in Albuquerque. Betty had migrated with her husband before their divorce and had remained in Albuquerque afterward, working at Aerospace, Inc. In 1982 her boyfriend, the father of her youngest child, as well as her work friends, had become her main support. All these Anglo single parents had well-paid jobs and were better able to support their families than some of their Hispana counterparts; and their age, marital experience, and long work history made them better able to cope, even though their support networks were smaller.

As working mothers face the contradictions of putting together their lives as workers and as mothers, constructing a support system constitutes crucial acts of mediation. The practice of holding down a full-time job and rearranging the household division of labor is augmented by the use of kin and friends for the occasional exchange of goods and services and, more important, for soliciting advice and emotional support. Unlike middle-class and upper-middle-class professional mothers, working-class women do not have discretionary income to spend on in-home day-care providers for their children or domestic workers to clean their houses. They are less able to afford expensive appliances (freezers, dishwashers, microwave ovens) to ease housework, and professional services ranging from tax accounting and bank loans to professional counseling are out of the range of their family budgets. The working mothers we interviewed used kin as occasional babysitters, borrowed money, clothes, and furniture from relatives, asked their husbands or brothers to fix their cars and help with the yard work, and leaned on sisters, friends, and husbands for emotional support.

In the everyday practice of asking for advice or borrowing and exchanging goods and services, these working mothers created women-centered support networks from their own primary kin (usually mothers and sisters) and, if married, their husbands' kin (mothers-in-law and sisters-in-law), plus their friends. Our data indicate that, contrary to the literature, working-class women have integrated support networks to include friends, especially friends established in the workplace. It was the sometimes extraordinary support of kin, friends, and even day-care providers that enabled some of them to better handle the contradictions of being working mothers.

[9]

Conclusion: Living with Contradictions

The central theme of this book has been the analysis of difference: the relationship between gender, class, and ethnicity. We have used a framework that emphasizes the social location of women: first in terms of local political economies, and second in terms of the mutual constitution of gender, class, ethnicity, and marital status. We have not emphasized identities or used class, ethnicity, and gender as labeling devices which when strung together set up hyphenated "types": working-class-Hispana-single mother, or middle-class-single-Anglo-professional woman. Our emphasis on practice has led us to see that such categories may slip and shift in importance as a woman moves through her life cycle, and that within a particular constructed analytic category such as "working class" or "Hispana" there is important variability. Rather than focusing on identity categories, then, we have looked for ways in which women's practices have converged or diverged.

As we focused on the contradictions that working mothers face in maintaining their commitment to both work and motherhood, the strategies that emerged in the actual practice of work, housework, and child care document the variability found among both Mexican-American and Anglo working families. Strategies and tactics help to mediate contradictions but rarely "resolve" them or cause them to disappear. Instead, women find themselves living in tension with the contradictions of their lives.

The Changing Dynamics of Social Location

We have located Mexican-American and Anglo women workers within the Albuquerque political economy, emphasizing the historical and structural dynamics that brought new sunbelt plants into the area's service and government economy in the 1970s and 1980s. We have proposed that Albuquerque stands as a fourth model of recent high-tech industrialization in the United States, quite different from the fledgling electronics industry in New York, or the more established industrial centers of Los Angeles and Silicon Valley, which each have an emphasis on immigrant workers, sub-contracting, and homework, as well as high-paying male jobs in research and development (in Silicon Valley) and large defense-related firms (in Los Angeles). Both frostbelt refugees and sunbelt spillovers relocated to Albuquerque, an economy dominated by government and service-sector employment, where many women's jobs are lower-paying than those available in the new industrial plants. Furthermore, the advent of new plants came during a recession when men's jobs, particularly in mining and construction, were vulnerable. From the perspective of women whose parents and even grandparents had been part of a family wage economy, manufacturing jobs represented not a process of proletarianization but a step up in an economy where many women had been earning only the minimum wage of $3.35 an hour. We suspect that the Albuquerque model might be equally appropriate for other small western cities such as Tucson, Colorado Springs, Fort Collins, and perhaps even the larger Phoenix in terms of the impact of industrialization on working-class women.

We have also learned, since the completion of our interviews in 1983, that there is a negative as well as a positive side to Albuquerque industrialization. At the national level, both the electronics and apparel industries have been hit hard by foreign competition since then. Over 200,000 apparel jobs were lost between 1975 and 1983 as more and more designers and retail chains began moving production to Hong Kong, Taiwan, Singapore, and South Korea (*New York Times*, July 15, 1986, p. D5). Trade bills to reduce imports, passed by the House and Senate in 1985 and 1987, were vetoed by President Reagan.

The apparel industry in Albuquerque felt the impact of international competition. Jeans, Inc., which manufactured blue jeans, closed in 1984, laying off 210 workers. Cowboy Clothes managed to maintain its work force over this period, partly because of the niche it had established in the western wear industry.[1] Leslie Pants did recover from the 1982–83 recession and by 1984 was employing 450 workers, full time. Nevertheless, between 1982 and 1992 the apparel labor force in New Mexico declined from 3,400 to 2,600. Even if Leslie Pants remains in business throughout the 1990s, the apparel industry in Albuquerque will not likely regain the level of employment it reached in 1982 (see *New Mexico Labor Market Review* from 1982 to 1992).

The electronics industry's periods of expansion and contraction in the 1980s make it clear that high-tech jobs can be unstable too. Defense-related electrical machinery plants remained relatively stable, but the semiconductor industry and those firms most directly involved in the manufacture of computers and electronic devices suffered from foreign competition, corporate buyouts, and changes in management policy. Computex laid off 300 workers in 1983; SystemsPlus expanded to 600 workers but then was forced to lay off 150 workers in 1985 as Japanese competition slowed down the computer chip industry. One of its plants was slow to build a new fabrication facility, and at least one other plant was never built. The labor force at Southwest Electronics was reduced from 1,000 to 500 between 1982 and 1987. More and more of its activities were transferred to a plant in Juarez, and eventually the Albuquerque plant was sold to a German company, which in 1992 announced that it would close its doors and move production to Florida—a loss of 300 jobs to the Albuquerque area.

By November 1991, New Mexico employment in electronics had reached a level of 6,500—2,000 more than in December 1982 and almost equaling peak employment of 6,600 before the 1984–85 downturn (*New Mexico Labor Market Review*, December 1991). Yet 400 jobs had been lost by September 1992, as the effects of the 1990–91 recession were beginning to be felt. Overall, it is not clear what the future of jobs for women in electronics will be in Albuquerque. Continued Japanese competition, especially in the semiconductor industry, could mean that American companies will hold on to a smaller share of the market, making projections for plant expansion unrealistic. Further, as events in eastern Europe and Russia make the de-

---

[1] We conducted an interview with one worker in each of these two plants, but they are not part of our sample.

[276]

fense buildup obsolete, military contracts will be trimmed and more electronics jobs will be eliminated. In late summer of 1992 one defense-dependent plant announced cutbacks of 300 jobs, perhaps signaling the transformation of Albuquerque from an offshoot of Silicon Valley to a "silicon desert."

Participative policies have had their ups and downs as well. At Computex during the 1985 layoffs the management eliminated flextime. With the closure of Jeans, Inc., the only other plant in Albuquerque that had instituted flextime, this aspect of new participative programs was completely eliminated for the industrial work force. The teams that had been put in place at SystemsPlus in 1983 were also dropped as the plant faced the computer industry recession in 1984–85. Changes in top management at the national headquarters of Howard Electronics led to a withdrawal of support for the Albuquerque plant's "high-involvement" philosophy; the plant manager and a number of key middle managers were removed, and four months later, in mid-1983, half of the plant's work force was laid off (Rehder 1985). By 1991, however, a new management had reintroduced a team structure, going much further even than Health-Tech in allowing teams to control their work environment. Individual teams set their own production goals, kept statistics on their productivity, and virtually eliminated the need for shop floor supervisors.

In 1992, Leslie Pants broke with tradition in the apparel industry and converted its assembly line organization to a team structure. Each team of thirty-six operators is organized into mini-teams of four to eight workers who each learn two or three operations and help one another maintain quality control. Management pays a flat hourly rate of $7.30 an hour, plus a bonus of thirty cents an hour if the team produces fewer than 2.9 flaws in every 100 pairs of pants. The company instituted the new system to improve quality and boost worker morale. Perhaps Leslie Pants will be an exception to the more general trend that although management may be willing to try participative techniques, they are often the first practices to be eliminated during times of financial hardship, or when supportive top managers are removed in corporations largely dedicated to more hierarchical arrangements.

Negative comments concerning participative management have come from a number of scholars and writers. Parker and Slaughter, for example (1988:16–19), argue that teams are often used to tighten up production which results in a speedup, but workers are expected

[277]

to do the time-motion studies themselves, rather than having them done by an "efficiency expert." Guillermo Grenier also concluded that the team structure was important in controlling workers: "While workers at [HealthTech] did participate in enforcing the rules and regulations of the plant, they had no say in designing the rules. Their participation was allowed only in areas that did not threaten managerial control. They participated in the work process much as slaves participated in slavery—as captives of an economic and social structure beyond their control. Indeed, by eliminating the potential for opposition, participation was utilized as a form of control" (1988:194).

Finally, a worker's compensation suit against Southwest Electronics made public the health hazards women may face in electronics workplaces. In August 1984 two women who had worked in the components department filed suit, claiming they had been exposed to cancer-causing substances. By December 1986 there were 115 plaintiffs, many of whom had done "potting" (a gluing operation that involved exposure to heated epoxy resins) and others who may have been exposed to a mixture of chemicals (a sort of gaseous "soup") that pervaded the plant, which had no local exhaust systems but only dilution ventilation. In one department, forty-nine women had lost their uteruses to cancer, tumors, or excessive bleeding; other workers had suffered neurological problems, particularly dizziness, memory loss, and numbness (*Albuquerque Journal*, February 22, 1987). The Southwest suit was settled out of court in June 1987; the plaintiffs received compensation for lost wages, medical costs, and some rehabilitation expenses. The terms of the agreement were confidential and all settlement documents were sealed (*Albuquerque Journal*, June 26, 1987; Fox 1991), but the case made it clear that there may be significant health hazards in sunbelt industrial work.

These three issues—(1) layoffs and job instability, (2) the potential manipulation of participative management policies by management or their elimination during economic downturns, and (3) the impact of exposure to chemicals on women's health—all focus on the down side of sunbelt industrialization and add to the problems and contradictions of combining work and family. By the early 1990s it was evident that working mothers faced a trade-off: good jobs with good wages and benefits in return for some job insecurity, the possibility that management was not as "open" as it initially appeared, and the risk of cancer, reproductive problems, or central nervous system damage.

Issues of Difference: Paths of Convergence and Divergence

Within a political economy (as one aspect of social location), class, gender, and ethnicity emerge as constructed differences—differences that split and divide individuals as one looks through the varied lenses of class, gender and ethnic background. Yet though they are analytically separable, they intertwine as women construct their lives. The interconnection begins with the ways in which women and men are differentially located in capitalist economies and the historical forces that have pulled men, women, and children of varying cultural and national backgrounds into particular urban settings. In other words, we can see the connection between class and gender as we pay attention to the ways capitalist economies both utilize and create divisions between men and women of the same working-class background.

Since the beginning of the industrial revolution, there has been a gender division of labor in both industries and local economies, with men in jobs that span a wide range of pay (from more highly skilled and steady to unskilled and sporadic), and women (whether the mill girls of the 1840s or current electronics workers) occupying a much narrower band of jobs, usually paid much less than men or in the same range as the lowest-paid males. As the division of labor historically developed in apparel and electronics, apparel became a female-dominated industry with male jobs reserved for the more highly paid managers, cutters, and machine repairmen. Electronics has contained a more gender-balanced but equally sex-segregated labor force: males hold positions ranging from top managers to engineers, research and development specialists, and lower-paid technicians; women are concentrated in the semiskilled assembly and clerical jobs. In the wider Albuquerque economy, working-class men are found in a wide range of small industrial, construction, transportation, and service jobs, but few of them are unionized, highly skilled, or highly paid.

Thus, when women are married or create households with male partners, the position of the family within the working class depends a great deal on the man's wage, relative to that of the woman. Women thus find their position in the family economy varying—as secondary providers, co-providers, mainstay providers, and, in the case of single parents, sole providers—depending on the husband's job history or the fate of the marriage.

Ethnicity becomes entwined with class and gender under the historical circumstances in which people of different cultural and national backgrounds are pulled into the same local economy. Patterns of migration thus feed into the constitution of a local labor force, and recruitment may be from a city's rural hinterland, from another region within a nation, or from other countries. Differences of language and culture may be relatively muted or accentuated, depending on how migrants are incorporated into a local labor force and on the relative ethnic segregation or integration of residential neighborhoods.

Our emphasis on local political economies led us to treat industries and urban areas historically and to examine the dialectic relationship between industrial development and the incorporation of women of different ethnic backgrounds into a local labor force. Migration is part of the story as well; in the case of Albuquerque, the city acts as a magnet for Hispano women and men from smaller villages and towns in New Mexico, just as it has attracted children of white retired military personnel, rural farmers, and small town tradespeople from other western and midwestern states.

Hispanas in our sample tended to come from New Mexico and had a larger proportion of their own or their husbands' kin network in Albuquerque. Anglos were more likely to have come from out of state. One might hypothesize that these migration patterns were cultural—that is, Hispanos choosing to stay closer to home, Anglos being more willing to travel—but we would argue, instead, that migration chains develop in all ethnic and regional groups and that once they develop, some members of the kin network follow others for jobs or other economic opportunities. New Mexican Hispanos have migrated to a number of different urban locations: to Barstow, Los Angeles, and Denver, for example, as well as to Albuquerque. The population of New Mexico has been dominantly Hispano since the colonial period, so it is not surprising that the Albuquerque working class has been recruited from the local region and this ethnic population. If we had conducted our research in Indianapolis or Iowa City, we would probably have seen similar patterns of in-state migration within a working class of European ancestry.

These dynamics have created a working class that is predominantly Hispano but has a significant proportion of Anglo members (as well as small numbers of blacks, Indians, and Southeast Asians). But the Hispana and Anglo women recruited to jobs in new sunbelt plants were not segregated into different departments or different skill levels. We suspect there may be greater differences between Anglo and Hispano men in some plants (for example, at Southwest Electronics the higher-paid GR-8 technicians were dominantly Anglo), yet throughout the economy substantial numbers of Anglo men are in jobs very similar to those occupied by Hispanos.

These locational and historical dynamics set the stage for what we found in both the workplace and the home as we examined the way women mediate the contradictions of job and family.

The Workplace

As noted above, gender was an important difference in the workplace: men and women were in different jobs at different levels of pay. This was particularly clear at Southwest Electronics, where men (primarily Anglos) dominated the jobs of machine setter and technician (grades 5, 6, and 8), while women were primarily assemblers, materials handlers, and quality control workers (grades 1, 2, and 4). There were also gender hierarchies at other plants where there were significant numbers of men (Aerospace, Computex, and SystemsPlus). At Aerospace, women were primarily employed in only three departments, while skilled male machinists made up the bulk of the labor force. Fortunately, women there benefited from the high-level union wage scale that included a narrow range of wages and consequently the highest pay for women in our study.

Not only are industrial jobs still gender-segregated, but there are differences in men's and women's work cultures as well. As Lamphere has argued elsewhere (1991), men often seem to be marginal to the female-dominated work culture. In addition, as women's industrial work culture becomes co-opted through plantwide activities and participative management schemes, men's work culture becomes fragmented or nonexistent. With the decline of large industrial male workplaces (auto factories, steel mills, mines) and the rise of more individualized service-sector jobs (truck driving, computer repair, warehouse work), men spend more time on the road, with customers rather than co-workers, and in isolated situations. Thus, at the level of both labor process and plantwide work culture, gender difference is a primary organizing principle within working-class jobs. Men's and women's work worlds are still divided.

Ethnicity, however, does not become a significant source of difference among women and does not account for women's strategies in the workplace. Hispana and Anglo women worked side by side in Albuquerque plants. A woman's position in the labor process, her struggles with her job, and her particular relationship with supervisors and other management proved more important in the development of strategies than was cultural identity—at least in the early 1980s. In any particular workplace, women developed individual coping strategies, collective strategies of resistance, or an ability to critique a participative management ideology as a result of the dialectical relationship between management policy and worker practice at that individual work site.

Thus the management at Leslie Pants was successful in co-opting worker resistance and keeping it at an individual level, whereas women at Southwest Electronics and Aerospace, Inc., were more successful in forging collective strategies of resistance to deal with the major contradiction between management's efforts to extract labor and women's attempts to control the conditions of their work. Likewise, women appreciated the particular constellation of management practices at both Howard Electronics and Computex (job rotation, flextime, plantwide meetings), whereas the labor process and team structure at HealthTech created conditions that led women to respond with collective resistance. The contradiction between management's ideology of participation and its actual practice was particularly sharpened during the union drive; hence, many women workers were able to see through the high-involvement philosophy and acknowledge that management control continued to be an important reality.

Women's position in the family and their role as mothers are not separated from their experiences or evaluation of what happens in the workplace. Our chapter on the family economy and marriage histories demonstrated the very important place of industrial jobs in the lives of working mothers and their children. Women stayed with these jobs because of their relative high wages and good benefits. They appreciated policies like flextime or the absence of time clocks because these made the contradictions between work and motherhood easier to live with. On the other hand, although they accepted jobs with unusual work schedules, they struggled with the difficulties that unconventional shifts caused in their efforts to arrange good child care during their working hours. Some women at HealthTech voted for the union because they hoped it would help them gain more control over the shift schedule. Other women voted against the union because the company created a climate of fear in which they felt that their own jobs were in jeopardy.

The Family

The issue of difference became more complex when we examined how working mothers coped with the contradictions between their roles as mothers and as workers by reallocating their reproductive labor. We examined three areas: (1) the reallocation of reproductive labor as it involved child care while the mother was at work; (2) the use of kin and friends to provide material and emotional support; and (3) the reallocation of tasks in the home.

In the first two areas we found that Anglo and Hispana women's behavioral strategies differed. These differences, however, seem best accounted for by the fact that Hispanas were more likely to have grown up in Albuquerque or another part of New Mexico, whereas, Anglo working mothers—even those who had come to Albuquerque as children—were from out of state and did not have their own or their husband's entire kin network close at hand. Thus, Hispanas were more likely to reallocate their reproductive labor by sharing child care with their husbands on a split-shift arrangement or by using close relatives as babysitters. Although 54 percent of our Anglo interviewees also used these two strategies, a greater proportion used home day-care providers and day-care centers (46 percent), compared with Hispana working mothers (33 percent). Migration patterns also accounted for differences in women's strategies in building a support system. Hispana wives and single mothers, more likely to be from Albuquerque or other parts of New Mexico, were able to forge networks involving sisters, mothers, and husband's kin, with friends—particularly those made at work—as an important adjunct. Anglo women often substituted friends for the kin (particularly sisters) who did not reside in Albuquerque.

In the third area, the division of housework and child care, there were fewer ethnic differences: just over 60 percent of both samples were traditional or semitraditional in their division of housework, while almost 40 percent were egalitarian or non-traditional. Yet it is also true that 42 percent of the Hispano couples, compared with 15 percent of the Anglos, participated in the traditional pattern; more Anglo couples (46 percent compared with 21 percent) had negotiated a semitraditional arrangement in which men did about 30 percent of the chores. With regard to daily child-care tasks, we found that Anglo couples were more likely to be semitraditional (62 percent to 38 percent of the Hispanos), while Hispanos were more likely to be egalitarian (33 percent to 15 percent for Anglos). Even our small numbers follow the national trend in indicating that both Hispano and Anglo husbands are more willing to share child-care chores than housework. We have argued that both the similarities and the differences are best accounted for not by ethnic or cultural background but by the relative importance of the wife as a provider within the household economy. Women who were secondary providers were more likely to be in households with traditional or semitraditional arrangements than were women who were coproviders or mainstay providers.

These conclusions, however, do not mean that cultural background and experience made no difference in these women's lives. By and large, their support networks, their babysitters, and their friends at work were selected from among members of their own ethnic group. The Hispanas lived in a world largely made up of Hispana mothers, sisters, other relatives, and friends; Anglo networks might involve kin and friends from a slightly wider set of backgrounds (regional or ethnic) but did not often include a large number of Hispanas. The major exceptions occurred in the intermarried couples, the three Hispana and four Anglo women married to men from the other category. Their kin networks included members of both categories, and they often had a much more integrated circle of friends, both inside and outside of work.

The Hispana women in our sample tended to come from rural backgrounds; their mothers were likely to have been housewives; they were overwhelmingly Catholic; and the Spanish language was of particular importance to them. Although most did not speak the language at home, they considered it an important part of their cultural heritage and hoped that their children would learn it. Many still had ties to rural villages in northern New Mexico, communities in the Rio Grande Valley, or towns and cities as far away as Carlsbad, New Mexico. In contrast, the women we have called Anglo came from a wide variety of backgrounds, were almost all from out of state (both rural and urban areas), and were more likely to be Protestant than Catholic. Although they had different cultural experiences to work with, Hispana and Anglo women in our study were forging converging strategies: that is, at the level of behavior, working mothers were constructing a set of practices that responded to similar situations. This was particularly true at work, where there seemed to be little difference between Hispana and Anglo women who had the same kinds of jobs, were members of the same department, or worked on the same assembly line.

Both Anglo and Hispana working mothers needed either to draw on the labor of their husbands, friends, and kin to replace their reproductive labor or to intensify their own labor by continuing to do housework and child care during nonwork hours. Hispanas and Anglos had different kin resources for building a support system, and these account for many of the differences we found in women's strategies for dealing with day care or utilizing a network of kin and friends. The points of convergence, however, emphasize the similarities in women's tactics and practices across ethnic boundaries, similarities grounded in the material realities of a *class* position.

We argue that difference needs to be understood in terms of a working mother's "social location" (Zavella 1991a) or, rather, her place in a local political economy and within a web of ethnicity- and gender-based social relations. Focusing on a local economy and the working mother's place in it helps us see how gender, class, and ethnicity intersect in women's lives and are mutually constituted. It is important for us to capture this specificity. Our approach to ethnic and racial difference focuses on behavioral strategies in response to material conditions, rather than exclusively on a cultural construction of ethnic identity.

Such a behavioral approach to ethnicity leads us to see convergences and divergences in behavior rather than to emphasize totalizing differences. At one level there were important commonalities among the Hispana and Anglo women we interviewed: most were committed working mothers who felt that they held good jobs and who needed their wages to support their families. At another level there were differences as Anglo and Hispano families forged support networks and found child care among persons of their own ethnic background. These differences, we argue, can best be explained by the kind of providing role each woman held in the family economy and by the local origin of most Hispanas. At a third level, our study demonstrates important differences *within* each ethnic category. Recognizing variability and commonality at these three different levels is more important than painting a portrait of *the* Mexican-American working mother or *the* working-class factory operative.

Industrial Women Workers in Comparative Perspective

Since the early 1970s it has been clear that women's work in industrial occupations needs to be seen in a global perspective. In the electronics and apparel industries in particular, but more recently also in automobiles and steel, a new international division of labor has been created. U.S. and Japanese corporations have established plants in the Third World, U.S. corporations have subcontracted with Third World companies, and European and Asian corporations have continued to expand at home and abroad. In the United States the result has been an era of "runaway shops" and regional restructuring, as industrial production declined in the East and Midwest and expanded in the South and West. Women's labor has been particularly important in this shift, since two of the industries most implicated in global restructuring have been apparel and electronics, both of which have hired female semiskilled operatives.

As scholars' attention turned to women in developing countries who were employed by the new industries, the focus was on consequences: did this industrial employment replicate early industrialism in the West? Did it provide new-found independence or autonomy for young female workers? Did it allow them to break ties with family and community? Critiquing earlier theories of modernization (with their assumption that industrial development has primarily positive effects), many theorists have argued that the increasing incorporation of women into industrial work, particularly in the Third World, has had very negative consequences, that it has made women economically vulnerable rather than integrating them into their societies' development and actualizing their potential. Those who argue the "exploitation thesis" have emphasized that women have little choice but to take jobs in modern plants where management-worker relations remain patriarchal and where the work itself is monotonous and repetitive (see Enloe 1983; Fernández Kelly 1983; Lim 1983; Nash 1983; Safa 1986).

Several of the same authors also stress that combining productive and reproductive roles in a "double day" constitutes another form of exploitation of the women entering the wage sector in Third World

[286]

countries. For example, in her study of working women in Singapore, Linda Lim says: "At the individual level, there are also many costs. Burdened by their reproductive role, and victimized by discrimination, women workers frequently do not achieve their full potential in employment. Their opportunities and incomes remain less than those of men, consigning them to a secondary and inferior economic role in the family as in the labour force" (1982:25–26).

While acknowledging the role of international capital, multi-national firms, and the state in creating the conditions for women's subordination in the labor market and in particular firms, we now have enough local studies to go beyond the exploitation thesis and explore a new set of questions. We are able to examine the different trajectories that local economies have taken, the different kinds of women workers new industries have attracted, and the strategies women themselves have developed in mediating the contradictions of family and work life. Many of the data in earlier studies are relevant to these issues, and even many exploitation theorists recognize that women workers are actors and not passive pawns (Enloe 1983: 420).

In Hong Kong, Singapore, Taiwan, and Malaysia, the electronics, apparel, and other light industries hired primarily young single women, first-generation workers from small villages or from families that had recently migrated to urban areas. Lydia Kung's study of Taiwanese factory women focuses on workers who lived in dormitories rather than at home; they viewed their work as an exchange of cash for labor, had low expectations for their situation, and accepted management's view of reality (1983:104–11). Kung does not provide enough data on the labor process and management-worker dynamics to show whether workers developed individual strategies and tactics in struggling with quotas or management policies. Janet Salaff's case studies of three Hong Kong working daughters suggests that there was little shop-floor resistance but that women did sometimes quit one job to find another with better wages and working conditions (1981:56–57).

Aihwa Ong, however, who describes the lives of Malay women electronics workers from Islamic village backgrounds, found them much more critical of Japanese management's control and pressures to produce. They engaged in indirect forms of resistance such as slowing production, losing their tempers, or crying when criticized by a foreman; at other times they damaged machinery or were pos-

[287]

sessed by village spirits in attacks that stopped production until a spirit-healer was able to exorcise the offended spirit (1987:164–65, 202–13). Ong also points out (1991:299) that the working daughters studied by Kung and Salaff, like those she interviewed in Malaysia, did contest in moral terms the categories and practices that management used. They might not have engaged in explicit resistance on the shop floor, but neither did they accept what they considered to be the dehumanizing aspects of factory work.

The Javanese "factory Daughters" studied by Diane Wolf (1992) were more defiant at home than in the workplace. In Javanese villages where land was scarce and peasant families poor, some families were not able to release their daughters from agricultural labor in order to let them engage in wage work. For daughters who did enter the paid labor force, wages were very low, and families often subsidized them by providing housing and meals or by sending food and other gifts to those living in factory dormitories. Furthermore, in Java with its bilateral kinship system and less patriarchal family structure, young girls were not dutiful workers, remitting 50 to 80 percent of their wages to parents. Instead, they were often defiant, working without their parents' permission, spending their meager wages on themselves, or perhaps buying luxury items for their families.

Clearly, single women are the most vulnerable and subordinate in their relationships with families. Usually daughters whose pay is important for their families' support may find it difficult to break away from patriarchal structures, and industrial firms often develop policies (from restrictive dormitories to bus services) that dovetail with family and community values supporting control over young women's behavior. National media images may also stigmatize working girls (Kung 1983:157–58; Ong 1987:181–82). Labor-force participation is a two-way street, however, and working daughters do not turn over all of their earnings to their families. They also invest in new forms of dress or makeup, and put off parental attempts to arrange marriages for them. Under particular economic and historical circumstances, such as those that developed in South Korea in the 1970s and 1980s (where female labor was vital to the economy, single women were living in isolated industrial estates fostering class consciousness, and conflict with both capital and a repressive state led to a growing labor movement), working daughters have engaged in militant tactics and strategies. South Korean industrial working women, including a large single population, have developed the most militant tactics of any female labor force in Asia. They have participated in strikes (including a hunger strike at one plant), developed an anticapitalist ideology, and emerged as a separate female wing of the labor movement (Ong 1991:302–04).

It is important not to overemphasize the roles of working daughters in these local economies, since there are substantial portions of married women and single mothers in the Asian labor forces as well. The contrast between working daughters, working single mothers, and working mothers with male partners emerges even more clearly in the literature on the U.S.-Mexico border. Here there are important differences between jobs in the apparel and electronics industries. Fernández Kelly (1983:55) found that 75 percent of *maquiladora* workers were single in the early 1980s, but apparel workers tended to be older and were more likely to be married and supporting their own children. Tiano (1987a:84) found similar differences between electronics and apparel workers, and stressed that the younger electronics workers were perhaps more occupationally mobile. More recently, Tiano has suggested that the *maquila* labor force is in flux, becoming more heterogeneous with the increasing participation of non-single women: "From a stage at which most employed women were working daughters who would eventually drop out of the formal labor force to enter the informal sector or devote their lives to full-time domestic tasks, it is moving toward a state in which many female workers are wives and mothers, and many women remain in paid employment over a larger proportion of their life course" (1991:58).

There is also evidence of resistance in the workplace among this mixed and changing labor force. Fernández Kelly (1983) provides an excellent description of getting a job in an apparel plant as well as of management's tactics to exhort workers to up their levels of productivity. However, the best account of women's tactics of resistance is Devon Peña's (1987:136–45). The literature on the U.S.-Mexican border tells a great deal about the role of the state and multinational capital in restricting women's strategies of resistance through legal controls on labor unions, policies that encourage labor migration so that workers can be easily replaced, and corporate strategies that include closing up and moving elsewhere at any sign of labor unrest. There are accounts of women's militancy on the border: for example, a vigil outside the closed Acapulco Fashions plant in Juarez in 1981 (Chapkis and Enloe 1983), and a 1983 strike over the doubling of quotas at another plant (Young 1987). This evidence, plus the material on strikes and walkouts in Asia (particularly South Korea), makes it clear that women workers are not passive pawns (Chapkis and Enloe 1983:91–97); nevertheless, as in the United States, firms and governments have often been successful in keeping women's strategies from coalescing beyond the individual level.

On the whole, the literature on Third World industrialization gives us a sense of the interrelationship between state policy, management strategies, and the youthful position of women workers as daughters in peasant or working-class families—all of which constrain women's militancy in the workplace and their autonomy within family structures. We also see cultural variability, however, between these labor forces (for example, between Malay and South Korean women's forms of resistance) and within them (between married and single women in Mexico, for example). It is clear that in labor forces dominated by working daughters, not just one but several trajectories exist for working women.

Working-Class Families in the United States

Single daughters are no longer the majority of the U.S. female work force. Working mothers now constitute a large proportion, and we need to keep in mind the new variety of ways in which women in industrial jobs have constructed their family lives: as members of dual-worker couples, as mothers returning to the labor force, as part-time workers, as single parents, as immigrant wives who have formed their families in other cultural contexts.

During the 1970s and 1980s, as industrial jobs particularly for women decreased, women found themselves unemployed (Rosen 1987), fighting rearguard actions to keep from receiving pay cuts in a declining industry (such as canning or textiles), or being victims of a plant closing. It is more difficult to find unionized workplaces where women can forge a work culture "in resistance," such as the apparel plant that Lamphere studied in 1977 (Lamphere 1985, 1987). Although we now have better documentation on women's struggles in service and clerical work (Bookman and Morgen 1988; Sacks 1988; Sacks and Remy 1984; Saltzman 1990), it is clear that union struggles are harder to win than they used to be. In Albuquerque, only Aerospace, Inc.—a plant organized by the machinists' union, paying high wages, and having an active group of female unionists—fit the model described by Lamphere in 1977. Changes in the NLRB and new tactics on the part of corporations to hire anti-union consultants and run a "tough legal campaign" (as well as to engage in illegal tactics) have made it difficult for women to engage in and win union drives (as the example of HealthTech demonstrated). We now have a clearer sense of how state power and management strategies have constrained women's group-level resistance in the workplace.

It is in the area of family life that we see the most change. The theme here is variability in the ways blue-collar women deal with the different trajectories that their working and marital lives take. Again, we see the importance of gradations within the working class, as well as of the way different ethnic and national populations have been pulled into local political economies.

Overall, when women enter the U.S. labor force, husbands in working-class families become more involved in reproductive labor at home. Working class men, like middle-class men, tend to do more child care than housework; however, we now have enough studies from different local political economies and representing Anglo, Mexican-American, and immigrant families to flesh out the circumstances in which men do more rather than less housework and child care. In other words, we can document a great deal of variability within the working class and get beyond stereotypes suggesting that working-class men (as opposed to middle-class and professional men) are Archie Bunker types who resist helping at home.

Immigrant men have changed least, but they tend to come from peasant and working-class cultures where women have not been employed for wages outside the household or where women's reproductive and productive work has not made them equal partners in the family economy. Yet even immigrant men tend to contribute more to housework and child care in the United States when they have working wives than they did in premigration contexts. Karen Hossfeld, who interviewed both Vietnamese and Mexican immigrant women working in electronics jobs in Silicon Valley, reports little change, but she does not provide much in the way of concrete data either on the questions she asked or the behavior she reports. She describes one case, the Rodriguez family, in which the husband was a sporadically employed construction worker and the wife held a full-time job in the electronics industry; the wife did all the housework, in addition to making tamales which she sold informally (1988a, chap. 7).

In contrast, Lamphere found that Portuguese and Colombian immigrant husbands in Central Falls, Rhode Island, often took care of young children while their wives worked (a split-shift arrangement) and did shopping, laundry, and some housework. Though they retained the ideology that the man was head of the household, they accepted their wives' employment as necessary and gradually began engaging in housework and child care. As in Albuquerque, these men were more willing to share the chores of child care than to perform such "female" tasks as cooking and cleaning (1987, chap. 6). For immigrants who married and had children before coming to the United States, and before most women had entered the labor force, women's employment brought less change than in our Albuquerque sample where we found egalitarian and even nontraditional patterns. Sherrie Grassmuck and Patricia Pessar also found that new immigrant women (from the Dominican Republic) had been able to renegotiate the household division of labor with their husbands. They argue, however, that women were relatively unwilling to jeopardize this new-found balance of power within the household by active resistance on the job, especially when such resistance could lead to job loss (1991:150–56).

Part-time or seasonal women workers have been relatively unsuccessful in obtaining changes in the family division of labor, as Zavella shows in her study of Chicana cannery workers. One-third of her twenty-four interviewees participated in a segregated division of labor where the wife was seen as primarily responsible for the housework and the care of the children; for two-thirds, the husbands and children helped, but there was no fundamental shift in responsibility (1987:137–38). Domestic workers might also fit this pattern: since their work is flexible, women can shorten their work week or fit their hours to family schedules, and husbands tend to regard domestic work as "not really a job." Mary Romero found that about half of twenty-five Chicana interviewees described a rigid sexual division of labor that defined inside housework as their responsibility. Many, however, pushed for a more equitable division of labor, with the result that some men did watch the children and help out with chores such as "starting dinner" (1992:32, 42). Glenn reports similar findings for Japanese-American (Nisei) domestic workers who raised their families during the 1930s and 1940s. Of nineteen Nisei working mothers, only four reported that their husbands helped with housecleaning on a regular basis, although many did all the outside chores such as gardening and house repairs. Glenn argues that although women would in theory have liked their husbands to help, in practice they did not want them to interfere and preferred to retain control over the skilled areas of cooking and housekeeping (1986:221–25).

When we look at native-born working-class women who hold full-time jobs, however, we seem to find far more variation: some families are moving only slowly toward re-allocating housework and child care; in others men are taking an equal share or possibly even doing the bulk of either the child-care chores or the housework. This seems to be happening among black, white, and Chicano/Hispano households, though subtle economic distinctions may account for some of the variability.

Arlie Hochschild's study includes two cases suggesting that there may be considerable variability within the black working class (1989: 128–41, 181–85). Ray Judson, a fork-lift driver, occasionally cared for his two-year-old son, and he would grill steaks outside on the barbecue; his wife challenged him to do more housework, and their conflicts over who would do "the second shift" eventually led to their separation. In contrast, Art Winfield, a thirty-five-year-old laboratory assistant, shared the care of his adopted five-year-old son and did the laundry, vacuuming, yard work, and half the cooking. In our terms, Ray Judson's wife was a secondary provider (earning $8.00 an hour to Ray's $13.50), while Art Winfield's wife, a legal secretary, was probably a coprovider. Hochschild did not find an overall correlation between the household division of labor and economics, but in these two cases, Ray's wife seemed to have less leverage for striking a bargain with a husband whose $30,000 a year made him the major provider. We clearly need additional data to document further this variability among working-class black families.

Among Chicanos, it is clear that wives' full-time wage work brings about changes in the household division of labor and more help from husbands (Ybarra 1982; Zinn 1980). Pesquera's study, however, indicates interesting differences between blue-collar and white-collar women in the extent of such changes. Pesquera's eight blue-collar interviewees had pushed hard to get their husbands to help with household chores, and half reported that cooking, cleaning, buying groceries, and doing laundry were shared. Clerical workers married to blue-collar men, on the other hand, reported that their husbands did much less housework. There was less difference in the area of

[handwritten marginal note: It's not only the income but the structure of the jobs — the demands]

[293]

child-care chores: half of both blue- and white-collar wives considered parenting a joint endeavor with husbands. Yet descriptions of daily routines indicated that women often did more than their husbands and that there were often struggles to get fathers to participate more fully in parenting (1985:140–49, 113–22).

Among the sixteen white families in Jane Hood's study of differences in the relative role of the wife as provider, the wives in the working-class families were more likely to be coproviders than secondary providers. The variations among these coproviders ranged from one family in which the husband did not help more but the teenage daughters did the housecleaning to two families with young children in which the parents shared child-care responsibility but the husband only "helped" with the housework. In the other five working-class couples (in two of which the wives were secondary providers and in three, coproviders), the husband helped but did not share equal responsibility for housework or child care. The two couples in the study who did share both parenting and housework equally were upper-middle-class families in which the husbands were professionals or managers (Hood 1983:85–109). Unlike our sample of working-class families (except for the Smiths; see Chapter 6), about half of these couples had older children who could be counted on to absorb some of the wife's housework. In addition, the wives had returned to the work force after staying at home for several years, whereas our interviewees had continued to work after their marriages and most had stayed out of the work force only for very short periods following the birth of their children.

All these studies indicate the presence of variability within the U.S. working class, as working mothers' strategies converge and diverge across ethnic boundaries. A woman's relative position as a coprovider, the age of her children, and her own willingness to engage in a struggle around issues of the "second shift" all seem related to the creation of more egalitarian patterns. On the other hand, patterns are very much in flux, and some men still engage in traditional behavior or "help out" with only a few female chores, thus perpetuating the double day for many wives.

Finally, we need to reemphasize the important differences between single and married working mothers. Our data show that women who are sole providers not only have much lower family incomes than households with male and female breadwinners but usually end up doing all of the housework and child care—unless they are living with relatives, and even in these cases, parenting is not shared. Tiano also found a big difference between single women and partnered mothers on the one hand, and single mothers and once-partnered mothers on the other.

> The economic insecurity to which their domestic statuses predisposed the single mothers and once-partnered women was reflected in their labor market vulnerability. Compelled to earn an income to support themselves and their dependents, yet facing recruitment barriers posed by their reproductive status, chronological maturity, and often limited educational attainment, they frequently were relegated to the apparel industry or to the most marginal jobs in the service sector. (Tiano 1992:56)

Although the single parents in our sample were not nearly so vulnerable, supporting children on a woman's income—given the wage differences between men and women—is very difficult and calls forth very different strategies and tactics both for finding living arrangements and day care and for building a support system.

The Difference that "Difference" Does Not Make

In examining data on working mothers in industrial occupations, both in the United States and abroad, we have come to see that different work and family trajectories characterize contrasting political economies. The shop floor strategies and family dynamics found where the labor force is primarily made up of working daughters (Malaysia, Hong Kong, Singapore) or is in flux (the U.S.-Mexico border) are quite different from those in the United States, where there are substantial portions of working mothers, both married and single. But even in the United States it is important to distinguish between immigrant working mothers, part-time working mothers, those who have re-entered the labor force, and those who have worked steadily throughout their childbearing years.

We have viewed difference—the intertwining of gender, class, and ethnicity—in relation to local political economies. In other words, we have tried to break apart dualistic notions of difference (dichotomous blocs of male versus female, Hispano versus Anglo,

[295]

single versus married, and working-class versus middle-class) and dissolve them into a more nuanced picture—a mosaic—emphasizing the converging and diverging strategies that are shaped as women migrate, marry, have children, take jobs, and later quit or change them. For example, we have emphasized the similarities between mainstay working wives such as Valerie Mondragon and Connie Mead, whose strategies around housework and child care were converging despite differences in their ethnic identities. And we have contrasted them with secondary providers such as Donna Garcia and coproviders such as Delores Baca, who share ethnic identity with Valerie but have forged quite different relationships with their husbands. Likewise, in the workplace we have seen that Mary Pike's tactics as she struggled to make the piece rate diverged from those of her co-worker Carrie Adams (another Anglo working mother), whose much different work practice eventually put her in the President's Club at Leslie Pants.

We would agree with Hochschild that there is a "stalled revolution" for working-class families, as well as for those of the middle and upper-middle classes. Some of our interviewees, such as Valerie Mondragon and Mary Pike, were able to push their husbands out of the "stall"; others, such as Delores Baca, were struggling without much success to get their husbands to take a greater role in housework; still others were like Geri Sandoval, who was able to share child-care chores with her husband but preferred to retain control over the housework because she had higher housekeeping standards. On the whole, however, men will need to participate a great deal more in both child care and housework before most couples can be called "egalitarian." In other words, many of the contradictions outlined in this book, especially those that involve replacing a woman's reproductive labor while she is at work, have not been resolved or completely mediated. Instead, women find themselves living in tension with the contradictions of their lives, however inventively they have worked out ways to involve husbands in domestic matters and to build supportive networks.

For the "stalled revolution" to get a push forward, we need important policy changes in both public and private domains: more affordable and higher-quality child care, a national parental leave policy, increased adoption of flextime and job sharing for young parents, better enforcement of health and safety standards, job training pro-

[296]

grams for women. The women workers we interviewed were committed to combining full-time employment with raising children, but more attention must be given to specific programs to make the industrial workplace a safer and more stable environment for employed women and to support their family choices.

Appendix

Mother's Providing Role, Occupation, Income, and Household Division of Labor

Pseudonym (Age)	Occupation	Hourly Wage
	Mexican Americans	
Delores Baca (25)	sewing machine operator (Leslie Pants)	$5.37
Albert (25)	stocker (supermarket chain)	$6.25
Thelma Barela (30)	plastics fabricator (Aerospace, Inc.)	$9.19
Ryan (31)	machine operator (trailer assembly firm)	$7.66
Lucia Benavides (39)	inspector, trimmer (Leslie Pants)	$6.61
Francisco (41)	maintenance man (public schools)	$4.60
Dolores Maes (24)	assembler (HealthTech)	$5.50
Carlos (24)	handyman I & II (city traffic dept.)	$6.80
Margaret Olguin (30)	assembler II (Computex)	$5.45
Avelino (31)	advertising salesman (Spanish radio station)	$600/mo. + comm.
Elena Ortega (33)	inspector II (Computex)	$6.39
Juan (26)	forklift operator (beverage warehouse)	$5.50
Josephine Perez (22)	electronics assembler (Computex)	$4.62
Manuel (26)	electronics assembler (Computex)	$5.11
Deborah Rivera (24)	modular tester (Southwest Electronics)	$6.25
Sabine (26)	modular tester (Southwest Electronics)	$7.74
Lucille Sanchez (33)	quality control, swaging (HealthTech)	$5.80
Mark (34)	salesman/driver (beverage company)	$6.50
Toni Sena (24)	sewing machine operator (Leslie Pants)	$5.00
Leo (27)	sheet-metal worker (air conditioning firm)	$5.10
Anita Alvarez (31)	electronics assembler (Howard Electronics)	$5.88
Art (34)	custodian	—

Annual Income	Children's Sex (Age)	Household	Child Care
$22,300	G (6 mo.)	traditional	semitraditional
$29,290[a]	G (8), B (6)	semitraditional	semitraditional
$13,450[b]	B (13), B (11), B (10), B (6), B (6)	egalitarian	semitraditional
$23,610	G (5)	traditional	traditional
$15,400	G (4), G (2)	egalitarian	semitraditional
$22,825	B (8), B (20 mo.)	egalitarian	semitraditional
$18,680	G (2), G (3 wk.)	traditional	traditional
$26,860	B (15 mo.)	egalitarian	semitraditional
$23,600	B (15), G (14), G (3)	traditional	semitraditional
$19,600[a]	G (22 mo.), G (10 mo.)	egalitarian	egalitarian
$11,300[c]	G (11) B (6) B (2)	no data	no data

Pseudonym (Age)	Occupation	Hourly Wage
Anglos		
Carrie Adams (24)	sewing machine operator (Leslie Pants)	$6.50
Roberto (24)	typewriter technician (college repair service)	$7.15
Linda Bennett (24)	sewing machine operator (Leslie Pants)	$6.50
Macky Garduno (29)	truck driver (plumbing supply)	$5.00 (55-hr/wk.)
Lynn Connelly (25)	inspector (Leslie Pants)	$4.50
Matthew (26)	supervisor (bedding manufacturer)	$7.50
Karen Leyba (23)	devices (HealthTech)	$5.00
Daniel (24)	mental health worker (mental health clinic)	$5.25
Mary Pike (22)	sewing machine operator (Leslie Pants)	$4.98–5.11
Don (23)	receiving (Leslie Pants)	$4.80
Ann Singleton (23)	assembler (Howard Electronics)	$5.92
Gene (26)	technician (local airport)	$7.50
Karen Smith (39)	inspector (Aerospace, Inc.)	$11.25
Rex (43)	machinist (Aerospace, Inc.)	$10.04
Maggie Todd (26)	timekeeper (payroll) (Southwest Electronics)	$6.71
Johnny (27)	machine setup (Southwest Electronics)	$6.89

Annual Income	Children's Sex (Age)	Household	Child Care
$27,370	G (14 mo.)	traditional	egalitarian
$29,000	G (3)	semitraditional	semitraditional
$20,020	G (3)	egalitarian	semitraditional
$15,280	G (2)	egalitarian	egalitarian
$19,000	G (4 mo.)	nontraditional	semitraditional
$27,925	G (2.5)	semitraditional	semitraditional
$45,000	B (21), B (18), G (12), B (7)	semitraditional	nontraditional
$27,000	B (13 mo.)	semitraditional	semitraditional

Pseudonym (Age)	Occupation	Hourly Wage
	Mexican Americans	
Prelinda Duran (41)	inspector (Computex)	$6.15
José (52)	dairy worker (local dairy)	$5.40
Nina Griego (31)	materials handler (Southwest Electronics)	$5.97
Allen (33)	shipping clerk (jewelry manufacturer)	$4.64
Valerie Mondragon (22)	swager, winder (HealthTech)	$5.30
Edward (21)	framer (construction)	$5.10
Marta Ortiz (28)	assembler (Southwest Electronics)	$5.48
Felipe (28)	laborer, wood shaver (wood shavings plant)	$4.50
Socorro Peña (30)	inspector (Computex)	$5.63
Lorenzo (31)	vehicle mechanic (construction firm)	$4.00
Lena Santos (23)	sewing machine operator (Leslie Pants)	$6.00
Jerry (25)	dry wall finisher (construction, seasonal)	$10.00
Lucy Valdez (28)	wire-prepper (Computex)	$5.58
Larry (33)	phone solicitor (handicapped industries)	$3.35
	Anglos	
Bonnie Anderson (30)	swager (HealthTech)	$5.55
Brett (30)	truck driver	$7.00
Sally Hall (22)	inspector (Leslie Pants)	$4.26–5.50
Guy (29)	machine mechanic (Leslie Pants)	$5.72
Connie Mead (34)	assembler III (Howard Electronics)	$5.55
Jack (34)	radio broadcaster (laid off)	$850/mo.
Jenny Phillips (19)	drill (HealthTech)	$5.00
Jesse (21)	farm helper (local dairy)	$3.35

Annual Income	Children's Sex (Age)	Household	Child Care
$22,180	B (3), B (1), B (26 wk.)	egalitarian	nontraditional
$18,180[a]	G (9), G (8), B (10 mo.)	egalitarian	nontraditional
$18,810[a]	G (21 mo.)	nontraditional	egalitarian
$19,160[d]	B (8), B (4)	traditional	egalitarian
$18,490[d]	G (7), B (3)	traditional	semitraditional
$27,520[d]	G (3)	semitraditional	semitraditional
$17,150[d]	B (7), B (5), B (4)	egalitarian	egalitarian
$15,900	B (6), B (4), B (6 mo.)	traditional	egalitarian
$16,100	G (2.5)	semitraditional	semitraditional
$17,000	B (10 mo.)	egalitarian	nontraditional
$12,440	B (14 mo.)	traditional	traditional

Pseudonym (Age)	Occupation	Hourly Wage
Mexican Americans		
Lorraine Delgado (24)	foil and overwrap (HealthTech)	$4.75
Jason (30)	supervisor (city water dept.)	$12.50
Donna Garcia (28)	skills trainer (SystemsPlus)	$7.00
Jimmy (31)	production supervisor (HealthTech)	$30,000/yr.
Jeanette Gilbert (32)	machine operator III (Computex)	$6.25
Ronald (33)	technician III (Computex)	$10.80
Inez Luna (23)	payroll clerk (Leslie Pants)	$6.25
Jake (26)	electrician	$12.50
Geri Sandoval (28)	circuit board repair (Southwest Electronics)	$5.96
Ray (29)	engineer specialist (phone company)	$10
Irene Tafoya (27)	materials handler (Southwest Electronics)	$5.76
William (25)	machinist (government agency)	$7.47
Leona Thomas (28)	electro-mechanical inspector (Computex)	$6.30
Carl (27)	Construction maintenance foreman (public utility)	$11.21
Anglo		
Vera Chandler (30)	winder (Southwest Electronics)	$5.68
Aris (39)	computer technician (national corporation)	$12.50

Annual Income	Children's Sex (Age)	Household	Child Care
$35,900	G (7)	traditional	traditional
$43,440	G (8), G (3)	traditional	nontraditional
$32,740	G (12), G (4)	semitraditional	semitraditional
$39,000	B (5 mo.)	semitraditional	egalitarian
$30,640	B (14 mo.)	traditional	semitraditional
$26,600	G (10), B (10 mo.)	semitraditional	egalitarian
$33,620	G (4), B (1)	semitraditional	egalitarian
$37,000	B (10), B (7)	semitraditional	semitraditional

Pseudonym (Age)	Occupation	Hourly Wage
Susan Anaya (28)	assembler (Southwest Electronics)	$5.46
Maria Apodaca (41)	sewing machine operator (Leslie Pants)	$3.50
Carmen Archuleta (28)	sewing machine operator (Leslie Pants)	$3.35
Regina Armenta (24)	foil and overwrap (HealthTech)	$5.20
Grace Estrada (21)	overwrap operator (HealthTech)	$5.10
Josie Gallegos (27)	sewing machine operator (Leslie Pants)	$6.33
Rosa Gomez (26)	assembler I (Southwest Electronics)	$5.48
Annette Griego (20)	swager (HealthTech)	$5.62
Linda Henry (37)	assembly operator (Howard Electronics)	$5.92
Corrine Maldonado (23)	trimmer and inspector (Leslie Pants)	$6.50
Betty Saiz (30)	materials handler (Southwest Electronics)	$5.76
Patricia Torres (30)	assembler II (Computex)	$5.50
Higher Income Sole Providers		
Laura Davidson (35)	stocker/processor (Aerospace, Inc.)	$9.40
Christina Espinosa (31)	fabricator (Aerospace, Inc.)	$9.75
Betty Thompson (37)	inspector (Aerospace, Inc.)	$9.75

[a]Husband unemployed for part of 1982 or 1983.
[b]Wife unemployed for part of 1982 or 1983.
[c]Wife's income only.
[d]Estimate may be high; husband unemployed for part of 1982–83, but we had no way of estimating lost wages.
[e]Includes $900 in child support.
[f]Includes $300 in child support.

Annual Income	Children's Sex (Age)	Household	Child Care
$12,230	B (8 mo.)	never married	separate household
$6,000	B (10), G (8), B (6)	husband away for five years	separate household
$6,375	B (2.5)	never married	with parents
$11,650	B (4)	divorced 1981	with cousin
$11,000	G (2)	divorced 1980	with parents
$12,000	B (13 mo.)	never married	separate household
$12,000	G (5)	never married	——
$12,000	B (4)	separated, then widowed 1980	with sister
$12,000	B (8), G (5)	divorced 1977	separate household
$8,000	B (5)	divorced 1977	with grandmother
$11,000 (child support:6 mos. @$150)	G (6), B (5)[e]	divorced 1977	separate household
$12,000 (child support:3 mos. @$100)	G (11), G (11), G (3)	never married	separate household
$19,000	B (16), G (14), B (2)	divorced (2 children by 1st husband, 1 by third)	separate household
$20,000	B (15), B (13)	divorced 1971	separate household
$22,000	B (17), B (15), B (14), G (11), G (2.5)	divorced boys' father; never married girls' father	separate household

Bibliography

Aldous, Joan, ed. 1982. *Two Paychecks: Life in Dual-Earner Families*. Beverly Hills, Calif.: Sage.

Anzaldúa, Gloria, ed. 1990. *Making Face, Making Soul—Haciendo Caras: Creative and Critical Perspectives of Women of Color*. San Francisco: Aunt Lute Foundation Books.

Arellano, Anselmo, and Josué Vigil. 1985. *Las Vegas Grandes on the Gallinas, 1835–1985*. Las Vegas, N.M.: Editorial Telerana.

Aries, Elizabeth J., and Fern L. Johnson. 1983. "Close Friendship in Adulthood: Conversational Content between Same-sex Friends." *Sex Roles* 9 (12): 1183–96.

Auerbach, Stevanne. 1975. "What Parents Want from Day Care." In *Child Care Services: Programs vs. Politics*, ed. Stevanne Auerbach and James A. Rivaldo, 137–52. New York: Human Sciences Press.

Avineri, Shlomo. 1968. *The Social and Political Thought of Karl Marx*. Cambridge: Cambridge University Press.

Bahr, Stephen J. 1974. "Effects on Power and Division of Labor in the Family." In *Working Mothers*, ed. Lois Hoffman and F. Ivan Nye, 167–85. San Francisco: Jossey-Bass.

Barth, Fredrik. 1959. *Political Leadership among Swat Pathans*. London: Athalone Press.

Beneria, Lourdes, and Martha Roldan. 1987. *The Crossroads of Class and Gender: Industrial Homework, Subcontracting, and Household Dynamics in Mexico City*. Chicago: University of Chicago Press.

Berk, Richard A., and Sarah Fenstermaker Berk. 1979. *Labor and Leisure at Home: Content and Organization of the Household Day*. Beverly Hills, Calif.: Sage.

Berk, Sarah Fenstermaker. 1985. *The Gender Factory: The Apportionment of Work in American Households*. New York: Plenum Press.

Bookman, Ann, and Sandra Morgen. 1988. *Women and the Politics of Empowerment*. Philadelphia: Temple University Press.

Bott, Elizabeth. 1957. *Family and Social Network: Roles, Norms, and External Relationships in Ordinary Urban Families*. London: Tavistock.

Bourdieu, Pierre. 1977. *Outline of a Theory of Practice*. Cambridge: Cambridge University Press.

Brasher, Stanley J. 1962. *Economic Analysis and Projection for Albuquerque, New Mexico*. A Study for the Planning Department, City of Albuquerque. Albuquerque: Planning Department.

Briggs, Charles L. 1988. *Competence in Performance: The Creativity of Tradition in Mexicano Verbal Art*. Philadelphia: University of Pennsylvania Press.

Briggs, Charles L., and John R. Van Ness, eds. 1987. *Land, Water, and Culture: New Perspectives on Hispanic Land Grants*. Albuquerque: University of New Mexico Press.

Burawoy, Michael. 1979. *Manufacturing Consent: Changes in the Labor Process under Monopoly Capitalism*. Chicago: University of Chicago Press.

Bureau of Business Research (BBR). 1949. *The Economy of Albuquerque, New Mexico*. Albuquerque: University of New Mexico and Federal Reserve Bank of Kansas.

Burma, John. 1954. *Spanish-Speaking Groups in the United States*. Durham, N.C.: Duke University Press.

Chapkis, Wendy, and Cynthia Enloe. 1983. *Of Common Cloth: Women in the Global Textile Industry*. Amsterdam: Transnational Institute.

Collier, Jane. 1974. "Women in Politics." In *Woman, Culture, and Society*, ed. Michelle Zimbalist Rosaldo and Louise Lamphere, 89–96. Stanford, Calif.: Stanford University Press.

——. 1988. *Marriage and Inequality in Classless Societies*. Stanford, Calif.: Stanford University Press.

Collier, Jane, and Michelle Z. Rosaldo. 1981. "Politics and Gender in Simple Societies" in *Sexual Meanings: The Construction of Gender and Society*, ed. Sherry Ortner and Harriet Whitehead, 275–329. Cambridge: Cambridge University Press.

Coltrane, Scott. 1990. "Birth Timing and the Division of Labor in Dual-Earner Families." *Journal of Family Issues* 11 (2): 157–81.

Davidson, Lynne R., and Lucile Duberman. 1982. "Friendship: Communication, and Interactional Patterns in Same-Sex Dyads." *Sex Roles* 8 (8): 809–22.

Davis, Angela. 1981. *Women, Race and Class*. New York: Random House.

Dawson, Deborah A. 1990. *Child Care Arrangements: Health of Our Nation's Children, United States, 1988*. Advance Data from Vital and Health statistics no. 187. Hyattsville, Md.: National Center for Health Statistics.

deBuys, William. 1985. *Enchantment and Exploitation: The Life and Hard Times of a New Mexico Mountain Range*. Albuquerque: University of New Mexico Press.

di Leonardo, Micaela. 1987. "The Female World of Cards and Holidays: Women, Families, and the work of Kinship." *Signs* 12 (3): 440–53.

Dornbusch, Sanford M., and Myra H. Strober, eds. 1988. *Feminism, Children, and the New Families.* New York: Guilford Press.

Dozier, Edward P. 1970. *The Pueblo Indians of North America.* New York: Holt, Rinehart & Winston.

Edwards, Richard C. 1979. *Contested Terrain: The Transformation of the Workplace in America.* New York: Basic Books.

Ehrenreich, Barbara, and Deirdre English. 1975. "The Manufacture of Housework." *Socialist Revolution* 26 (Oct.–Dec.); reprinted in *Capitalism and the Family*, ed. Mina Caulfield et al., 7–42. San Francisco: Agenda.

Enloe, Cynthia. 1983. "Women Textile Workers in the Militarization of Southeast Asia." In *Women, Men, and the International Division of Labor*, ed. June Nash and Maria Patricia Fernández Kelly, 407–25. Albany: State University of New York Press.

Fernández Kelly, Maria Patricia. 1983. *For We Are Sold, I and My People: Women and Industry in Mexico's Frontier.* Albany: State University of New York Press.

Fernández Kelly, Maria Patricia, and Anna M. Garcia. 1988. "Economic Restructuring in the United States: Hispanic Women in the Garment and Electronics Industries." *Women and Work: An Annual Review* 3:49–65.

Fernández Kelly, Maria Patricia, and Saskia Sassen. 1991. "A Collaborative Study of Hispanic Women in the Garment and Electronics Industries." Final Report presented to the Ford, Revson, and Tinker Foundations. Typescript, distributed by the Center for Latin American and Caribbean Studies, New York University.

Firth, Raymond. 1962. *Essays on Social Organization and Values.* London School of Economics Monograph 28. London: Athalone Press.

Fox, Margery, Margaret Gibbs, and Doris Auerback. 1985. "Age and Gender Dimensions of Friendship." *Psychology of Women Quarterly* 9 (4): 489–502.

Fox, Steve. 1991. *Toxic Work: Women Workers at GTE Lenkurt.* Philadelphia: Temple University Press.

Freedman, Estelle B. 1990. "Theoretical Perspectives on Sexual Difference: An Overview." In *Theoretical Perspectives on Sexual Difference*, ed. Deborah L. Rhode, 257–62. New Haven: Yale University Press.

Freeman, Richard B., and James L. Medoff. 1984. *What Do Unions Do?* New York: Basic Books.

Gagnier, Regenia. 1990. "Feminist Postmodernism: The End of Feminism or the Ends of Theory?" In *Theoretical Perspectives on Sexual Difference*, ed. Deborah L. Rhode, 21–30. New Haven: Yale University Press.

Galarza, Ernesto. 1972. "Mexicans in the Southwest: A Culture in Process." In *Plural Society in the Southwest*, ed. Edward H. Spicer and Raymond H. Thompson, 261–97. New York: Arkville Press, for the Weatherhead Foundation.

Gallese, Liz Roman. 1985. *Women Like Us: What Is Happening to the Women of the Harvard Business School, Class of '75—the Women Who Had the First Chance to Make It to the Top.* New York: New American Library, Signet Books.

[313]

Giddens, Anthony. 1979. *Central Problems in Social Theory: Action, Structure, and Contradiction in Social Analysis.* Berkeley: University of California Press.

Glasmeier, Amy K., Peter Hall, and Ann R. Markusen. 1983. "Recent Evidence on High-Technology Industries' Spatial Tendencies: A Preliminary Investigation." Working Paper no. 417, Institute of Urban and Regional Development, University of California, Berkeley.

Glenn, Evelyn Nakano. 1985. "Racial Ethnic Women's Labor: The Intersection of Race, Gender, and Class Oppression." *Review of Radical Political Economics* 17 (3): 86–108.

——. 1986. *Issei, Nisei, War Bride: Three Generations of Japanese American Women in Domestic Service.* Philadelphia: Temple University Press.

Gluckman, Max. 1955. *Custom and Conflict in Africa.* Oxford: Blackwell.

Goldscheider, Frances K., and Linda J. Waite. 1991. *New Families, No Families? The Transformation of the American Home.* Berkeley: University of California Press.

Gonzales, Phillip B. 1986. "Spanish Heritage and Ethnic Protest in New Mexico: The Anti-Fraternity Bill of 1933." *New Mexico Historical Review* 61 (4): 281–99.

——. 1991. "Americans . . . Set Apart: Ethnic Diffidence and Categorical Awareness among a Chicano Sub-type." Typescript. University of New Mexico, Department of Sociology.

——. 1993a. "Historical Poverty, Restructuring Effects and Integrative Ties: Mexican American Neighborhoods in a Peripheral Sunbelt Economy." In *Beyond the Underclass Debate: Latino Communities in the United States,* ed. Rachel Pinderhuges and Joan Moore. New York: Russell Sage.

——. 1993b. "The Ethnopolitics of Affirmative Action: Hispanic Regents versus the President at the University of New Mexico." In *Contemporary Chicano Politics,* ed. David Montejano. Albuquerque: University of New Mexico Press. Forthcoming.

Grant, Alexander, and Company. 1982. *The Fifth Study of General Manufacturing Business Climates of 48 Contiguous States of America.*

Grassmuck, Sherrie, and Patricia Pessar. 1991. *Between Two Islands: Dominican International Migration.* Berkeley: University of California Press.

Green, Susan S. 1983. "Silicon Valley's Women Workers: A Theoretical Analysis of Sex-Segregation in the Electronics Industry Labor Market." In *Women, Men, and the International Division of Labor,* ed. June Nash and Maria Patricia Fernández Kelly, 273–331. Albany: State University of New York Press.

Grenier, Guillermo. 1988. *Inhuman Relations: Quality Circles and Anti-Unionism in American Industry.* Philadelphia: Temple University Press.

Haas, Linda. 1982. "Determinants of Role-Sharing Behavior: A Study of Egalitarian Couples." *Sex Roles* 8 (7): 747–70.

Hartmann, Heidi I. 1981. "The Family as the Locus of Gender, Class, and Political Struggle: The Example of Housework." *Signs* 6 (3): 366–94.

Hochschild, Arlie, with Anne Machung. 1989. *The Second Shift: Working Parents and the Revolution at Home.* New York: Viking Penguin.

Holmstrom, Lynn. 1972. *The Two-Career Family.* Cambridge, Mass.: Schenkman.

Hood, Jane C. 1983. *Becoming a Two-Job Family: Role Bargaining in Dual Worker Households.* New York: Praeger.

Hood, Jane C., and Susan Golden. 1979. "Beating Time/Making Time: The Impact of Work Scheduling on Men's Family Roles." *Family Coordinator*, October, pp. 575–82.

hooks, bell. 1984. *Feminist Theory: From Margin to Center.* Boston: South End Press.

Hossfeld, Karen J. 1988a. "Divisions of Labor, Divisions of Lives: Immigrant Women Workers in Silicon Valley." Ph.D. diss. University of California, Santa Cruz.

———. 1988b. "Sex, Race, and Class in Silicon Valley: Immigrant Women Workers and the High-Tech Division of Labor." Manuscript.

Huber, Joan, and Glenna Spitze. 1981. "Wives' Employment, Household Behaviors, and Sex-Role Attitudes." *Social Forces* 60 (1): 150–69.

Hurtado, Aida. 1989. "Relating to Privilege: Seduction and Rejection in the Subordination of White Women and Women of Color." *Signs* 14 (4): 833–55.

Kahn, Alfred J., and Sheila B. Kamerman. 1987. *Child Care: Facing the Hard Choices.* Dover, Mass.: Auburn House.

Katz, Naomi, and David S. Kemnitzer. 1983. "Fast Forward: The Internationalization of Silicon Valley." In *Women, Men, and the International Division of Labor*, ed. June Nash and Maria Patricia Fernández Kelly, 332–45. Albany: State University of New York Press.

———. 1984. "Women and Work in Silicon Valley: Options and Futures." In *My Troubles Are Going to Have Trouble with Me: Everyday Trials and Triumphs of Women Workers*, ed. Karen Sacks and Dorothy Remy, 209–18. New Brunswick. N.J.: Rutgers University Press.

Keefe, Susan E. 1984. "Real and Ideal Extended Familism among Mexican Americans and Anglo Americans: On the Meaning of 'Close' Family Ties." *Human Organization* 43:65–70.

Keefe, Susan E., and Amado M. Padilla. 1987. *Chicano Ethnicity.* Albuquerque: University of New Mexico Press.

Keller, John F. 1983. "The Division of Labor in Electronics." In *Women, Men, and the International Division of Labor*, ed. June Nash and Maria Patricia Fernández Kelly, 346–73. Albany: State University of New York Press.

Kung, Lydia. 1983. *Factory Women in Taiwan.* Ann Arbor: UMI Research Press.

Kutsche, Paul. 1979. *The Survival of Spanish American Villages.* Colorado College Studies no. 15. Colorado Springs: Research Committee, Colorado College.

Kutsche, Paul, and John R. Van Ness. 1981. *Cañones: Values, Crisis, and Survival in a Northern New Mexico Village.* Albuquerque: University of New Mexico Press.

Lamb, Michael 1986. "The Changing Roles of Fathers." In *The Father's Role*, ed. Michael Lamb. 3–28. New York: Wiley.

Lamphere, Louise. 1974. "Strategies, Cooperation, and Conflict among Women in Domestic Groups." In *Woman, Culture, and Society*, ed. Michelle Zimbalist Rosaldo and Louise Lamphere, 97–112. Stanford, Calif.: Stanford University Press.

——. 1979. "Fighting the Piece-Rate System: New Dimensions of an Old Struggle in the Apparel Industry." In *Case Studies on the Labor Process*, ed. Andrew Zimbalist 257–76. New York: Monthly Review Press.

——. 1985. "Bringing the Family to Work: Women's Culture on the Shop Floor." *Feminist Studies* 11(3): 519–40.

——. 1987. *From Working Daughters to Working Mothers: Immigrant Women in a New England Industrial Community.* Ithaca: Cornell University Press.

——. 1990. "Comments on Joan Scott: The Evidence of Experience." Paper presented at symposium "Anthropology's Interlocutors." American Anthropological Association Meetings, New Orleans, November 30.

——. 1991. "The Gendered Nature of the Workplace: Comparing Male and Female Experiences." Paper presented at symposium "Women's Work Cultures." American Anthropological Association Meetings, Chicago, November 23.

Lamphere, Louise, and Guillermo Grenier. 1988. "Women, Unions, and 'Participative Management': Organizing in the Sunbelt." In *Women and the Politics of Empowerment*, ed. Ann Bookman and Sandra Morgen, 227–56. Philadelphia: Temple University Press.

LaRossa, Ralph, and Maureen Mulligan LaRossa. 1981. *Transition to Parenthood: How Infants Change Families.* Beverly Hills, Calif.: Sage Publications.

Leach, Edmund. 1954. *Political Systems of Highland Burma.* Reprint. Boston: Beacon Press, 1965.

Lieberson, Stanley. 1961. "A Societal Theory of Race and Ethnic Relations." *American Sociological Review* 21 (December 1961): 902–10. (Reprinted in *Majority and Minority: The Dynamics of Racial and Ethnic Relations*, ed. Norman R. Yetman and C. Hoy Steele, 45–53. Boston: Allyn & Bacon, 1975.)

Lim, Linda. 1978. *Women Workers in Multinational Corporations: The Case of the Electronics Industry in Malaysia and Singapore.* Michigan Occasional Papers no. 9. Ann Arbor: University of Michigan Women's Studies Program.

——. 1982. *Women in the Singapore Economy.* ERC Occasional Papers Series. Singapore: Chopmen.

——. 1983. "Capitalism, Imperialism, and Patriarchy: The Dilemma of Third-World Women Workers in Multinational Factories." In *Women, Men, and the International Division of Labor*, ed. June Nash and Maria Patricia Fernández Kelly, 70–91. Albany: State University of New York Press.

Lorde, Audre. 1984. *Sister Outsider: Essays and Speeches.* New York: Crossing.

Luckingham, Bradford. 1982. *The Urban Southwest: A Profile History of Albuquerque, El Paso, Phoenix, Tucson.* El Paso: Texas Western Press.

Malecki, E. J. 1985. "Technological Imperatives and Modern Corporate Strategy." In *Production, Work, Territory: The Geographical Anatomy of Industrial Capitalism*, ed. Allen J. Scott and Michael Storper, 67–79. Boston: Allen & Unwin.

Marx, Karl. 1845. Selections from "Theses on Feuerbach." In *Selected Writings in Sociology and Social Philosophy*, trans. T. B. Bottomore, 67–69. New York: McGraw-Hill, 1964.

Mayo, Elton 1933. *The Human Problems of an Industrial Civilization*. New York: Macmillan.

Model, Suzanne. 1982. "Housework by Husbands: Determinants and Implications." In *Two Paychecks: Life in Dual-Earner Families*, ed. Joan Aldous, 193–205. Beverly Hills, Calif.: Sage.

Moraga, Cherrie, and Gloria Anzaldua, eds. 1981. *This Bridge Called My Back: Writings by Radical Women of Color*. Watertown, Mass.: Persephone.

Nash, June. 1983. "The Impact of the Changing International Division of Labor on Different Sectors of the Labor Force." In *Women, Men, and the International Division of Labor*, ed. June Nash and Maria Patricia Fernández Kelly, 2–38. Albany: State University of New York Press.

Nash, June, and Maria Patricia Fernández Kelly. 1983. *Women, Men, and the International Division of Labor*. Albany: State University of New York Press.

Oakley, Ann. 1974. *Woman's Work: The Housewife, Past and Present*. New York: Pantheon Books.

Ong, Aihwa. 1987. *Spirits of Resistance and Capitalist Discipline: Factory Women in Malaysia*. Albany: State University of New York Press.

———. 1991 "The Gender and Labor Politics of Postmodernity." *Annual Review of Anthropology* 20: 279–310.

Oppenheimer, Alan J. 1969. *The Historical Background of Albuquerque*. Albuquerque: Urban Development Institute of the University of Albuquerque with City Planning Department.

Ortner, Sherry. 1984. "Theory in Anthropology since the Sixties." *Comparative Studies in Society and History* 26(1):126–65.

Ortner, Sherry, and Harriet Whitehead. 1981. *Sexual Meanings: The Cultural Construction of Gender and Sexuality*. Cambridge: Cambridge University Press.

Parker, Mike, and Jane Slaughter. 1988. *Choosing Sides: Unions and the Team Concept*. A Labor Notes Book. Boston: South End Press.

Peña, Devon. 1987. "'Tortuosidad': Shop Floor Struggles of Female Maquiladora Workers." In *Women on the U.S.-Mexico Border: Responses to Change*, ed. Vicki L. Ruiz and Susan Tiano, 129–54. Boston: Allen & Unwin.

Perkins, Dennis N. T., Veronica Nieva, and Edward Lawler. 1983. *Managing Creation: The Challenge of Building a New Organization*. New York: Wiley.

Perrigo, Lynn. 1985. *Hispanos: Historic Leaders in New Mexico*. Santa Fe, N.M.: Sunstone Press.

Pesquera, Beatriz M. 1985. "Work and Family: A Comparative Analysis of Professional, Clerical, and Blue-Collar Chicana Workers." Ph.D. diss., University of California, Berkeley.

Pleck, Joseph. 1985. *Working Wives, Working Husbands*. Beverly Hills, Calif.: Sage.

Pogrebin, Letty Cottin. 1987. *Among Friends: Who We Like, Why We Like Them, and What We Do about It*. New York: McGraw-Hill.

Rapoport, Rhona, and Robert N. Rapoport. 1971. *Dual-Career Families*. London: Penguin.

Rapoport, Rhona, and Robert N. Rapoport, with Janice M. Bumstead, eds. 1978. *Working Couples*. New York: Harper & Row.

Rehder, Robert R. 1985. "Stifling Innovation and Change." *Training and Development Journal*, July, pp. 60–64.

Rhode, Deborah L. 1990. *Theoretical Perspectives on Sexual Difference*. New Haven: Yale University Press.

Robinson, John P. 1977. *How Americans Use Time: A Social-Psychological Analysis of Everyday Behavior*. New York: Praeger.

Robinson, John P., et al. 1988. *The Rhythm of Everyday Life: How Soviet and American Citizens Use Their Time*. Boulder, Colo.: Westview Press.

Roethlisberger, Fritz J., William J. Dickson, and Harold A. Wright. 1939. *Management and the Worker: An Account of a Research Program Conducted by the Western Electric Company, Hawthorne Works, Chicago*. Cambridge, Mass.: Harvard University Press.

Rollins, Judith. 1985. *Between Women: Domestics and Their Employers*. Philadelphia: Temple University Press.

Romero, Mary. 1992. *Maid in the U.S.A.* New York: Routledge.

Rosaldo, Renato. 1989. *Culture and Truth: The Remaking of Social Analysis*. Boston: Beacon Press.

Rosen, Ellen I. 1987. *Bitter Choices: Blue Collar Women In and Out of Work*. Chicago: University of Chicago Press.

Rubin, Lillian. 1976. *Worlds of Pain: Life in the Working-Class Family*. New York: Basic Books.

——. 1985. *Just Friends: The Role of Friendship in Our Lives*. New York: Harper & Row.

Ruiz, Vicki L. 1983. "By the Day or the Week: Mexicana Domestic Workers in El Paso." In *Women on the U.S.-Mexico Border: Responses to Change*, ed. Vicki L. Ruiz and Susan Tiano, 61–76. Boston: Allen & Unwin.

Ruiz, Vicki L., and Susan Tiano. 1987. *Women on the U.S.-Mexico Border: Responses to Change*. Boston: Allen & Unwin.

Sacks, Karen Brodkin. 1988. *Caring by the Hour: Women, Work and Organizing at Duke Medical Center*. Urbana: University of Illinois Press.

Sacks, Karen Brodkin, and Dorothy Remy, eds. 1984. *My Troubles Are Going to Have Trouble with Me: Everyday Trials and Triumphs of Women Workers*. New Brunswick, N.J.: Rutgers University Press.

Safa, Helen I. 1986. "Runaway Shops and Female Employment: The Search for Cheap Labor." In Eleanor Leacock, Helen I. Safa, et al., *Women's Work*, 58–74. South Hadley, Mass.: Bergin & Garvey.

Salaff, Janet W. 1981. *Working Daughters of Hong Kong: Filial Piety or Power in the Family*. Cambridge: Cambridge University Press.

Saltzman, Cynthia. 1990. "Unseen Women at the Academy." In *Uncertain Terms: Negotiating Gender in American Culture*, ed. Faye Ginsburg and Anna Lowenhaupt Tsing, 152–68. Boston: Beacon Press.

Sanjek, Roger, ed. 1990. *Fieldnotes: The Makings of Anthropology*. Ithaca: Cornell University Press.

Scott, Joan. 1991. "The Evidence of Experience." *Critical Inquiry* 17(4): 773–97.

Shaiken, Harley, and Stephen Herzenberg. 1988. *Automation and Global Production: Automobile Engine Production in Mexico, the United States, and Canada*. San Diego: Center for U.S.-Mexican Studies, University of California, San Diego.

Shapiro-Perl, Nina. 1979. "The Piece Rate: Struggle on the Shop Floor. Evidence from the Costume Jewelry Industry in Providence, Rhode Island." In *Case Studies on the Labor Process*, ed. Andrew Zimbalist, 277–98. New York: Monthly Review Press.

——. 1984. "Resistance Strategies: The Routine Struggle for Bread and Roses." In *My Troubles Are Going to Have Trouble with Me: Everyday Trials and Triumphs of Women Workers*, ed. Karen Brodkin Sacks and Dorothy Remy, 193–208. New Brunswick, N.J.: Rutgers University Press.

Skold, Karen, P. Siegel, and M. Lawrence. 1983. *Child Care in Santa Clara County*. Stanford, Calif.: Institute for Research on Women and Gender, Stanford University.

Snow, Robert T. 1983. "The New International Division of Labor and the U.S. Work Force: The Case of the Electronics Industry." In *Women, Men, and the International Division of Labor*, ed. June Nash and Maria Patricia Fernández Kelly, 39–69. Albany: State University of New York Press.

Stacey, Judith. 1990. *Brave New Families: Stories of Domestic Upheaval in Late Twentieth Century America*. New York: Basic Books.

Stack, Carol. 1974. *All Our Kin: Strategies for Survival in a Black Community*. New York: Harper & Row.

Staines, Graham L., and Joseph H. Pleck. 1983. *The Impact of Work Schedules on the Family*. Ann Arbor: University of Michigan, Institute for Social Research.

Swerdlow, Amy, and Hanna Lessinger, eds. 1983. *Class, Race, and Sex: The Dynamics of Control*. Boston: G. K. Hall.

Taplin, Ruth. 1986. "Women in World Market Factories: East and West." *Ethnic and Racial Studies* 9 (2): 168–95.

Thompson, Edward. P. 1966. *The Making of the English Working Class*. New York: Vintage Press.

Thorne, Barrie. 1990. "Children and Gender: Constructions of Difference." In *Theoretical Perspectives on Sexual Difference*, ed. Deborah L. Rhode, 100–13. New Haven: Yale University Press.

Tiano, Susan. 1987a. "Maquiladoras in Mexicali: Integration of Exploitation." In *Women on the U.S.-Mexico Border: Responses to Change*, ed. Vicki L. Ruiz and Susan Tiano, 77–101. Boston: Allen & Unwin.

——. 1987b. "Women's Work and Unemployment in Northern Mexico." In *Women on the U.S.-Mexico Border: Responses to Change*, ed. Vicki L. Ruiz and Susan Tiano, 17–39. Boston: Allen & Unwin.

——. 1991. "Household Composition, Domestic Status, and Women's Work Trajectories," chap. 6. Typescript.

Turner, Victor. 1957. *Schism and Continuity in an African Society: A Study of Ndembu Life.* Manchester: Manchester University Press.

U.S. Bureau of the Census. 1960a, 1970a, 1980a. *Census of Population: Detailed Population Characteristics,* vol. 1, pt. 33, *New Mexico.* Washington, D.C.: Government Printing Office.

——. 1960b, 1970b, 1980b. *Census of Population: Detailed Population Characteristics, United States Summary.* Washington, D.C.: Government Printing Office.

——. 1963a, 1982a. *Census of Manufactures: Geographic Area Series, New Mexico.* Washington, D.C.: Government Printing Office.

——. 1963b. *Census of Manufactures,* vol. 1, *Subject and Special Statistics.* Washington, D.C.: Government Printing Office.

——. 1982b. *Trends in Child Care Arrangements of Working Mothers.* Prepared by Marjorie Lueck, Ann C. Orr, and Martin O'Connell. Current Population Reports, ser. P-23, no. 117. Washington, D.C.: Government Printing Office.

——. 1987. *Statistical Abstract of the United States.* Washington, D.C.: Government Printing Office.

U.S. Bureau of Labor Statistics. 1977. *Technological Change and Its Labor Impact in Five Industries.* Bulletin no. 1961. Washington, D.C.: Government Printing Office.

——. 1982. *Study on Electronics Industry.* Washington, D.C.: U.S. Government Printing Office.

——. 1991. *Employment and Earnings Characteristics of Families.* Bulletin USDL 91–373. Washington, D.C.: Government Printing Office.

Uttal, Lynet. 1990. The Parent–Childcare Provider Relationship: The Crucial Link between Employment and Family Responsibilities with Special Attention to the Effects of Race and Class Dynamics. Diss. prospectus, University of California, Santa Cruz.

Vanek, Joan. 1974. "Time Spent in Housework." *Scientific American* 231 (November): 116–120.

Wagner, Roland M., and Diane M. Schaffer. 1980. "Social Networks and Survival Strategies: An Exploratory Study of Mexican American, Black, and Anglo Female Family Heads in San Jose, California." In *Twice a Minority: Mexican American Women,* ed. Margarita B. Melville, 173–90. St. Louis, Mo.: C. V. Mosby.

Winnie, William W., Jr. 1960. "The Spanish Surname Criterion for Identifying Hispanos in the Southwestern United States: A Preliminary Evaluation." *Social Forces* 38:363–66.

Wolf, Diane. 1992. *Factory Daughters: Gender, Household Dynamics, and Rural Industrialization in Java.* Berkeley: University of California Press.

Wolf, Margery. 1974. "Chinese Women: Old Skills in a New Context." In *Woman, Culture, and Society,* ed. Michelle Zimbalist Rosaldo and Louise Lamphere, 157–72. Stanford, Calif.: Stanford University Press.

Wright, Paul H. 1982. "Men's Friendships, Women's Friendships and the Alleged Inferiority of the Latter." *Sex Roles* 8 (1): 1–20.

Yanagisako, Sylvia Junko. 1977. "Women-Centered Kin Networks in Urban Bilateral Kinship." *American Ethnologist* 4 (2): 207–26.

——. 1989. "The Changing Gender Politics of Italian Family Firms." Unpublished paper, Stanford University.

Yanagisako, Sylvia Junko, and Jane Collier. 1990. "The Mode of Reproduction in Anthropology." In *Theoretical Perspectives on Sexual Difference*, ed. Deborah L. Rhode, 131–41. New Haven: Yale University Press.

Yancey, William L., Eugene P. Ericksen, and Richard N. Juliani. 1976. "Emergent Ethnicity: A Review and Reformulation." *American Sociological Review* 41 (3): 391–402.

Ybarra, Lea. 1982. "When Wives Work: The Impact on the Chicano Family." *Journal of Marriage and the Family* 44 (1): 169–78.

Young, Gay. 1987. "Gender Identification and Working-Class Solidarity among Maquila Workers in Ciudad Juarez: Stereotypes and Realities." In *Women on the U.S.-Mexico Border: Responses to Change*, ed. Vicki L. Ruiz and Susan Tiano, 105–27. Boston: Allen & Unwin.

Young, Michael, and Peter Willmott. 1957. *Family and Kinship in East London.* New York: Penguin Books.

Zavella, Patricia. 1987. *Women's Work and Chicano Families: Cannery Workers of the Santa Clara Valley.* Ithaca: Cornell University Press.

——. 1991a. "Mujeres in Factories: Race and Class Perspectives on Women, Work, and Family." In *Gender at the Crossroads of Knowledge: Feminist Anthropology in the Post-modern Era*, ed. Micaela di Leonardo, 312–36. Berkeley: University of California Press.

——. 1991b. "Reflections on Diversity among Chicanas." *Frontiers* 12 (2): 763–85.

Zinn, Maxine Baca. 1980. "Employment and Education of Mexican-American Women: The Interplay of Modernity and Ethnicity in Eight Families." *Harvard Educational Review* 50 (1): 47–62.

Zinn, Maxine Baca, Lyn Weber Cannon, Elizabeth Higginbotham, and Bonnie Thornton Dill. 1986. "The Costs of Exclusionary Practices in Women's Studies." *Signs* 11 (2): 290–303.

Index

Index

Transportation equipment, 46n
Transportation sector, 55

Unions, 86, 130, 167
at participative plant, 149, 153–54, 164
and plant culture, 91, 105, 109, 120, 126–29
and use of resistance strategies, 112–13, 117, 171–72, 174–81, 291

Van Ness, John R., 24n

Wages, 43, 90, 124, 150, 163, 168
of Anglo husbands, 68, 78, 79, 205, 210
of coproviders, 64–67, 71, 202, 205, 210
effects of unionization on, 121, 122
gender differences in, 50–55, 88, 130
and hiring policy, 111–12
of Hispano husbands, 74, 77, 195, 202
impact of recession on, 62
of mainstay providers, 73, 200
paid for child care, 229, 232–34, 236, 238, 239
piece-rate system, 97–104, 109, 110, 114–15
profit-sharing, 106–7
quota/bonus system, 116–17, 142–44, 154–55
of secondary providers, 78–79, 195
of sole providers, 80, 82, 84, 86, 87, 213, 216
of women in Albuquerque, 60–61
Waite, Linda J., 5
Whitehead, Harriet, 19
Willmott, Peter, 245
Wolf, Diane, 19, 288
Women
employment of, in relationship to family economy, 59, 68, 217

family income contribution of, 60 (table 14)
as proportion of labor force, 11–12, 32, 35–36, 46–50, 51–52, 55–57
See also Anglos; Child care; Coprovider; Hispanos; Household division of labor; Mainstay provider; Secondary provider; Sole provider
Work culture. *See* Plant culture
Work history, 59, 62
of Anglos, 68–72, 74–76
of coproviders, 63–72
of Hispanos, 63–68, 72–74, 76–79, 81–87
of husbands, 69–70, 73–75, 77–79
of mainstay providers, 72–76
of secondary providers, 76–80
of sole providers, 80–87
Working class, 5–6, 12–14, 56, 279
and household division of labor, 184, 185, 217, 218, 291–94
importance of wives' earnings to family economy, 54–55, 76
resources of, compared with middle class, 245
Workplace division of labor
based on ethnicity, 94
based on gender, 92, 93, 110, 121–22, 129–30, 140–41, 279
international, 286
Work practice. *See* Practice; Strategies and tactics
Work shifts, impact of. *See* Child care; Household division of labor

Yanagisako, Sylvia, 19, 245
Yancey, William L., 25
Young, Michael, 245

Zavella, Patricia, xii, xiii, 12, 246, 247, 249, 292

Anthropology of Contemporary Issues

A SERIES EDITED BY

ROGER SANJEK
